WORKERS' COUNCILS

ANTON PANNEKOEK

T0163966

AK PRESS

EDINBURGH · LONDON · OAKLAND

Workers' Councils
By Anton Pannekoek

©2003 AK Press in this format
All rights reserved.

First published in English by:
Southern Advocate for Workers' Councils,
Melbourne, Australia, 1948

ISBN: 1-902593-56-1

Edited with an introduction and bibliography by Robert F. Barsky,
Yale University (2002–3) and University of Western Ontario; with
contributions by Noam Chomsky, MIT; Ken Coates, Bertrand
Russell Peace Foundation, and Peter Hitchcock, CUNY

AK Press
674-A 23rd Street
Oakland, CA 94612-1163
USA
(510) 208-1700
www.akpress.org
akpress@akpress.org

AK Press
PO Box 12766
Edinburgh, EH8 9YE
Scotland
(0131) 555-5165
www.akuk.com
ak@akedin.demon.uk

The addresses above would be delighted to provide you with the latest complete AK catalog, featuring several thousand books, pamphlets, zines, audio
products, video products, and stylish apparel published & distributed by
AK Press. Alternatively, check out our websites for the complete catalog, latest
news and updates, events, and secure ordering.

Library of Congress Cataloging-in-Publication Data
A catalog record for this title is available from the Library of
Congress.

Cover design by John Yates

TABLE OF CONTENTS

INTERVIEWS

WORKERS' COUNCILS

I. THE TASK

II. THE FIGHT

III. THE FOE

IV. THE WAR (1944)

V. THE PEACE (1947)

Introduction, by Robert Barsky

Workers' Councils is good, solid, working-class literature."
– Noam Chomsky

This text of Anton Pannekoek's *Workers' Councils,* which is based on the 1950 Melbourne edition, questions the legitimacy of wage labor and the subordination to authority in the workplace. Ideas relating to these crucial issues are not presented here as a series of convoluted arguments rooted in language games. Rather, this book sets out in clear and unequivocal terms previously-discussed methods for re-organizing the workplace to meet the needs of ordinary people who both man the machines, and purchase the products they produce.

One might think, given the first paragraph, that this book will be a welcome re-edition of a well-known text. Today, however, this book is part of a large corpus of neglected works which consider, from a so-called "radical" perspective, very basic issues of concern to a general reading public. Like so much related work by anarchists, communists, socialists, wobblies, or others who have thought about relations of power in the workplace, it ought to be better known. Anyone who has ever worried about how factories are organized, what role unions play in determining factory output, why workers have so little say on shop floors, and how it is that people can speak of "post-industrialization" given the vast number of items produced each day in factories and shops, will find considerable value in reading these texts. More specialized audiences, such as people who have come across the work of Gramsci, Lenin, Marx or Trotsky will be surprised, I think, by the pertinence of Pannekoek's views. People familiar with more recent versions of Marxist analysis will be relieved to discover a writer more obviously engaged in the concerns of ordinary working people, rather than some version of dialectical writing that has been tainted with the will for postmodern obscurity. This is a text that is made to be read for its insight, but it's also a text that offers a framework for change which, although at times in need of updating, rings true in many places. Finally, people who know of Anton Pannekoek as an astronomer, and an historian of science, will be pleasantly surprised that he is yet another example of those great scientists who have worked on, or given their name to, progressive political work.

On the other hand, there's no question that people less familiar with the issues raised in this book, or with works by other persons concerned with similar things, such as Karl Korsch, Rosa Luxemburg, or, more recently, Zellig Harris, will find the book challenging at times. As Ken Coates notes in his interview, younger readers will need to have a strong historical sense to cut through Pannekoek's writing, but it is indeed worth the effort. And this effort will be assisted considerably, in my opinion, by the insights offered herein by

Noam Chomsky, Ken Coates and Peter Hitchcock. It was Chomsky who originally suggested to Mark Pavlick the need for a new edition of this book, and
in his fascinating interview he draws attention to the ways in which we can re-
cast questions about wage-earners, globalization, and free trade with reference
to this type of book. For Chomsky, *Workers' Councils* isn't an ideologically-
charged Marxist text, but is instead a sensible approach to critical concerns
about the challenges of being a working person in contemporary society. By
taking this tack, Chomsky helps drive home the point that ordinary workers,
not ideologues, have fought over the years for decent wages, fair settlements,
acceptable living conditions, and equality. These people, and the movements
they have supported, are constantly bashed or ignored by those who like to
equate concerns for human beings with radicalism or utopianism, as a means
of pandering to the rich and the powerful and promoting their own agendas.

Mark Pavlick, who started the Chomsky discussion circle in Washington
DC, and who has been concerned with the types of issues raised in this book
for several decades, suggested that I pursue the project. I have relied upon
Mark's wisdom and suggestions throughout this long process. His new collec-
tion of unpublished and early Chomsky texts (forthcoming from Common
Courage Press) will further demonstrate the value of this book for current
debates. Ken Coates has been a tireless correspondent and a wise source of
information he has collected, in his many writings and his priceless reminis-
cences. My dear friend Peter Hitchcock, who has doggedly pursued work on
the "workers of the world" from a range of cultural, economic, and historical
perspectives adds a whole new dimension to this work by discussing
Pannekoek's views about Chinese workers, and by providing a framework for
thinking about Pannekoek in the contemporary working-persons setting.
Finally, I should add that this book appears as I put the final touches upon a
biography of Zellig Harris, Noam Chomsky's teacher, and the author of a book
(published posthumously) called *The Transformation of Capitalist Society.* Readers
interested in different models for re-thinking workplace inequality and factory
inefficiency would derive significant benefit from some of Harris's insights.
Even more dramatic given the current crisis of capitalism is the appearance of
Seymour Melman's monumental tome, *After Capitalism: From Managerialism to
Workplace Democracy,* an up-to-date example of how truly radical thinking can
contribute not only to productive freedom in the workplace, but to a better
society. My frequent discussions with Chomsky, Coates, Hitchcock and
Melman on such fundamental topics as worker organizations brings significant
light to a context that is darkened by an ever-widening gap between the haves
and the have-nots, the workers and those who can afford to buy the goods, the
First and the Third Worlds, at a time when "security" can serve as an excuse
for more militarism and more illegitimate intrusion into people's lives, rather

than better organizations of those institutions which we rely upon to survive from one day to the next.

I owe words of thanks to the Social Sciences and Humanities Research Council, the University of Western Ontario, and Yale University, and, in particular, to Doug Kneale, Michael Holquist, Kathleen Okruhlik, and Elise Snyder. Tyler Tokaryk's assistance in the final edit was invaluable. And finally, my thanks again to Patricia Foxen, my love and inspiration.

Robert F. Barsky
New Haven, CT

Robert F. Barsky and Noam Chomsky

ROBERT BARSKY: *Why should we re-publish Pannekoek's work today?*

NOAM CHOMSKY: There is a spread, for the first time in many years, of a significant public challenge first of all to the existence of the corporation, a very questionable type of economic organization, and more deeply, there's questioning of the legitimacy of wage labor and the subordination to authority in the workplace. This is what Anton Pannekoek is talking about in *Workers' Councils*. Herein, he draws from very deep traditions, all over the West, which sometimes have no connection to Marxism or any radical tradition; for example, the Republican Party of the United States. In the 1860s, the Republican Party was opposed to wage labor, which it regarded as not different from chattel slavery. That was a standard view in the independent workers movement. And if you read material from the American working class press in the 1850s, which was run by young women from the farms and by laborers from downtown Boston, and others, it's the same perceptions and convictions. It comes from their own sense of what they call republicanism, that is, that free men and women don't sell themselves, they don't enter servitude to a monarchical authority, which is how they regarded the industrial system. You can even read editorials in the *New York Times* from this period which denounce wage labor. The Knights of Labor,[1] the main United States labor union in the 19th Century, was also committed to collective worker ownership. Even in the early days of the American Federation of Labor in the 1890s, you had members discussing this. These were very deeply-rooted ideas, and they come straight out of 18th century conceptions of natural rights, the rights of free people, which in those days mostly meant free men. The working class press at that time was run by women, to a large extent, though, and it contained the same ideas, and we see it again in the Homestead Strike in the 1890s. It took a long time to drive them out of peoples' heads, and then never completely disappeared. So there's a resonance today, when you talk about them to working class groups, at least in the United States. All this has real meaning, and here in *Workers' Councils* we have an intelligent exposition with an historical background, coming out of a different tradition, the European socialist tradition, which feeds into this, and provides a backing, which can stimulate it and lead to extremely important developments.

RB: *This book contains general ideas as well as specific details about how to transform society. Is there still some value in the more technical details of this book for the contemporary world?*

NC: Things have changed, but I don't think that the fundamentals have. So let's take information technology, which is new. The information technology itself is kind of neutral. It can, and is being used to dominate and control the workforce. But you can also use it to provide real time information to people on the shop floor, to enable people to make global decisions about plant activities by themselves, without managers. There's an interesting study of this in David Noble's work [*Progress Without People, Forces of Production*], and indeed it's exactly what he was talking about. When automation came along, and especially numerical processing and computer control of machine tools, the early efforts to apply them were done under the auspices of the military, because that way it was essentially cost-free. So it could have gone either direction; the technology that was available could have been used to increase managerial control and de-skill mechanics, which was done, or it could have been used to eliminate managerial control and to put control into the hands of skilled workers. The decision to do the first and not the second was not based on economic motives, as Noble points out pretty successfully, but was made for power reasons, in order to maintain managerial control and a subordinate workforce. There was evidence that firms could have made more money by working the other way, that is, according to capitalist principles. The fact that this didn't occur is a good example of what happens throughout the workforce.

RB: *The view we hear most often is that without managerial control, no progress would be possible; Pannekoek's book, and what you've just said, suggest the opposite, that managers have impeded progress.*

NC: It might well be, and this goes back to the early 19th Century. If you look at 19th Century materials about the early Industrial Revolution in the United States—I haven't looked but I'm sure that it would be the same in England—repeatedly there are cases where decisions were made not on narrow economic grounds—profit—but on grounds of subordination and domination, to organize production in particular ways. This actually caused problems for American industries in the 1970s, when they were falling behind Europe and Japan; it was in considerable part because of the hierarchical system of US production, with layers and layers of management, which took decisionmaking away from the hands of working people, people who can make these decisions more effectively than managers. Europe and Japan had other techniques, like quality control groups, so there was some devolution of decisionmaking there, although not much, but it too turned out to be more efficient than the American system. That led to calls for what was called the "re-industrialization of America" that went on in the 1980s, when the Reagan administration essentially closed the American market in major industries, assuming that otherwise they were going to be wiped out by Japanese competition. What happened during this period was that there was a re-constitution of the steel industry, the auto industry, the semi-conductor industry, and so on, maintaining the heavy layers of control, but moving more towards the lean production style of the Japanese and

German manufacturing. This was a response to the de-skilling of the American workforce. This is discussed in the technical literature, including work by outstanding economists like Robert Solow and others, who point out that the United States does not provide the technical training and the skill training that is standard for most of the population, meaning the workforce, in places like Germany and Japan. In an era of production in which skills really matter, where the repetitive tasks can be done by robots, you only need people to do more skilled work. If you haven't developed fundamental skills in the population, like basic literacy, numeracy, vocational education and so on, then you'll fall behind. A friend of mine who has worked on the free school movement, and is now involved in educational innovation projects at the university level in Massachusetts, has pointed out that the technical schools are often much more imaginative and free in the way that education proceeds than are the universities, because they just have to train people to do things. The sciences are like that as well; you train people, they work with you, and that is the way people learn.

RB: *Pannekoek describes this very issue of worker management of production and interests in ways that follow this model employed in the sciences.*

NC: Pannekoek of course was a well-known astronomer. Sciences have to work like that, and they have for a long time. Those ideas come straight out of the Enlightenment, actually, notably Rousseau, Humboldt, and back even further. It gets picked up in the left-Marxist traditions, and the independent working class traditions, which have separate roots. They go in parallel, and they have been suppressed in parallel, but they can re-emerge and interact with one another.

RB: *What about another parallel, between the anarcho-syndicalists and the Council Communists? Both share some of these ideas, and both have influenced, and been influenced by, Anton Pannekoek.*

NC: Anarcho-syndicalists and Council Communists were at this time almost indistinguishable. In fact, they cooperated pretty closely; if you look at the literature on the reactions to the Spanish revolution, the anarchist revolution, the Council Communists were, like the anarcho-syndicalists, very positive. Important figures from the two sides, Karl Korsch and Rudolph Rocker, were saying about the same things.

RB: *But Pannekoek in this book is hard on the union movement, saying that they at times replicate the society, notably hierarchical relationship to workers.*

NC: They do.

RB: *In that sense his sympathy for anarcho-syndicalism may be somewhat mitigated.*

NC: It depends upon what kind of union we're talking about. The union is the collective organization of the workers, which takes over production and distribution, and so on, and interacts with communities. In this sense the union is a combination of Pannekoek-style council communism, anarcho-syndicalism, and Kropotkin's emphasis on community organization. That combination makes great sense. After all, a work place is not just a work place, it's also in a community. The community has a role to play and what it does to the people in it has important effects on the community, as on others who are not in the workplace itself or the local community. Those kind of interactions have to be an essential part of any society based upon voluntary association.

RB: *So this would apply as much to housing as to the workplace?*

NC: Indeed. One of the successful anarchist-initiated developments in Canada is the major housing cooperative in Montreal, which is a good model for lots of things.

RB: *Where Pannekoek is less clear is on the relationship between the large institutions required for, say, the distribution of resources required for all workers' councils, such as power or water. Is this a flaw?*

NC: I'm personally skeptical about detailed descriptions of the future society; I just don't think we know enough. And this applies as well to fine detailed descriptions, for example, Diego Abad de Santillan's 1937 book, *After the Revolution*. De Santillan was close to the Spanish anarchists, and he wrote a very detailed description of how they should organize society after the revolution. It was very critical of the Spanish anarchists, and of what they were doing, and in his book you'll find an extremely detailed account of what he thought the society ought to look like. In my view, though, it's too detailed; we don't know enough. The kinds of questions you're asking here are very serious, but the answers to them will be learned by experiment; you try, you see how it works, and then you try other things. Nobody is smart enough to plan a society. You can talk about some of the principles upon which a society should work, and you can set up guidelines as to how to implement them, and how to experiment with them, and there are probably many different ways of doing them. There's no reason to believe that there's only one right answer; there are lots of different answers, with advantages and disadvantages, and people have to choose between them on the basis of experience, what has happened to others, and so on. This is true in every area. Take for example the problem of controlling criminal activity. Any society, no matter what it is, will contain people you are afraid of. What do you do with people you're afraid of? For one reason or another, they cannot become part of the functioning society. This is true of families, true in communities, true in the world. So you have to have ways of dealing with it. You want to find the most humane, and least punitive mode of doing this, but it's hard to believe that there won't be any crime or anti-social behavior. Humans are just to complicated. Every one of us has anti-social tendencies, and under certain circumstances, some of them will come out, and when they do, they have to be controlled. You can see that with your own children. But there are no formulas for how to do it, any more than there are formulas for raising your children. These are things that have to be worked out through experience, and institutions have to be constructed to deal with them. Once constructed, they then have to be tested, modified, and examined, with skepticism, in an experimental spirit. This applies as well to schools, and everything else.

RB: *One message of this text is that you can exercise control over your own future, and you can be productive while satisfying your own interests. So even when Pannekoek is critical, as he is of the unions, he remains optimistic about our ability to set up a society in which people can productively pursue their own interests.*

NC: Pannekoek's criticism of unions is historically specific. He's talking about the unions that existed, not necessarily working-class associations, which could be different. Even at the time, I think that the criticism was too harsh, since the unions were spearheading reformist social democratic initiatives, which were extremely important for people. That's why the unions are under such vicious attack, and have been ever since the 1940s; there are efforts to try to diminish or destroy the possibilities that flow from the initiatives that they supported, and which aimed for democratization and the improvement of human life. Those are not insignificant things; as a result, people can get health care, education, opportunities to control their own communities, and that is all good, even if it's not workers' control. Yes, unions reproduce the structure of society in bad ways, but then you deal with that.

RB: *Is Pannekoek's work consistent with Zellig Harris's ideas, which have now been published in his posthumous 1997 book* The Transformation of Capitalist Society?[2] *There are obvious points of overlap in terms of workers control,[3] but how close are they?*

NC: Zellig Harris's work draws from these circles. Harris and Paul Mattick were close friends, and Mattick comes straight out of Pannekoek's tradition; indeed, he was responsible for making Pannekoek's ideas known, or at least for distributing the original Pannekoek book. So sure, this is coming from exactly the same background. Harris moves in different directions, though, because he's thinking of ESOPs [Employee Shared Ownership Plans], and other techniques by which workers' control can be introduced, that is, by mechanisms that actually exist within the capitalist society. There are things that can be done in that framework, and in fact there are major entities that are technically under workers' control, like United Airlines, which in principal is under workers', and not management, control. And pension funds are under workers' control in principle, by no means in practice. If devices like that are used in order to take over part of the functioning of society, then that is a move in the direction that Pannekoek is talking about. It makes use as always of what is available, which can be a good idea, as far as it goes.

RB: *The other function that this book could perhaps play is to counteract the endlessly-repeated theme that in today's world there's no alternative to the status quo.*

NC: That is really nothing other than cheap propaganda, and it is successful among people who benefit from it. There's nothing surprising about that. The same people could have told you that there's no alternative to fascism. If you look at the early period of corporatization, say the early part of the 20th century, you see that it was understood to be a radical attack on classical liberalism. Corporatization essentially undercut the crucial core idea of classical liberalism, that rights inhere in people, that rights are something that people have. It held, in contrast, that rights are something that organic entities have. In some respects, fascism, Bolshevism, and corporatization have the same intellectual roots, neo-Hegelian ideas about the rights of organic entities. They come from the same texts, German philosophy of the late nineteenth century. This was proposed by progressives, who recognized, very clearly, that it was going to destroy the freedoms of people in the United States, but it had to be done. It's interesting to read people like Woodrow Wilson in this regard. He was a progressive, in the early 20th Century, and he said corporatization was absolutely necessary; but he was also very clear about it. He said that the old America, of free independent people, is gone. From now on, people are going to be the servants of corporate entities. It was nice to have a free society, but, goodbye. Goodbye, because there was no alternative. And in a certain sense, that was correct. The market systems were terribly destructive, you couldn't let them continue to function. They had to be administered, and business, of course, wanted to administer them itself. So they administer them themselves internally, through conglomerates of one sort or another, trusts, corporations, whatever. From a theoretical point of view any business firm, a mom and pop grocery store for example, is a market failure. The business firm has a technical description in modern economics: it's a local solution to market imperfections when the transaction costs are too high. In ordinary language, the firm is a market imperfection because it is administering economic interactions internally, and not through the market. When you go from a mom and pop grocery store to General Electric, you're talking about an enormous market imperfection. And it's a recognition by the capitalists themselves that the markets are simply too destructive to function, so we have to administer and control them. That was the "there is no alternative" idea of the early 20th Century, and it simply continues. There's an interesting theology about trade that has been developed, and here economists have a lot to answer for. Trade is being held up as some kind of holy thing that you have to maximize, but of course trade has no value in itself. It's a value to the extent that it has positive welfare effects. Otherwise it's not a value, it's not like freedom, for example. The claim is that the new form of what is misleadingly called globalization increases trade, and that's good. Well, the fact of the matter is that even in the way that they measure trade, globalization doesn't increase it. So the growth in trade is not faster than it was during the Bretton Woods period, say. Furthermore, if you take a look at what is called trade, you find that by any reasonable measure, trade may in fact be declining. The reason is that an enormous part of what is called trade is centrally-managed. So intra-firm trade, trade within a single corporation, is considered trade. If General Motors moves parts from Indiana to Illinois for assembly, and then back to Texas to sell, you don't call this trade. But you do call it trade when you move it across the border to Mexico and back. And that's no small part; US trade with Mexico is probably more than 50% intra-firm. And that's only a piece of it. When you do out-sourcing, that is, in order to destroy unions and get the cheapest possible labor, and disposable labor, and when you forget about environmental effects, and so on, a standard device is out-sourcing. In that case you don't produce your own batteries, or something, you out-source them to some small company that doesn't have to obey work standards, or whatever it may be. This is often in foreign countries. A good deal of what is called trade is the interaction through out-sourcing, and that is centrally managed. Beyond that, the whole economy, everywhere, is moving towards oligopoly, which means several huge corporations dominating a particular component of the economy. Corporations partially compete, but they also partially cooperate. If you look at the auto industry, you'll see that it has narrowed considerably from what it was 20 or 30 years ago. Furthermore, if you look at the companies, you'll see that they partially own each other, and they work on joint projects together, and they have the same representatives on their Boards of Directors, and so on. All of this ends up being kind of a mercantilist system, in which what Adam Smith would have called 'trade' is a small component of what is going on. You can't assign numbers to it, and the reason for this is that corporations are totalitarian institutions, and they don't tell you what they are doing, any more than the Kremlin told you what it was doing. There's a way to find out what corporations are doing, though; in the US, Congress has subpoena power, and it can, if it wanted to, open the books. One of the major efforts of union leaders in the 1950s was to open the books; they said, "tell us what you're doing, don't be fascistic or Stalinist". Well, the unions lost that one, but the right remains there. The public has the right to force them to open the books and to discover what is going on. Is there trade? Let's forget about whether trade is good or bad, because it's not obvious, but the question is, is it really happening? Or is what is happening to a large extent nothing other than centrally-administered interaction with high-levels of managerial control in what amounts to a global mercantilist system? In parts of this system, like aircraft production, you can see this clearly. There's presently a dispute between Brazil and Canada, which is kind of comical, because they are arguing about subsidies to airline manufacturers. Okay, these are two little midgets bickering about subsidies. In the meantime, the commercial aircraft industry is in the hands of two corporations, Boeing and Airbus. Both of them are state-subsidized, and neither of them could exist without massive subsidies. Boeing was an offshoot of the United States Airforce, which is where much of the technology is developed, so we all end up flying around in modified army transport planes. Now it's down to those two companies, and that is the biggest civilian export. Automobile manufacturers are down to about half a dozen firms, all of them inter-linked. And that is the direction that everything is going. So if you care about what is actually happening, the economy is moving towards totalitarian control, or mercantilistic control, and the claim is, as it has been since the late 19th Century, there is no alternative. And in a sense there isn't, if the only alternative is markets, which are too destructive, so you have to have administration. But then there's the obvious question: why does the administration have to be totalitarian? You could say the same thing about governmental structures. In some respects they may be more efficient when they have totalitarian features, but that's not an argument for them.

RB: *You've just done a truly radical analysis!*

NC: None of this is profound, anybody can understand this. As soon as you decode a little bit of the propaganda, you can say yes, that is what is right in front of us.

RB: *That's certainly the impression one has in reading* Workers' Councils, *that there's an obvious validity and a clear-headed presentation.*

NC: It is obvious in the sense that children could understand it. It's not like quantum physics. You don't have to have a profound understanding of deep subjects in order to grasp what it's about, just ordinary common sense, a willingness to look at the facts that are available to us. Of course one quickly discovers that many of these facts are not available to us, because they are kept secret. They are kept secret in principle within quasi-totalitarian institutions.

RB: *Another way that they are kept secret is that texts like this one which talk about these ideas are so hard to find. And yet when we read a book like* Workers' Councils, *we find it very understandable and useful.*

NC: This particular book was last printed in the 1950s, and back then, who read it? 25 people? And it is not filled with Marxist jargon. Pannekoek of course is a Marxist, but you didn't have to know that, you could read it and

forget the Marxist framework. As such, it's good, solid, working-class literature.

Notes on Robert F. Barsky and Noam Chomsky Interview

1. For a sense of this organization, see
http://www.spartacus.schoolnet.co.uk/USAknights.htm
2. Zellig S. Harris, *The Transformation of Capitalist Society*, Lanham MD, Rowman and
Littlefield, 1997.
3. To address this obvious lacuna, I have recently completed *Zellig's America: Linguistics,
Radical Politics and Zionism in the Twentieth Century*, Cambridge; London: The MIT Press,
2003.

Robert F. Barsky and Ken Coates

ROBERT BARSKY: *The world has changed considerably since the middle of the 20th century, when* Workers' Councils *was first published—or has it? Pannekoek describes problems facing workers organizations which are still with us today, and many of the conditions which prevailed when this text was produced still reign, if not in our own countries, in many regions of the Third World. But does the method of social organization proposed here still seem topical to you?*

KEN COATES: The world of work has changed enormously since the middle of the last century. Concentration means that greater powers of capital are ranged against more fragmented, and even isolated work forces. This process has been complex. It has entailed, amongst other things, a movement of manufacturing away from traditional centers to newly-industrial countries, commonly employing very low paid workers, often in unsafe and primitive conditions. But even when conditions have been more advanced, the result has been dire in the traditional centers, entailing a great increase in structural unemployment. In response, we have seen a growth of non-manual, part-time, and short-term employment. A large scale shift into service industries has changed the pattern of labor organization, generating a sharp growth in service unions. The movement of capital into the service sector has threatened and is threatening public sector services. The scale of mechanization has commonly reduced the size of individual work forces, and rendered the organization of trade unions more difficult, between individual plants, sectors of production, and transnational outposts. Simply to describe the complexities of workers' organization in modern companies thus requires a very complex matrix. Accordingly, it is clear that the powers of capital today require a more inventive and far more cosmopolitan response from unions.

RB: *Isn't it the case that some of these creative approaches have come from outside the unions, particularly more recently?*

KC: There has been a blossoming of voluntary organizations concerning themselves with the adverse impact of industry, whether on the global environment, or on local social amenities, or on human and social rights. This flowering of civil society has begun to make possible overall criticism of the present structure of society, through, amongst other initiatives, the Porto Alegre process, which has joined labor unions into its framework.

RB: *You have worked your whole life with the labor movement, but you were also elected to the European Parliament, which must have felt a long way from the shop floor; do you still find yourself confronted with the principle issues which were of concern to you when first you started your union struggles?*

KC: I was not re-elected to the European Parliament in 1999, although I did previously work for ten years in that area. I spent the first five years as Chairman of the Sub-Committee on Human Rights, working within conventional Parliamentary structures across the whole range of human rights issues. In my second term, I stepped down from that responsibility which has been very onerous indeed, because I wished to devote myself much more actively to the problem of mass unemployment in Europe. I had agitated for the establishment of a Temporary Committee on Employment, charged with the task of preparing the Parliament's response to European unemployment. When that Committee was formed in 1994, I became its *Rapporteur,* and drafted its two reports, both of which were carried by overwhelming majorities. But both were ignored by the Council of Ministers, leaving the Parliament's opinions completely sidelined. The proposals upon which we had agreed were broadly neo-Keynesian within the framework which had been proposed by Jacques Delors, the President of the European Commission. That the European governments flatly rejected all such proposals was a very clear indication in the middle 1990s that neo-liberalism was in the driving seat in the European institutions, and that the conventional postwar social democratic perspectives were now seriously challenged. That the challenge sometimes came form social democratic governments themselves did not make our political responses any easier.

RB: *You in fact used the facilities and the clout to pursue work relating to civil society, the type of work one would expect to find in a parliament, but one which has been so profoundly overshadowed of late by the combination of militarism and neo-liberalism.*

KC: During all my ten years in the Parliament, I tried to make use of its facilities in order to develop greater scope for European civil society. This is not the sum of 'n' national civil societies: the existence of strong pensioners' associations in England or Greece does not in itself add up to a greater capacity by pensioners to defend their interests at the European level. To try to assist in more rapid convergence, I proposed the convening of a European Pensioners' Parliament. Under the sponsorship of the Socialist Group of MEPs, a full-scale European Parliament of pensioners was convened, drawn from every country in the European Union. The pensioners were able to agree on a comprehensive charter of joint demands, and the whole process greatly increased interaction and networking between existing national movements. It was followed by a second Pensioners' Parliament under the auspices of the European Parliament itself. As a result of these initiatives, disabled people approached me, and, with some difficulty, there were able to organize a Disabled Peoples' Parliament, which had a very dramatic effect in strengthening the co-operation of organizations or people with disabilities all across the area of the European Union. Once we had been blocked in our attempt to enforce job-creating policies, throughout the European Union, we convened two full-scale assemblies of unemployed people, within the same general perspective.

RB: *Do you feel that your approach to workers' concerns has evolved considerably through time, or do the same truisms apply? Are there texts, by, say, Noam Chomsky, Antonio Gramsci, David Noble or Bertrand Russell which remain for you basic texts for those interested in these issues? How does Anton Pannekoek's work resonate as regards these other figures?*

KC: Obviously my approach to the development of the freedom of working people has evolved, but there are certain constants which are very evident. Yes, these may be embodied in certain texts. But it is a most remarkable text which can reflect the heaving mix of concerns which express themselves through living social movements. Pannekoek's work stands out well in this respect, with the reservation that I mark out in my response to your next question. In the Institute for Workers' Control, which I helped to establish during the 1960s, our approach did not follow, in any conventional way, the dissemination of any particular texts. Of course, we drew upon all the teachers you mention: but we also derived most of our practice from the British worker's education movement. As a result, we sought to develop collective responses by groups of workers who worked out their own ideas about how they might go forward. Such groups were helped by workers' educationalists such as Michael Barratt Brown and Tony Topham, who provoked groups of steel workers, miners, dockers, and bus men into generating their own detailed proposals for industrial democracy in their industries. These proposals vary considerably, not only in relation to the different industrial conditions in the areas concerned, but also in relation to the range of ideas upon which particular groups of workpeople could draw. Some of these ideas shared affinities with, say, the Guild Socialists; others were closer to the industrial unions. But such study as took place was the better informed because workers had themselves struggled directly with the problems which had troubled the pioneers in an earlier generation.[1]

RB: *Anton Pannekoek exhibits a deep suspicion about trade unions in this text, fearful that they might reproduce the very structures they have been set up to combat. What do you think about this part of his work?*

KC: The suspicion of trade unions was very common, among trade unionists themselves. You will recall Tom Mann's very famous outburst, at the beginning of his life as a militant engineer:

> "How long, how long, will you be content with the present half-hearted policy of your Unions? I readily grant that good work has been done in the past by the Unions, but, in Heaven's name, what good purpose are they serving now? All of them have large numbers out of employment even when their particular trade is busy.

None of the important societies have any policy other than that of endeavoring to keep wages from falling. The true Unionist policy of aggression seems entirely lost sight of: in fact the average unionist of today is a man with a fossilized intellect, either hopelessly apathetic, or supporting a policy that plays directly into the hands of the capitalist exploiter."[2]

But although down the years new generations of trade union members have echoed this frustration, it is equally true that down the years they have made great gains, without passing beyond the capitalist forms of organization. Indeed, the English meaning of the words "Workers' Control" captures a more complex reality. When they succeed in controlling hiring and firing, workers have not established their rule over the enterprise. But they have effectively restricted the powers of the employer to do as he wishes. The whole history of trade union agitation is the story of the encroachment of powers by the workpeople's collectives, and the circumscription of what used to be seen as the employer's prerogatives. In this sense, trade unions have been a part of the historical separation of powers, and have limited the arbitrary capacity of employers to govern the work places as they wish. This process was actually fostered by successive Governments before and during the First World War, in an effort to encourage industrial peace. It advanced with giant strides during the Second World War, when Ernest Bevin, one of the principal agitators between 1914 and 1918, became Minister of Labor in the coalition Government, and imposed a regime of joint consultation on often recalcitrant employers. This was full of ambiguities, as was Bevin's later and much more expanded contribution, which saw him aiding in the reconstruction of the German trade union movement, while he was the British Foreign Secretary in the post-war Labor Government. Wiseacres claimed that the structure of the Transport and General Workers' Union had been transplanted into Germany as a result.

RB: *How did you approach this problem in your own work?*

KC: We had long discussions about this. Could it grow over into full-scale self-management, in which workers could determine the objectives of the enterprises in which they worked, and establish new forms of self-government? Revolutionaries such as Lenin and Trotsky changed their views about the role of trade unions with experience. At times, Trotsky shared Pannekoek's impatience. But at other times, as in his polemic with Thalheimer, he was strongly insistent on workers' control as a negative constriction of employer power, firmly to be demarcated from workers' self-management. During a famous post-revolutionary controversy, Lenin made great play of the importance of trade unions as educational bodies, at the same time that he developed a sharp doctrine of separation of powers, with the intention of curbing bureaucratic authoritarianism in the institutions of the revolution. The idea of the Workers' and Peasants' Inspectorate accepted that the workers needed effective instruments to control their own representatives. Not only was this insight understood by the Yugoslavs when they set out to develop the institutions of self-management, but extensive experiments were made with the intention of acting upon it. Much of the internal history of trade unions has been about asserting and re-asserting this principle. At the very beginning of Webb's History, we learn about how the trade unions controlled their own funds from peculation by greedy treasurers, by keeping them in boxes with three locks, just as the Church and Chapel funds had been safeguarded by previous generations. The treasurer could only access the union's money, with the co-operation of those auditors who kept the other keys, and ensured probity in the dispensation of cash.

RB: *In England I met a representative from a large bookseller who said that Noam Chomsky's work is sold primarily to younger people (16-25 years of age), which might lead us to suggest all sorts of things about disillusionment with contemporary society. Can you imagine that even despite the differences in tone, approach and style that this same group of people will find Anton Pannekoek's work compelling?*

KC: Chomsky is preaching democracy to people who have to make sense of the oppressions of the 21st Century. Young people will need to have a strong historical sense to cut through the earlier arguments of Pannekoek, who was addressing those problems of which we have been speaking. I think it is worth the effort.

RB: *You have been working for a long time in the Bertrand Russell Peace Foundation, and in some ways have continued to work in ways consistent with his approach. Is it appropriate to consider what, if any relations exist between the work of Russell and Pannekoek?*

KC: I don't think that Russell knew of Pannekoek, although this could be checked out at the archives at McMaster University.[3] Russell's own little book, *Roads to Freedom*[4], is still worth reading, and has a lively chapter on the syndicalist revolt, which is mainly inspired by the CGT [Confédération Générale du Travail] in France, the De Leonists in the United States, and the IWW [International Workers of the World]. It draws heavily on the work of G. D. H. Cole in England.

RB: *Someone who has in effect picked up the types of questions they both address is Seymour Melman, whose new book,* After Capitalism,[7] *deals with the need for workplace reform to address the US's march towards an economic model of managerialism which ominously resembles in important ways the USSR's "planned economy." He said to me recently that he hopes to someday write his memoirs, which he hopes to call* I never changed my mind!. *I think that he's referring here to his basic approach to issues, and the fundamental values which guide his thinking about fundamental issues concerning, for example, workplace* *democracies. Have you "changed your mind" about the types of issues discussed in here, and if so, in which ways?*

KC: No, I agree with Seymour Melman, and on the big things I feel more convinced than ever I did that the domination of one man or woman by another is a crime against our future. If anything, I've become more extreme in this view, but I have long believed that a truly human society will be one in which no-one has ever taken an order or performed an action without knowing why. On the other hand, what most people mean when they speak of "changing their minds" is not modifying their deep convictions, but, simply, learning about conjunctural matters. On the whole that is a good idea! "When circumstances change I change my mind. What do you do?" said J. M. Keynes.

Notes on Robert F. Barsky and Ken Coates Interview

1. A brief guide to this conflicting mass of doctrines can be found in *Industrial Democracy in Great Britain*, MacGibbon and Kee, 1967, eds. Ken Coates and Tony Topham.
2. Ken Coates and Tony Topham, *The Making of the Transport and General Workers' Union*, Blackwell, 1991, volume 1, part 1, p. 42.
3. http://www.mcmaster.ca/russdocs/russell.htm
4. *Roads to Freedom: Socialism, Anarchism, and Syndicalism.* London, 1918.
5. Seymour Melman, *After Capitalism: From Managerialism to Workplace Democracy*, NY: Knopf, 2001.

Robert F. Barsky and Peter Hitchcock

ROBERT BARSKY: *This is an unusual text in some ways, a long pamphlet, a peda-gogical guide to modifying workers' relations, a polemical essay, and a kind of popular his-tory of the working class and its relations to land and machine owners. You yourself have worked a lot on working class fictions and non-fictions, tell me how you see the genre in which Pannekoek writes, and how this effects the substance of the argument.*

PETER HITCHCOCK: I think it would be interesting to explore the text as a kind of fiction, as it reflects on the fictive being of working-class subjectivity for instance. Then again there is the question of Chinese fictions (fictions about China) and this is perhaps more pertinent on this occasion. Here Pannekoek is polemical to a degree that threatens the foundation of the argument. Part of the problem is simply the form: the pamphlet mode allows for sweeping general-ization, some of which is deserving and would be supportable if necessary, but there is also a sense that the critique of Japanese imperialism, for example, an imperialism that directly affects China, can only be made precisely because of the elisions that it forces. Often the survey proceeds in a highly deterministic and functionalist manner (a few upper class folks study in Europe and voila, a Japanese bourgeoisie is born!) or Pannekoek offers comparisons that are either empty or unsupportable ("The working classes in the country, as well as in the towns, lived in a state of hopeless misery, of squalor and despair, surpassing the worst conditions in Europe of olden times"). This does not mean, however, that Pannekoek's provocation is completely unfounded. Dismissing claims that Japanese expansionism was born of population pressures, Pannekoek responds that incursions into China were largely economic, and focused on iron ore extraction in the north and cotton production in and around Shanghai. This much remains true in the links of imperialism and capitalism: strategic interests tend to be the profitable ones.

RB: *One way in which this book still resonates is in its analysis of the relationship between these links you mention, between imperialism and capitalism. But in certain sections he seems to undermine the importance of the peasant population, and when he does talk about it, draws a sharp line between peasants in China and in Europe, just as he distinguishes very strongly between the bourgeoisie in both places. How does this rather complex set of compar-isons play into the development of his version of Marxism?*

PH: On this question I think Pannekoek bears comparison to his Chinese counterparts who, like him, were struggling hard over the differences and uneven developments of class formation and antagonism on a world scale. In fact, as Arif Dirlik has pointed out, Chinese Marxists before the rise of the Chinese Communist Party were more likely to favor an anarcho-Marxism much closer to Kropotkin than to Marxist-Leninism. That the latter would triumph has tended to obscure the influence of the former which might have provided Pannekoek himself with a provocation to explore the question of comparison in a deeper way. The whole history of "socialism with Chinese characteristics" pivots on the specific character of the Chinese peasantry, and this specificity was much discussed long before the Russian Revolution made its mark. Part of the significance of Pannekoek on this score is that he earnestly acknowledges the differences even if he does not sufficiently elaborate the implications that proceed from them. For those one would have to read Mao.

RB: *You are particularly interested in the plight of Chinese workers, and this area is seldom discussed when we consider Pannekoek's work. Why is this an important section for Pannekoek, and how might it be of continued interest to people interested in current events in the region?*

PH: The section devoted to China replays familiar mantras but only because they touch on certain historical truths. The decline and fall of the Qing was a complex and messy process, fueled by ruling class arrogance, corruption, and a naive isolationism. In the nineteenth century the Chinese military was clearly in need of massive modernization but even after humiliating defeats at the hands of the British navy the nation state clung to older pastimes. The gross exploitation of the Chinese by foreign colonial powers with their "concessions" and price fixing of imports only exacerbated the social contradictions of Chinese modernity. As Pannekoek notes, this opened the possibility of socialist organization (he mentions Sun Yatsen in this regard) and a nationalist movement from below but it simultaneously paved the way for further intervention in China by those willing to compete for its potential surplus value. When we say that the days of high imperialism and colonial powers are gone this does not mean that imperialism does not participate in today's struggles over surplus value. It is a different kind of imperialism but one that is earnestly knocking on China's door.

RB: *How does Pannekoek contribute to the long debates about the relationship between China and the Soviet Union, and what in your sense does this bring to his argument?*

PH: Not surprisingly, Pannekoek also casts a jaundiced eye on Soviet interest in China after 1917 and this makes for blanket statements rather than nuance. While no one doubts Soviet manipulation of China's emerging Left, Pannekoek gives the impression that Mao and the early communists were simply dupes with no agency of their own: "The C.P. of China had been instructed from Moscow that the Chinese revolution was a middle-class revolution, that the bourgeoisie had to be the future ruling class, and that the workers simply had to assist her against feudalism and bring her into power." Cynics will say that even after the demise of the Soviet Union the Chinese communists are still following this model but the class, geopolitical, and indeed spatial coordinates of modern China are not so easily drawn. Still, it remains the case that Japan's invasion owed a great deal to the factional warring of the republican period in China when communist inspired peasant revolution wrestled with the Kuomintang nationalist-fueled modernization narrative across vast stretches of eastern and southern China. Even though the Qing tried vainly to resuscitate its fortunes by allying itself with the Japanese in Manchuria, Pannekoek is right to focus on the peculiarities of China's urban bourgeoisie as a land-owning class and thus more easily vilified as those most likely to maintain peasant subjection. Japanese imperialism did indeed necessitate a united front but it was only after Chiang Kai-shek's brief capture in the Xian incident of 1936 that this necessity gained greater purchase.

RB: *It seems important to discuss how the West dealt with this formidable alliance between the Soviet Union and China, and what role can we ascribe, in Pannekoek's reading, to the relationship between workers of the world and nationalism?*

PH: While the Soviets nurtured their relationship with the Chinese Communist Party, the United States and the West played the China card towards the nationalists. The KMT drew on fears of communism to advance its particular brand of "democracy" and its earlier atrocities went largely unpunished. The gamble was clearly that nationalism was a small price to pay if foreign capital could reassert itself through a form of neo-colonial trade. It should be noted, however, that Pannekoek overlooks the fact that the Japanese war machine was also being fueled by the West, including the United States, and that this form of risk management continued right up to Pearl Harbor.

RB: *In this sense, though, Pannekoek's book is out of date, although there are moments at which we find marks of a prescient analysis. Surprisingly enough, it's in the questions about "class" that we find some of the more interesting predictions. And his concern with the conditions appropriate for the installation of capitalism in China have also borne the test of time, if the massive number of consumer goods bearing the 'made in China' ensign is any indication.*

PH: Hindsight, of course, tarnishes Pannekoek's commentary significantly. The world war demonstrably did not mean the rise of China as a new capitalist world power: the communists won, and so the ironies of history decreed that the defeated Japanese would assume that mantle in Asia. One cannot blame Pannekoek for this misdiagnosis since it is in the nature of political punditry that such shortfalls must occur. What is interesting, however, is Pannekoek's vision of future class relations which, for all the wackiness and muddleheadedness of his reading, now appears wonderfully prescient. Thus, while China's war debt did not immediately make it subject to American influence, the notion now that "American capital....will have the lead in building up its industry" does not seem farfetched (especially if one tracks foreign direct investment and joint venture activity). Similarly, Pannekoek's note that China has "fertile soil, capable of producing an abundance of products" is hyperbolic (particularly in light of demographics) but his qualification "requiring security by wide scientific care and regulation of the water, by constructing dikes and excavating and normalizing rivers" remains a pertinent issue (to which we would have to add the question of hydropower and projects like the Three Gorges Dam). The class implications of such activities are for Pannekoek quite pronounced: "The ideals and aims for which the working masses of China are fighting will, of course, not be realized. Landowners, exploitation and poverty will not disappear; what disappears are the old stagnant, primitive forms of misery, usury and oppression. The productivity of labor will be enhanced; the new forms of direct exploitation by industrial capital will replace the old ones. The problems facing Chinese capitalism will require central regulations by a powerful government. That means forms of dictatorship in the central government, perhaps complemented by democratic forms of autonomy in the small units of district and village." Pannekoek believed he was writing of a turning point in history—one in which the goals of social transformation would come sharply into view. For all sorts of reasons (including the Cold War, Maoism, Americanization and globalization) historical crisis has taken a different route.

RB: *Pannekoek points to elements of the Chinese workers' character, suggesting that it is filled with promise for revolutionary change. For instance: "With the growth of industry the fight of the industrial workers will spring up. With the strong spirit of organization and great solidarity shown so often by the Chinese proletarians and artisans, even a rise more rapid than in Europe of a powerful working class movement may be expected." In your work there, have you had this same sentiment, or is this another way in which Pannekoek was a bit too optimistic?*

PH: Here Pannekoek's optimistic will shines through, but we could have done with a bit more intellectual pessimism. Nevertheless, the importance he notes in Chinese class formation remains a burning issue, perhaps more so now. Historically we might now say that the biggest muzzle on working-class political action was provided, paradoxically, by "actually existing socialism." There are many holes in such an argument, but even if it were the case the alibi is running a little thin. Basically labor organization in the PRC was deemed superfluous (by the Party) as long as significant surpluses were largely redistributed. This did not stop class formation and antagonism (the Party understood that the task was to make communism not simply to announce its achievement) but with economic differences, comparatively small worker protest was not acute. That is not the case today where extremes of poverty and wealth have come much more clearly into view. Labor organization is still stifled and for now at least the capitalists and the communists are smiling at each other across the table.

RB: *So Pannekoek's analysis is still pertinent?*

PH: For all the rhetorical blather and ideological shortcuts these passages read like cuneiform on capital's pillars. Perhaps the words will not outlast the form, but the fact that they were etched at all reminds us that both are historical. As we try to historicize a present in which capital divides and unites China and the United States, the class war of which Pannekoek wrote is both anachronistic and vital. What is out of time in worker councils is on time in terms of capital relations, and that paradox provides different names for self organization in the current crisis, another uneven development, perhaps, that Pannekoek would have appreciated.

J.J. Lebel and Paul Mattick[1]

J. J. LEBEL: *What relevance does Pannekoek's book have in Europe today? Do you think that the analytic memory and theory of the past experience of council communism, as Pannekoek expresses them, can be "heard" and understood by workers here today?*

PAUL MATTICK: A book, such as Pannekoek's, is not in need of immediate relevance. It concerns itself with a historical period; with past occurrences as well as possible future experiences, in which the phenomenon of workers' councils appearing and disappearing points to a trend of development in workers' class struggle and its changing objectives. Like anything else, forms of class struggle are historical in the sense that they make their appearance long before their full realization becomes an actual possibility. In an embryonic form, for example, trade unions arose spontaneously as instruments of working class resistance to capitalist exploitation at the very beginning of capitalism's development, only to disappear again because of objectively determined hindrances to their further development. Yet, their temporary irrelevance did not hinder their full unfolding under changed conditions, which then determined their character, possibilities and limitations. Similarly, workers' councils made their appearance under conditions which precluded the release of all their revolutionary potentialities. The content of the social upheavals in which the first workers' councils arose was not adequate to their organizational form. The Russian workers' councils of 1905 and 1917, for instance, fought for a constitutional bourgeois democracy and for trade union goals such as the eight-hour day and higher wages. The German workers' councils of 1918 gave up their momentarily-won political power in favor of the bourgeois National Assembly and the illusory evolutionary path of German social democracy. In either case, the workers' councils could only eliminate themselves as their organizational form contradicted their limited political and social goals. Whereas, in Russia, it was the objective unreadiness for a socialist revolution, in Germany it was the subjective unwillingness to realize socialism by revolutionary means, which accounted for the decay and, finally, the forced destruction of the council movement. Nonetheless, it had been the workers' councils, not the traditional labor organizations, which secured the success of the revolutionary upheavals however limited they proved to be. Although the workers' councils revealed that the proletariat is quite able to evolve revolutionary instrumentalities of its own-either in combination with the traditional labor organizations, or in opposition to them-at the time of their formation they only had very vague concepts, or none at all, of how to consolidate their power and use it in order to change society. Thus they fell back upon the political instrumentalities of the past. The question of whether or not the council idea, as elaborated by Pannekoek, could be understood and taken up by the workers today, is a rather strange one, because the council idea implies no more, but also no less, than the self organization of the workers wherever and whenever this becomes an inescapable necessity in the struggle for their immediate needs, or for farther-reaching goals, which can either no longer be reached by, or are in fact opposed by, traditional labor organizations such as the trade unions and political parties. In order to take place at all, a particular struggle within a factory, or an industry, and the extension of the struggle over wider areas and larger numbers, may require a system of workers' delegates, committees of action, or workers' councils. Such struggles may or may not find the support of the existing labor organizations. If not, they will have to be carried on independently, by the fighting workers themselves, and imply their self-organization. Under revolutionary circumstances, this may well lead to a wide spread system of workers' councils, as the basis for a total reorganization of the social structure. Of course, without such a revolutionary situation, expressing a social crisis condition, the working class will not concern itself with the wider implications of the council system, even though it might organize itself for particular struggles by way of councils. Pannekoek's description of the theory and practice of workers' councils relates thus to no more than the workers' own experiences. But what they experience they can also comprehend and, under favorable conditions, apply in their struggle within and against the capitalist system.

JJL: *How do you think Pannekoek's book came about and in what relationship to his practice (in Germany or Holland)? Do you think his book and his essay on trade unionism (in* Living Marxism*) apply to present-day conditions?*

PM: Pannekoek wrote his book on workers' councils during the Second World War. It was a summing-up of his life's experience of the theory and practice of the international labor movement and of the development and transformation of capitalism within various nations and as a whole. It ends with the temporary triumph of a revived, though changed, capitalism, and with the utter subjugation of working class interests to the competitive needs of rival capitalist systems preparing for new imperialistic conflicts. Unlike the ruling classes, which adapt themselves quickly to changed conditions, the working class, by still adhering to traditional ideas and activities, finds itself in a powerless and apparently hopeless situation. And as socioeconomic changes only gradually change ideas, it may still take considerable time before a new labor movement–fitted to the new conditions–will arise. Although the continued existence of capitalism, in either its private or state-capitalist forms, proved that the expectation of the growth of a new labor movement in the wake of the Second World War was premature, the continued resilience of capitalism does not remove its immanent contradictions and will therefore not release the workers from the need to put an end to it. Of course, with capitalism still in the saddle, the old labor organizations, parliamentary parties and trade unions, could also be maintained. But they are already recognized, and recognize themselves, as part and parcel of capitalism, destined to go down with the system on which their existence depends. Long before it became an obvious fact, it was clear to Pannekoek that the old labor movement was a historical product of the rising capitalism, bound to this particular stage of development, wherein the question of revolution and socialism could only be raised but not answered. At such a time, these labor organizations were destined to degenerate into tools of capitalism. Socialism depended now on the rise of a new labor movement, able to create the preconditions for proletarian self-rule. If the workers were to take over the production process and determine the distribution of their products, they needed, even prior to this revolutionary transformation, to function and to organize themselves in an entirely different manner than in the past. In both forms of organization, the parliamentary parties and the trade unions, the workers delegate their power to special groups of leaders and organizers, who are supposed to act on their behalf, but actually only foster their own separate interests. The workers lost control over their own organizations. But even if this had not been so, these organizations were totally unfit to serve as instruments for either the proletarian revolution or the construction of socialism. Parliamentary parties were a product of bourgeois society, an expression of the political democracy of laissez-faire capitalism and only meaningful within this context. They have no place in socialism, which is supposed to end political strife by ending special interests and social class relations. As there is no room, nor need for political parties in a socialist society, their future superfluity already explains their ineffectiveness as an instrument of revolutionary change. Trade unions, too, have no functions in socialism, which does not know of wage relations and which organizes its production not with regard to specific trades and industries but in accordance with social needs. As the emancipation of the working class can only be brought about by the workers themselves, they have to organize themselves as a class, in order to take and to hold power. Regarding present conditions, however, which are not as yet of a revolutionary nature, the council form of working-class activities does not directly betray its wider-reaching revolutionary potentialities, but is a mere expression of the accomplished integration of the traditional labor organizations into the capitalist system. Parliamentary parties and trade unions lose their limited effectiveness when it is no longer possible to combine an improvement of workers' living standards with a progressive expansion of capital. Under conditions which preclude a sufficient capitalist accumulation, that is, under conditions of economic crisis, the reformist activities of political parties and trade unions cease to be operative and these organizations abstain from their supposed functions, as they would now endanger the capitalist system itself. They will rather try to help sustain the system, up to the point of directly sabotaging the workers aspirations for better living and working conditions. They will help capitalism overcome its crisis at the expense of the workers. In such a situation, the workers, unwilling to submit to the dictates of capital, are forced to resort to activities not sanctioned by official labor organizations, to so-called wildcat strikes, factory occupations and other form of direct actions outside the control of the established labor organizations. These self-determined activities, with their temporary council structure, indicate the possibility of their radical application under arising revolutionary situations, replacing the traditional organizational forms, which have become a hindrance for both the struggle for immediate needs and for revolutionary goals.

JJL: *Can you give a few practical and concrete examples of how workers' councils functioned (in Russia, Germany, Hungary etc.), and how they differed from traditional party or union organizations? What are the basic differences? How do party and council or union clash?*

PM: As every strike, demonstration, occupation or other kinds of anticapitalist activity which ignores the official labor organizations and escapes their controls, takes on the character of independent working class action, which determines its own organization and procedures, may be regarded as a council movement; so, on a larger scale, the spontaneous organization of revolutionary upheavals, such as occurred in Russia in 1905 and 1917, in Germany in 1918, and later—against the state-capitalist authorities—in Hungary, Czechoslovakia and Poland, avail themselves of workers' councils as the only form of working class actions possible under conditions in which all established institutions and organizations have become defenders of the status quo. These councils arise out of necessity, but also because of the opportunity provided by the capitalist production processes, which are already the "natural" forms of working class activities and organization. Here the workers are "organized" as a class against the capitalist class; the place of exploitation is also the vehicle for their resistance to capitalist oppression. "Organized" by their rulers in factories, industries, armies, or in separate working-class districts, workers turned these "organizations" into their own, by utilizing them for their independent endeavors and under their own leadership. The latter was elected from their midst, and was at all times recallable. Thus the historically evolved divergence between the institutionalized labor organizations and the working class at large was done away with, and the apparent contradiction between organization and spontaneity resolved. Until now, to be sure, workers' councils have found their limitations in the limits of spontaneous actions under unfavorable conditions. They have been the sporadic expression of sporadic movements, as yet incapable of turning their potential for becoming the organizational structure of non-exploitative relations into reality. The basic difference between the council movement and the traditional labor organizations is, that whereas the latter lose their functions in a decaying capitalism and have nothing to contribute to the construction of socialism, the former not only become the only form of effective working-class actions regardless of the state in which capitalism finds itself, but are, at the same time, the pre-figuration of the organizational structure of socialist society.

JJL: *Do you see any similarity (in intent, result, or form) between council communism and present day workers' struggles in the US and Europe? Do you think any recent events indicate a significant and qualitative evolution towards a different type of society? Or, do you think the recent outstanding struggles (May '68, Lordstown, LIP etc) are just more of the same old programmed modernizations of capitalism?*

PM: There is, without doubt, a connection between the recent expressions of self-determined working-class actions, such as the French movement of May 1968, the occupation of LIP, but also the rebellions of the workers in East-Germany, Poland and even Russia, and the "instinctive" as well as conscious recognition that the forms of action represented by the concept and the reality of workers' councils is the necessary requirement of workers' struggles under prevailing conditions. Even unofficial strikes in the USA may be regarded as a first expression of a developing class consciousness, directing itself not only against the obvious capitalist enemy but also against the capitalistically-integrated official labor movement. However, traditions are still powerful and the institutions nourished by them constitute part of capitalism's resilience. It seems to require far more catastrophic situations than those recently experienced to release the full power of spontaneous mass actions, overrunning not just the defenders of capitalism but the system itself. In so far as recent and forthcoming workers' struggles escaped or escape the influence and control of the capitalist authorities, which the leadership of the official labor movement also belong to, they were and will be movements that cannot be integrated into the capitalist system and therefore constitute real revolutionary movements.

JJL: *If new general strikes (such as May '68) or other mass revolutionary movements come up, do you think they can evolve towards workers' councils, away from parties and unions? How? What do you think can be done to get rid of parties and unions which prohibit self-organization and direct democracy?*

PM: In a general crisis of capitalism there is always the possibility that the social movements resulting from it will go beyond the obstacles placed in their way by traditional forms of economic and political activity, and proceed in accordance with new necessities which include the need for effective forms of organization. However, just as capitalism will not abdicate of its own accord, the existing labor organizations will try their utmost to keep control of these social movements and direct them towards goals favorable to themselves. In the "best" case—should they fail to help secure the status quo—they will direct a possible revolutionary upheaval into state-capitalist channels, in order to maintain social production relations which would not only allow for their further existence, but would also transform their organizations into instrumentalities of a modified capitalist system, and their bureaucracies into a new ruling class. In brief, if anything at all, they would attempt to turn a potential socialist revolution into a state-capitalist revolution, with results such as are represented by the so-called socialist nations. They may succeed in such endeavors, however that is the most pressing reason for both advocating and trying to set up workers' councils in any revolutionary situation, and for attempting to concentrate in them all the power needed for working self-determination. Social control through workers' councils is one future possibility among others. The probability of its realization is perhaps less than the probability of a state capitalist transformation. But as the latter is not a solution to the problem inherent in social exploitation relations, a possible state-capitalist revolution would merely postpone, but not eliminate, the need for another revolution with socialism as its goal.

JJL: *Do you think councils are still, today, the basic pattern for a communist society or must they be updated to fit present day conditions?*

PM: Communism will be a system of workers' councils or it will not exist. The "association of free and equal producers," which determines its own production and distribution, is thinkable only as a system of self-determination at the point of production, and the absence of any other authority than the collective will of the producers themselves. It means the end of the state, or any state-based system of exploitation. It must be a planned production, without the intervention of exchange relations and the vicissitudes of the market system. The regulation of the social character of production must discard fetishistic value and price relations, and must be carried out in terms of the economy of time, with direct labor-time as a measure of calculation, where calculation is still required. A presupposition of such a development is the absence of a central government with political power of its own. The central institutions of the council system are mere enterprises among others, without a special apparatus to assert their will outside the consent of other councils or of other enterprises. The structure of the system must be such as to combine central regulation with the self-determination of the producers. Whereas, under the conditions of underdevelopment which faced the first councils after a successful political revolution (the reference is to Russia in 1917, it was practically impossible to realize a communist society based on workers' councils; the prevailing conditions in the developed capitalist nations allow much more for the actualization of socialism via the council system. It is precisely the more advanced form of capitalism, with its advanced technology, high productivity, and network of communication, which offers a material base for the establishment of communism based on a system of workers' councils. The council idea is not a thing of the past, but the most realistic proposition for the establishment of a socialist society. Nothing which has evolved during the last decades has robbed it of its feasibility; on the contrary, it has merely substantiated the non-utopian character of the workers' councils and the probability of the emergence of a truly communist society.

Notes on J.J. Lebel and Paul Mattick Interview

1. This interview was given in February 1975. It was never published. Initially it was aimed to be part of a radio program on workers' councils which never went on the air. A French translation was added to the second French edition of Workers' Councils (Spartacus, November 1982). Reprinted from Vol. 4 "Workers Councils"–Anton Pannekoek (ECHANGES), where it appeared as an appendix

WORKERS' COUNCILS

PREFACE

Anton Pannekoek's original Dutch text was undertaken in 1941 during the occupation of Holland by the Germans, and completed after the War, in 1946. It was published in Dutch in 1946 and then translated by the author, with some modifications and additions, for serial publication from 1947–49 in the Australian monthly *Southern Advocate for Workers' Councils*. The book form of the English language version was used as the basis of the present text, although some minor corrections have been made to improve readability. I wish to thank Rachael Rakes, Jeff Rector, John Yates and the members of the AK Press for their devotion and excellent work.

Robert F. Barsky

I. The Task

1. LABOR

In the present and coming times, now that Europe is devastated and mankind is impoverished by world war, it impends upon the workers of the world to organize industry, in order to free themselves from want and exploitation. It will be their task to take into their own hands the management of the production of goods. To accomplish this great and difficult work, it will be necessary to fully recognize the present character of labor. The better their knowledge of society and of the position of labor in it, the less difficulties, disappointments and setbacks they will encounter in this striving.

The basis of society is the production of all goods necessary to life. This production, for the most important part, takes place by means of highly developed technics in large factories and plants by complicated machines. This development of technics, from small tools that could be handled by one man, to big machines handled by large collectives of workers of different kind, took place in the last centuries. Though small tools are still used as accessories, and small shops are still numerous, they hardly play a role in the bulk of the production.

Each factory is an organization carefully adapted to its aims; an organization of dead as well as of living forces, of instruments and workers. The forms and the character of this organization are determined by the aims it has to serve. What are these aims?

In the present time, production is dominated by capital. The capitalist, possessor of money, founded the factory, bought the machines and the raw materials, hires the workers and makes them produce goods that can be sold. That is, he buys the labor power of the workers, to be spent in their daily task, and he pays to them its value, the wages by which they can procure what they need to live and to continually restore their labor power. The value a worker creates in his daily work in adding it to the value of the raw materials, is larger than what he needs for his living and receives for his labor power. The difference that the capitalist gets in his hands when the product is sold, the surplus-value, forms his profit, which, in so far as it is not consumed, is accumulated into new capital. The labor power of the working class thus may be compared with an ore mine, that in exploitation gives out a produce exceeding the cost bestowed on it. Hence the term exploitation of labor by capital. Capital itself is the product of labor; its bulk is accumulated surplus-value.

Capital is master of production; it has the factory, the machines, the produced goods; the workers' work at its command; its aims dominate the work and determine the character of the organization. The aim of capital is to make profit. The capitalist is not driven by the desire to provide his fellow-men with the necessities of life; he is driven by the necessity of making money. If he has a shoe factory he is not animated by compassion for the painful feet of other people; he is animated by the knowledge that his enterprise must yield profit and that he will go bankrupt if his profits are insufficient. Of course, the normal way to make profit is to produce goods that can be sold at a good price, and they can be sold, normally, only when they are necessary and practical consumption-goods for the buyers. So the shoemaker, to produce profits for himself, has to produce well-fitting shoes, better or cheaper shoes than others make. Thus, normally, capitalist production succeeds in what should be the aim of production, to provide mankind with its life necessities. But the many cases, where it is more profitable to produce superfluous luxuries for the rich or trash for the poor, or to sell the whole plant to a competitor who may close it, show that the primary object of present production is profit for the capital.

This object determines the character of the organization of the work in the shop. First it establishes the command by one absolute master. If he is the owner himself, he has to take care that he does not lose his capital; on the contrary he must increase it. His interest dominates the work; the workers are his "hands," and they have to obey. It determines his part and his function in the work. Should the workers complain of their long hours and fatiguing work, he points to his task and his solicitudes that keep him busy till late in the night after they have gone home without concerning themselves any more. He forgets to tell, what he hardly understands himself, that all his often strenuous work, all his worry that keeps him awake at night, serves only the profit, not the production itself. It deals with the problems of how to sell his products, how to outrival his competitors, how to bring the largest possible part of the total surplus-value, into his own coffers. His work is not a productive work; his exertions in fighting his competitors are useless for society. But he is the master and his aims direct the shop.

If he is an appointed director he knows that he is appointed to produce profit for the shareholders. If he does not manage to do so, he is dismissed and replaced by another man. Of course, he must be a good expert, he must understand the technics of his branch, to be able to direct the work of production. But still more he must be expert in profit-making. In the first place he must understand the technics of increasing the net-profit, by finding out how to produce at least cost, how to sell with most success and how to beat his rivals. This every director knows. It determines the management or business. It also determines the organization within the shop.

The organization of the production within the shop is conducted along two lines, of technical and of commercial organization. The rapid development of technics in the last century, based upon a wonderful growth of science, has improved the methods of work in every branch. Better technics is the best weapon in competition, because it secures extra profit at the cost of the rivals. This development increased the productivity of labor, it made the goods for use and consumption cheaper, more abundant and more varied, it increased the means of comfort, and, by lowering the cost of living, i.e., the value of labor power, enormously raised the profit of capital. This high stage of technical development brought into the factory a rapidly increasing number of experts, engineers, chemists, physicists, well versed by their training at universities and laboratories in science. They are necessary to direct the intricate technical processes, and to improve them by regular application of new scientific discoveries. Under their supervision act skilled technicians and workers. So the technical organization shows a carefully regulated collaboration of various kinds of workers, a small number of university-trained specialists, a larger number of qualified professionals and skilled workers, besides a great mass of unskilled workers to do the manual work. Their combined efforts are needed to run the machines and to produce the goods.

The commercial organization has to conduct the sale of the product. It studies markets and prices, it advertises, it trains agents to stimulate buying. It includes the so-called scientific management, to cut down costs by distributing men and means; it devises incentives to stimulate the workers to more strenuous efforts; it turns advertising into a kind of science taught even at universities. It is not less, it is even more important than technics to the capitalist masters; it is the chief weapon in their mutual fight. From the view-point of providing society with its life necessities, however, it is an entirely useless waste of capacities.

But also the forms of technical organization are determined by the same motive of profit. Hence the strict limitation of the better paid scientific experts to a small number, combined with a mass of cheap unskilled labor. Hence the structure of society at large, with its low pay and poor education for the masses, with its higher pay—so much as higher education demands for the constant filling of the ranks—for a scientifically trained minority.

These technical officials have not only the care of the technical processes of production. Under capitalism they have also to act as taskmasters of the workers. Because under capitalism production of goods is inseparably connected with production of profit, both being one and the same action, the two characters of the shop-officials, of a scientific leader of production and of a commanding helper of exploitation, are intimately combined. So their position is ambiguous. On the one hand they are the collaborators of the manual workers, by their scientific knowledge directing the process of transformation of the materials, by their skill increasing the profits, they also are exploited by capital. On the other hand they are the underlings of capital, appointed to hustle the workers and to assist the capitalist in exploiting them.

It may seem that not everywhere the workers are thus exploited by capital. In public-utility enterprises, for instance, or in co-operative factories. Even if we leave aside the fact that the former, by their profit, often must contribute to the public funds, thus relieving the taxes of the propertied class, the difference with other business is not essential. As a rule co-operatives have to compete with private enterprises; and public utilities are controlled by the capitalist public by attentive criticism. The usually borrowed capital needed in the business demands its interest, out of the profits. As in other enterprises there is the personal command of a director and the forcing up of the tempo of the work. There is the same exploitation as in every capitalist enterprise. There may be a difference in degree; part of what otherwise is profit may be used to increase the wages and to improve the conditions of labor. But a limit is soon reached. In this respect they may be compared with private model enterprises where sensible broad-minded directors try to attach the workers by better treatment, by giving them the impression of a privileged position, and so are rewarded by a better output and increased profit. But it is out of the question that the workers here, or in public utilities or co-operatives, should consider themselves as servants of a community, to which to devote all their energy. Directors and workers are living in the social surroundings and the feelings of their respective classes. Labor has here the same capitalist character as elsewhere; it constitutes its deeper essential nature under the superficial differences of somewhat better or worse conditions.

Labor under capitalism in its essential nature is a system of squeezing. The workers must be driven to the utmost exertion of their powers, either by hard constraint or by the kinder arts of persuasion. Capital itself is in a constraint; if it cannot compete, if the profits are inadequate, the business will collapse. Against this pressure the workers defend themselves by a continual instinctive resistance. If not, if they willingly should give way, more than their daily labor power would be taken from them. It would be an encroaching upon their funds of bodily power, their vital power would be exhausted before its time, as to some extent is the case now; degeneration, annihilation of health and strength, of themselves and their offspring, would be the result. So resist they must. Thus every shop, every enterprise, even outside the times of sharp conflict, of strikes or wage reductions, is the scene of a constant silent war, of a perpetual struggle, of pressure and counter-pressure. Rising and falling under its influence, a certain norm of wages, hours and tempo of labor establishes itself, keeping them just at the limit of what is tolerable and intolerable (if intolerable the total of production is effected). Hence the two classes, workers and capitalists, while having to put up with each other in the daily course of work, in deepest essence, by their opposite interests, are implacable foes, living when not fighting, in a land of armed peace.

Labor in itself is not repulsive. Labor for the supplying of his needs is a necessity imposed on man by nature. Like all other living beings, man has to exert his forces to provide for his food. Nature has given them bodily organs and mental powers, muscles, nerves and brains, to conform to this necessity. Their wants and their means are harmoniously adapted to one another in the regular living of their life. So labor, as the normal use of their limbs and capacities, is a normal impulse for man and animal alike. In the necessity of providing food and shelter there is, to be sure, an element of constraint. Free spontaneousness in the use of muscles and nerves, all in their turn, in following every whim, in work or play, lies at the bottom of human nature. The constraint of his needs compels man to regular work, to suppression of the impulse of the moment, to exertion of his powers, to patient perseverance and self-restraint. But this self-restraint, necessary as it is for the preservation of oneself, of the family, of the community, affords the satisfaction of vanquishing impediments in himself or the surrounding world, and gives the proud feeling of reaching self-imposed aims. Fixed by its social character, by practice and custom in family, tribe or village, the habit of regular work grows into a new nature itself, into a natural mode of life, a harmonious unity of needs and powers, of duties and disposition. Thus in farming the surrounding nature is transformed into a safe home through a lifelong heavy or placid toil. Thus in every people, each in its individual way, the old handicraft gave to the artisans the joy of applying their skill and fantasy in the making of good and beautiful things for use.

All this has perished since capital became master of labor. In production for the market, for sale, the goods are commodities which besides their utility for the buyer, have exchange-value, embodying the labor implemented; this exchange-value determines the money they bring. Formerly a worker in moderate hours—leaving room for occasional strong exertion—could produce enough for his living. But the profit of capital consists in what the worker can produce in surplus to his living. The more value he produces and the less the value of what he consumes, the larger is the surplus-value seized by capital. Hence his life-necessities are reduced, his standard of life is lowered as much as possible, his hours are increased, the tempo of his work is accelerated. Now labor loses entirely its old character of pleasant use of body and limbs. Now labor turns into a curse and an outrage. And this remains its true character, however mitigated by social laws and by trade-union action, both results of the desperate resistance of the workers against their unbearable degradation. What they may attain is to turn capitalism from a rude abuse into a normal exploitation. Still then labor, being labor under capitalism, keeps its innermost character of inhuman toil: the workers compelled by the threat of hunger to strain their forces at foreign command, for foreign profit, without genuine interest, in the monotonous fabrication of uninteresting or bad things, driven to the utmost of what the overworked body can sustain, are used up at an early age. Ignorant economists, unacquainted with the nature of capitalism, seeing the strong aversion of the workers from their work, conclude that productive work, by its very nature, is repulsive to man, and must be imposed on unwilling mankind by strong means of constraint.

Of course, this character of their work is not always consciously felt by the workers. Sometimes the original nature of work, as an impulsive eagerness of action, giving contentment, asserts itself. Especially in young people, kept ignorant of capitalism and full of ambition to show their capacities as first-rate workers, feeling themselves moreover possessor of an inexhaustible labor-power. Capitalism has its well-advised ways of exploiting this disposition. Afterwards, with the growing solicitudes and duties for the family, the worker feels caught between the pressure of the constraint and the limit of his powers, as in tightening fetters he is unable to throw off. And at last, feeling his forces decay at an age that for middle-class man is the time of full and matured power, he has to suffer exploitation in tacit resignation, in continuous fear of being thrown away as a worn-out tool.

Bad and damnable as work under capitalism may be, still worse is the lack of work. Like every commodity, labor-power sometimes finds no buyer. The problematic liberty of the worker to choose his master goes hand in hand with the liberty of the capitalist to engage or to dismiss his workers. In the continuous development of capitalism, in the founding of new enterprises and the decline or collapse of old ones, the workers are driven to and fro, are accumulated here, dismissed there. So they must consider it good luck even, when they are allowed to let themselves be exploited. Then they perceive that they are at the mercy of capital. That only with the consent of the masters they have access to the machines that wait for their handling.

Unemployment is the worst scourge of the working class under capitalism. It is inherent in capitalism. As an ever returning feature it accompanies the periodical crises and depressions, which during the entire reign of capitalism ravaged society at regular intervals. They are a consequence of the anarchy of capitalist production. Each capitalist as an independent master of his enterprise is free to manage it at his will, to produce what he thinks profitable or to close the shop when profits are failing. Contrary to the careful organization within the factory there is a complete lack of organization in the totality of social production. The rapid increase of capital through the accumulated profits, the necessity to find profits also for the new capital, urges a rapid increase of production flooding the market with unsaleable goods. Then comes the collapse, reducing not only the profits and destroying the superfluous capital, but also turning the accumulated hosts of workers out of the factories, throwing them upon their own resources or on meagre charity. Then wages are lowered, strikes are ineffective, the mass of the unemployed presses as a heavy weight upon the working conditions. What has been gained by hard fight in times of prosperity is often lost in times of depression. Unemployment was always the chief impediment to a continuous raising of the life standard of the working class.

There have been economists alleging that by the modern development of big business this pernicious alternation of crises and prosperity would disappear. They expected that cartels and trusts, monopolizing as they do large branches of industry, would bring a certain amount of organization into the anarchy of production and smooth its irregularities. They did not take into account that the primary cause, the yearning for profit, remains, driving the organized groups into a fiercer competition, now with mightier forces. The incapacity of modern capitalism to cope with its anarchy was shown in a grim light by the world crisis of 1930. During a number of long years production seemed to have definitely collapsed. Over the whole world millions of workers, of farmers, even of intellectuals were reduced to living on the doles, which the governments by necessity, had to provide: From this crisis of production the present war crisis took its origin.

In this crisis the true character of capitalism and the impossibility to maintain it, was shown to mankind as in a searchlight. There were the millions of people lacking the means to provide for their life necessities. There were the millions of workers with strong arms, eager to work; there were the machines in thousands of shops, ready to whirl and to produce an abundance of goods. But it was not allowed. The capitalist ownership of the means of production stood between the workers and the machines. This ownership, affirmed if necessary by the power of police and State, forbade the workers to touch the machines and to produce all that they themselves and society needed for their existence. The machines had to stand and rust, the workers had to hang around and suffer want. Why? Because capitalism is unable to manage the mighty technical and productive powers of mankind to conform to their original aim, to provide for the needs of society.

To be sure, capitalism now is trying to introduce some sort of organization and planned production. Its insatiable profit-hunger cannot be satisfied within the old realms; it is driven to expand over the world, to seize the riches, to open the markets, to subject the peoples of other continents. In a fierce competition each of the capitalist groups must try to conquer or to keep to themselves the richest portions of the world. Whereas the capitalist class in England, France, Holland made easy profits by the exploitation of rich colonies, conquered in former wars, German capitalism with its energy, its capacities, its rapid development, that had come too late in the division of the colonial world, could only get its share by striving for world-power, by preparing for world-war. It had to be the aggressor, the others were the defenders. So it was the first to put into action and to organize all the powers of society for this purpose; and then the others had to follow its example.

In this struggle for life between the big capitalist powers the inefficiency of private capitalism could no longer be allowed to persist. Unemployment now was a foolish, nay, a criminal waste of badly needed manpower. A strict and careful organization had to secure the full use of all the labor power and the fighting power of the nation. Now the untenability of capitalism showed itself just as grimly from another side. Unemployment was now turned into its opposite, into compulsory labor. Compulsory toil and fighting at the frontiers where the millions of strong young men, by the most refined means of destruction mutilate, kill, exterminate, "wipe out" each other, for the world-power of their capitalist masters. Compulsory labor in the factories where all the rest, women and children included, are assiduously producing ever more of these engines of murder; whereas the production of the life necessities is constricted to the utmost minimum. Shortage and want in everything needed for life and the falling back to the poorest and ugliest barbarism is the outcome of the highest development of science and technics, is the glorious fruit of the thinking and working of so many generations! Why? Because notwithstanding all delusive talk about community and fellowship, organized capitalism, too, is unable to handle the rich productive powers of mankind to their true purpose, using them instead for destruction.

Thus the working class is confronted with the necessity of itself taking the production in hand. The mastery over the machines, over the means of production, must be taken out of the unworthy hands that abuse them. This is the common cause of all producers, of all who do the real productive work in society, the workers, the technicians, the farmers. But it is the workers, chief and permanent sufferers from the capitalist system, and moreover, majority of the population, on whom it impends to free themselves and the world from this scourge. They must manage the means of production. They must be masters of the factories, masters of their own labor, to conduct it at their own mill. Then the machines will be put to their true use, the production of abundance of goods, to provide for the life necessities of all.

This is the task of the workers in the days to come. This is the only road to freedom, this is the revolution for which society is ripening. By such a revolution the character of production is entirely reversed; new principles will form the basis of society. First, because the exploitation ceases. The produce of the common labor will belong to all those who take part in the work. No surplus-value to capital any more; ended is the claim of superfluous capitalists to a part of the produce.

More important still than the cessation of their share in the produce is the cessation of their command over the production. Once the workers are masters over the shops, the capitalists lose their power of leaving in disuse the machines, these riches of mankind, precious product of the mental and manual exertion of so many generations of workers and thinkers. With the capitalists disappears their power to dictate what superfluous luxuries or what rubbish shall be produced. When the workers have command over the machines they will apply them for the production of all that the life of society requires.

This will be possible only by combining all the factories, as the separate members of one body, into a well organized system of production. The connection that under capitalism is the fortuitous outcome of blind competition and marketing, depending on purchase and sale, is then the object of conscious planning. Then, instead of the partial and imperfect attempts at organization of modern capitalism, that only lead to fiercer fight and destruction, comes the perfect organization of production, growing into a world-wide system of collaboration. For the producing classes cannot be competitors, only collaborators.

These three characteristics of the new production mean a new world. The cessation of the profit for capital, the cessation of unemployment of machines and men, the conscious adequate regulation of production, the increase of the produce through efficient organization, give to each worker a larger quantity of product with less labor. Now the way is opened for a further development of productivity. By the application of all technical progress the produce will increase in such a degree that abundance for all will be joined to the disappearance of toil.

2. LAW AND PROPERTY

Such a change in the system of labor implies a change of Law. Not, of course, that new laws must first be enacted by Parliament or Congress. It concerns changes in the depth of society [in the customs and practice of society], far beyond the reach of such temporary things as Parliamentary acts. It relates to the fundamental laws, not of one country only, but of human society, founded on man's convictions of Right and Justice.

These laws are not immutable. To be sure, the ruling classes at all times have tried to perpetuate the existing Law by proclaiming that it is based on nature, founded on the eternal rights of man, or sanctified by religion. This, for the sake of upholding their prerogatives and dooming the exploited classes to perpetual slavery. Historical evidence, on the contrary, shows that law continually changed in line with the changing feelings of right and wrong.

The sense of right and wrong, the consciousness of justice in men, is not accidental. It grows up, irresistibly, by nature, out of what they experience as the fundamental conditions of their life. Society must live; so the relations of men must be regulated in such a way—it is this that law provides for—that the production of life-necessities may go on unimpeded. Right is what is essentially good and necessary for life. Not only useful for the moment, but needed generally; not for the life of single individuals, but for people at large, for the community; not for personal or temporal interests, but for the common and lasting weal. If the life-conditions change, if the system of production develops into new forms, the relations between men change, their feeling of what is right or wrong changes with them, and the law has to be altered.

This is seen most clearly in the laws regulating the right of property. In the original savage and barbarian state the land was considered as belonging to the tribe that lived on it, hunting or pasturing. Expressed in our terms, we should say that the land was common property of the tribe that used it for its living and defended it against other tribes. The self-made weapons and tools were accessories of the individual, hence were a kind of private property, though not in our conscious and exclusive sense of this word, in consequence of the strong mutual bonds amongst the tribesmen. Not laws, but use and custom regulated their mutual relations. Such primitive peoples, even agricultural peoples in later times (as the Russian peasants of before 1860) could not conceive the idea of private ownership of a tract of land, just as we cannot conceive the idea of private ownership of a quantum of air.

These regulations had to change when the tribes settled and expanded, cleared the forests and dissolved into separate individuals (i.e., families), each working a separate lot. They changed still more when handicraft separated from agriculture, when from the casual work of all, it became the continual work of some; when the products became commodities, to be sold in regular commerce and to be consumed by others than the producers. It is quite natural that the farmer who worked a piece of land, who improved it, who did his work at his own will, without interference from others, had the free disposal of the land and the tools; that the produce was his; that land and produce were his property. Restrictions might be needed for defense, in mediaeval times, in the form of possible feudal obligations. It is quite natural that the artisan, as the only one who handled his tools, had the exclusive disposal of them, as well as of the things he made; that he was the sole owner.

Thus private ownership became the fundamental law of a society founded on small-scale working-units. Without being expressly formulated it was felt as a necessary right that whoever exclusively handled the tools, the land, the product, must be master of them, must have the free disposal of them. Private ownership of the means of production belongs as its necessary juridical attribute to small trade.

It remained so, when capitalism came to be master of industry. It was even more consciously expressed, and the French Revolution proclaimed liberty,

equality and property the fundamental Rights of the citizen. It was private ownership of the means of production simply applied, when, instead of some
apprentices, the master-craftsman hired a larger number of servants to assist
him, to work with his tools and to make products for him to sell. By means of
exploiting the labor-power of the workers, the factories and machines, as private property of the capitalist, became the source of an immense and ever
growing increase of capital. Here private ownership performed a new function
in society. As capitalist ownership it ascertained power and increasing wealth to
the new ruling class, the capitalists, and enabled them strongly to develop the
productivity of labor and to expand their rule over the earth. So this juridical
institute, notwithstanding the degradation and misery of the exploited workers,
was felt as a good and beneficent, even necessary institution, promising an
unlimited progress of society.

This development, however, gradually changed the inner character of the
social system. And thereby again the function of private ownership changed.
With the joint-stock companies the twofold character of the capitalist facto-
ry-owner, that of directing the production and that of pocketing the
surplus-value, is splitting up. Labor and property, in olden times intimately
connected, are now separated. Owners are the shareholders, living outside the
process of production, idling in distant country-houses and maybe gambling at
the exchange. A shareholder has no direct connection with the work. His property does not consist in tools for him to work with; his property consists simply in pieces of paper, in shares of enterprises of which he does not even know
the whereabouts. His function in society is that of a parasite. His ownership
does not mean that he commands and directs the machines; this is the sole right
of the director. It means only that he may claim a certain amount of money
without having to work for it. The property in hand, his shares, are certificates
showing his right–guaranteed by law and government, by courts and police–to
participate in the profits; titles of companionship in that large Society for
Exploitation of the World, that is capitalism.

The work in the factories goes on quite apart from the shareholders. Here
the director and the staff have the care all day, to regulate, to run about, to
think of everything, the workers are working and toiling from morning till
evening, hurried and abused. Everybody has to exert himself to the utmost to
render the output as large as possible. But the product of their common work
is not for those who did the work. Just as in olden times burgesses were ran-
sacked by gangs of wayside robbers, so now people entirely foreign to the production come forward and, on the credit of their papers (as registered owners
of share scrip), seize the chief part of the produce. Not violently; without having to move as much as a finger they find it put on their banking account, automatically. Only a poor wage or a moderate salary is left for those who together did the work of production; all the rest is dividend taken by the sharehold-

ers. Is this madness? It is the new function of private ownership of the means of production. It is simply the praxis of old inherited law, applied to the new forms of labor to which it does no longer fit.

Here we see how the social function of a juridical institute, in consequence of the gradual change of the forms of production, turns into the very reverse of its original aim. Private ownership, originally a means to give everybody the possibility of productive work, now has turned into the means to prevent the workers from the free use of the instruments of production. Originally a means to ascertain to the workers the fruits of their labor, it now turned into a means to deprive the workers of the fruits of their labor, for the benefit of a class of useless parasites.

How is it, then, that such obsolete law still holds sway over society? First, because the numerous middle-class and small-business people, the farmer and independent artisans cling to it, in the belief that it assures them their small property and their living; but with the result that often, with their mortgaged holdings, they are the victims of usury and bank-capital. When saying: I am my own master, they mean: I have not to obey a foreign master; community in work as collaborating equals lies far outside their imagination. Secondly and chiefly, however, because the power of the State, with its police and military force, upholds old law for the benefit of the ruling class, the capitalists.

In the working class, now, the consciousness of this contradiction is arising as a new sense of Right and Justice. The old right, through the development of small trade into big business, has turned into wrong, and it is felt as a wrong. It contradicts the obvious rule that those who do the work and handle the equipment must dispose of it in order to arrange and execute the work in the best way. The small tool, the small lot could be handled and worked by a single person with his family. So that person had the disposal of it, was the owner. The big machines, the factories, the large enterprises can only be handled and worked by an organized body of workers, a community of collaborating forces. So this body, the community, must have the disposal of it, in order to arrange the work according to their common will. This common ownership does not mean an ownership in the old sense of the word, as the right of using or misusing at will. Each enterprise is, but part, the total productive apparatus of society; so the right of each body or community of producers is limited by the superior right of society, and has to be carried out in regular connection with the others.

Common ownership must not be confounded with public ownership. In public ownership, often advocated by notable social reformers, the State or another political body is master of the production. The workers are not masters of their work, they are commanded by the State officials, who are leading and directing the production. Whatever may be the conditions of labor, however human and considerate the treatment, the fundamental fact is that not the workers themselves, but the officials dispose of the means of production, dispose of the product, manage the entire process, decide what part of the produce shall be reserved for innovations, for wear, for improvements, for social expenses, what part has to fall to the workers, what part to themselves. In short, the workers still receive wages, a share of the product determined by the masters. Under public ownership of the means of production, the workers are still subjected to and exploited by a ruling class. Public ownership is a middle-class program of a modernized and disguised form of capitalism. Common ownership by the producers can be the only goal of the working class.

Thus the revolution of the system of production is intimately bound up with a revolution of Law. It is based on a change in the deepest convictions of Right and Justice. Each production-system consists of the application of a certain technique, combined with a certain Law regulating the relations of men in their work, fixing their rights and duties. The technics of small tools combined with private ownership means a society of free and equal competing small producers. The technics of big machines combined with private ownership, means capitalism. The technics of big machines, combined with common ownership, means a free collaborating humanity. Thus capitalism is an intermediate system, a transitional form resulting from the application of the old Law to the new technics. While the technical development enormously increased the powers of man, the inherited law that regulated the use of these powers subsisted nearly unchanged. No wonder that it proved inadequate, and that society fell to such distress. This is the deepest sense of the present world crisis. Mankind simply neglected in time to adapt its old law to its new technical powers. Therefore it now suffers ruin and destruction.

Technique is a given power. To be sure, its rapid development is the work of man, the natural result of thinking over the work, of experience and experiment, of exertion and competition. But once established, its application is automatic, outside our free choice, imposed like a given force of nature. We cannot go back, as poets have wished, to the general use of the small tools of our forefathers. Law, on the other hand, must be instituted by man with conscious design. Such as it is established, it determines freedom or slavery of man towards man and towards his technical equipment.

When inherited law, in consequence of the silent growth of technics, has turned into a means of exploitation and oppression, it becomes an object of contest between the social classes, the exploiting and the exploited class. So long as the exploited class dutifully acknowledges existing law as Right and Justice, so long its exploitation remains lawful and unchallenged. When then gradually in the masses arises a growing consciousness of their exploitation, at the same time new conceptions of Right awaken in them. With the growing feeling that existing law is contrary of justice, their will is roused to change it and to make their convictions of right and justice the law of society. This means that the sense of being wronged is not sufficient. Only when in great masses of the workers this sense grows into such clear and deep convictions of Right that they permeate the entire being, filling it with a firm determination and a fiery enthusiasm, they will be able to develop the powers needed for revolving the social structure. Even then this will be only the preliminary condition. A heavy and lengthy struggle to overcome the resistance of the capitalist class defending its rule with the utmost power, will be needed to establish the new order.

3. SHOP ORGANIZATION

Thus the idea of their common ownership of the means of production is beginning to take hold of the minds of the workers. Once they feel the new order, their own mastery over labor to be a matter of necessity and of justice, all their thoughts and all their actions will be consecrated to its realization. They know that it cannot be done at once; a long period of fight will be unavoidable. To break the stubborn resistance of the ruling classes the workers will have to exert their utmost forces. All the powers of mind and character, of organization and knowledge, which they are capable of mustering must be developed. And first of all they have to make clear to themselves what it is they aim at, what this new order means.

Man, when he has to do a work, first conceives it in his mind as a plan, as a more or less conscious design. This distinguishes the actions of man from the instinctive actions of animals. This also holds, in principle, for the common struggles, the revolutionary action of social classes. Not entirely, to be sure; there is a great deal of unpremeditated spontaneous impulse in their outbursts of passionate revolt. The fighting workers are not an army conducted after a neatly conceived plan of action by a staff of able leaders. They are a people gradually rising out of submissiveness and ignorance, gradually coming to con-sciousness of their exploitation, again and again driven to fight for better liv-ing conditions, by degrees developing their powers. New feelings spring up in their hearts, new thoughts arise in their heads, how the world might and should be. New wishes, new ideals, new aims fill their mind and direct their will and action. Their aims gradually take a more concise shape. From the simple strife for better working conditions, in the beginning, they grow into the idea of a fundamental reorganization of society. For several generations already the ideal of a world without exploitation and oppression has taken hold of the minds of the workers. Nowadays the conception of the workers themselves master of the means of production, themselves directing their labor, arises ever more strong-ly in their minds.

This new organization of labor we have to investigate and to clarify to our-selves and to one another, devoting to it the best powers of our mind. We can-not devise it as a fantasy; we derive it from the real conditions and needs of present work and present workers. It cannot, of course, be depicted in detail; we do not know the future conditions that will determine its precise forms. Those forms will take shape in the minds of the workers then facing the task. We must content ourselves for the present to trace the general outlines only, the leading ideas that will direct the actions of the working class. They will be as the guiding stars that in all the vicissitudes of victory and adversity in fight, of success and failure in organization, keep the eyes steadily directed towards the great goal. They must be elucidated not by minute descriptions of detail, but chiefly by comparing the principles of the new world with the known forms of existing organizations.

When the workers seize the factories to organize the work an immensity of new and difficult problems arises before them. But they dispose of an immensity of new powers also. A new system of production never is an artificial structure erected at will. It arises as an irresistible process of nature, as a convulsion moving society in its deepest entrails, evoking the mightiest forces and passions in man. It is the result of a tenacious and probably long class struggle. The forces required for construction can develop and grow up in this fight only.

What are the foundations of the new society? They are the social forces of fellowship and solidarity, of discipline and enthusiasm, the moral forces of self-sacrifice and devotion to the community, the spiritual forces of knowledge, of courage and perseverance, the firm organization that binds all these forces into a unity of purpose, all of them are the outcome of the class fight. They cannot purposely be prepared in advance. Their first traces arise spontaneously in the workers out of their common exploitation; and then they grow incessantly through the necessities of the fight, under the influence of experience and of mutual inducement and instruction. They must grow because their fullness brings victory, their deficiency defeat. But even after a success in fighting attempts at new construction must fail, so long as the social forces are insufficient, so long as the new principles do not entirely occupy the workers' hearts and minds. And in that case, since mankind must live, since production must go on, other powers, powers of constraint, dominating and suppressing forces, will take the production in their hands. So the fight has to be taken up ever anew, till the social forces in the working class have reached such a height as to render them capable of being the self-governing masters of society.

The great task of the workers is the organization of production on a new basis. It has to begin with the organization within the shop. Capitalism, too, had a carefully planned shop-organization; but the principles of the new organization are entirely different. The technical basis is the same in both cases; it is the discipline of work imposed by the regular running of the machines. But the social basis, the mutual relations of men, are the very opposite of what they were. Collaboration of equal companions replaces the command of masters and the obedience of servants. The sense of duty, the devotion to the community, the praise or blame of the comrades according to efforts and achievements, as incentives take the place of fear for hunger and perpetual risk of losing the job. Instead of the passive utensils and victims of capital, the workers are now the self-reliant masters and organizers of production, exalted by the proud feeling of being active co-operators in the rise of a new humanity.

The ruling body in this shop-organization is the entirety of the collaborating workers. They assemble to discuss matters and in assembly take their decisions. So everybody who takes part in the work takes part in the regulation of the common work. This is all self-evident and normal, and the method seems to be identical to that followed when under capitalism groups or unions of workers had to decide by vote on the common affairs. But there are essential differences. In the unions there was usually a division of task between the officials and the members; the officials prepared and devised the proposals and the members voted. With their fatigued bodies and weary minds the workers had to leave the conceiving to others; it was only in part or in appearance that they managed their own affairs. In the common management of the shop, however, they have to do everything themselves, the conceiving, the devising, as well as the deciding. Devotion and emulation not only play their role in everybody's work-task, but are still more essential in the common task of regulating the whole. First, because it is the all-important common cause, which they cannot leave to others. Secondly, because it deals with the mutual relations in their own work, in which they are all interested and all competent, which therefore commands their profound considerations, and which thorough discussion must settle. So it is not only the bodily, but still more the mental effort bestowed by each in his participation in the general regulation that is the object of competition and appreciation. The discussion, moreover, must bear another character than in societies and unions under capitalism, where there are always differences of personal interest. There in his deeper consciousness everybody is concerned with his own safeguarding, and discussions have to adjust and to smooth out these differences in the common action. Here, however, in the new community of labor, all the interests are essentially the same, and all thoughts are directed to the common aim of effective co-operative organization.

In great factories and plants the number of workers is too large to gather in one meeting, and far too large for a real and thorough discussion. Here decisions can only be taken in two steps, by the combined action of assemblies of the separate sections of the plant, and assemblies of central committees of delegates. The functions and the practice of these committees cannot exactly be ascertained in advance now; they are entirely new, an essential part of the new economic structure. When facing the practical needs the workers will develop the practical structure. Yet something of their character may, in general lines, be derived by comparing them with bodies and organizations known to us.

In the old capitalist world central committees of delegates are a well-known institution. We have them in parliaments, in all kinds of political bodies and in leading boards of societies and unions. They are invested with authority over their constituents, or even rule over them as their masters. As such it is in line with a social system of a working mass of people exploited and commanded by a ruling minority. Now, however, the task is to build up a form of organization for a body of collaborating free producers, actually and mentally controlling their common productive action, regulating it as equals after their own will—a quite different social system. Again in the old world we have union councils administering the current affairs after the membership, assembling at greater intervals, have fixed the general policy. What these councils then have to deal with are the trifles of the day, not vital questions. Now, however, basis and essence of life itself are concerned, the productive work, that occupies and has to occupy everybody's mind continually, as the one and greatest object of their thoughts.

The new conditions of labor make these shop-committees something quite different from everything we know in the capitalist world. They are central, but not ruling bodies, they are no governing board. The delegates constituting them have been sent by sectional assemblies with special instructions; they return to these assemblies to report on the discussion and its result, and after further deliberation the same or other delegates may go up with new instructions. In such a way they act as the connecting links between the personnels of the separate sections. Neither are the shop-committees bodies of experts to provide the directing regulations for the non-expert multitude. Of course, experts will be necessary, single or in bodies, to deal with the special technical and scientific problems. The shop-committees, however, have to deal with the daily proceedings, the mutual relations, the regulation of the work, where everybody is expert and at the same time an interested party. Among other items it is up to them to put into practice what special experts suggest. Nor are the shop-committees the responsible bodies for the good management of the whole, with the consequence that every member may shift his part of responsibility upon the impersonal collectivity. On the contrary, whereas this management is incumbent upon all in common, single persons may be consigned special tasks which to fulfill with their entire capacity, in full responsibility, whilst they carry all the honors for the achievement.

All members of the personnel, men and women, younger and older, who take part in the work, as equal companions take their part in this shop-organization, in the actual work as well as in the general regulation. Of course, there will be much difference in the personal tasks, easier or more difficult according to force and capacities, different in character according to inclination and abilities. And, of course, the differences in general insight will give a preponderance to the advice of the most intelligent. At first, when as an inheritance of capitalism there are large differences in education and training, the lack of good technical and general knowledge in the masses will be felt as a heavy deficiency. Then the small number of highly trained professional technicians and scientists must act as technical leaders, without thereby acquiring a commanding or socially leading position, without gaining privileges other than the estimation of their companions and the moral authority that always attaches to capacity and knowledge.

The organization of a shop is the conscious arrangement and connection of all the separate procedures into one whole. All these interconnections of mutually adapted operations may be represented in a well-ordered scheme, a mental image of the actual process. As such it was present in the first planning and in the later improvements and enlargements. This image must be present in the minds, of all the collaborating workers; they all must have a thorough acquaintance with what is their own common affair. Just as a map or a graph fixes and shows in a plain, to everyone intelligible picture the connections of a complicated totality, so here the state of the total enterprise, at every moment, in all its developments must be rendered visible by adequate representations. In numerical form this is done by bookkeeping. Bookkeeping registers and fixes all that happens in the process of production: what raw materials enter the shop, what machines are procured, what product they yield, how much labor is bestowed upon the products, how many hours of work are given by every worker, what products are delivered. It follows and describes the flow of materials through the process of production. It allows continually to compare, in comprehensive accounts, the results with the previous estimates in planning. So the production in the shop is made into a mentally controlled process.

Capitalist management of enterprises also knows mental control of the production. Here, too, the proceedings are represented by calculation and bookkeeping. But there is this fundamental difference that capitalist calculation is adapted entirely to the viewpoint of production of profit. It deals with prices and costs as its fundamental data; work and wages are only factors in the calculation of the resulting profit on the yearly balance account. In the new system of production, on the other hand, hours of work is the fundamental datum, whether they are still expressed, in the beginning, in money units, or in their own true form. In capitalist production calculation and bookkeeping is a secret of the direction, the office. It is no concern of the workers; they are objects of exploitation, they are only factors in the calculation of cost and produce, accessories to the machines. In the production under common ownership the bookkeeping is a public matter; it lies open to all. The workers have always a complete view of the course of the whole process. Only in this way they are able to discuss matters in the sectional assemblies and in the shop-committees, and to decide on what has to be done. The numerical results are made visible, moreover, by statistical tables, by graphs and pictures that display the situation at a glance. This information is not restricted to the personnel of the shop; it is a public matter, open to all outsiders. Every shop is only a member in the social production, and also the connection of its doings with the work outside is expressed in the book-keeping. Thus insight in the production going on in every enterprise is a piece of common knowledge for all the producers.

4. SOCIAL ORGANIZATION

Labor is a social process. Each enterprise is part of the productive body of society. The total social production is formed by their connection and collaboration. Like the cells that constitute a living organism, they cannot exist isolated and cut off from the body. So the organization of the work inside the shop is only one-half of the task of the workers. Over it, a still more important task, stands the joining of the separate enterprises, their combination into a social organization.

Whereas organization within the shop already existed under capitalism, and had only to be replaced by another, based on a new foundation, social organization of all the shops into one whole is, or was until recent years, something entirely new, without precedent. So utterly new, that during the entire nineteenth century the establishing of this organization, under the name of "socialism" was considered the main task of the working class. Capitalism consisted of an unorganized mass of independent enterprises—"a jostling crowd of separate private employers," as the program of the Labor Party expresses it—connected only by the chance relations of market and competition, resulting in bankruptcies, overproduction and crisis, unemployment and an enormous waste of materials and labor power. To abolish it, the working class should conquer the political power and use it to organize industry and production. This State-socialism was considered, then, as the first step into a new development.

In the last years the situation has changed in so far that capitalism itself has made a beginning with State-run organization. It is driven not only by the simple wish to increase productivity and profits through a rational planning of production. In Russia there was the necessity of making up for the backwardness of economic development by means of a deliberate rapid organization of industry by the bolshevist government. In Germany it was the fight for world power that drove to State control of production and State-organization of industry. This fight was so heavy a task that only by concentrating into the hands of the State the power over all productive forces could the German capitalist class have a chance of success. In national-socialist organization property and profit—though strongly cut for State needs—remain with the private capitalist, but the disposal over the means of production, their direction and management has been taken over by the State officials. By an efficient organization the unimpaired production of profits is secured for capital and for the State. This organization of the production at large is founded on the same principles as the organization within the factory, on the personal command of the general director of society, the Leader, the head of the State. Wherever Government takes control over industry, authority and constraint take the place of the former freedom of the capitalist producers. The political power of the State officials is greatly strengthened by their economic power, by their command over the means of production, the foundation of society.

The principle of the working class is in every respect the exact opposite. The organization of production by the workers is founded on free collaboration: no masters, no servants. The combination of all the enterprises into one social organization takes place after the same principle. The mechanism for this purpose must be built up by the workers.

Given the impossibility to collect the workers of all the factories into one meeting, they can only express their will by means of delegates. For such bodies of delegates in later times the name of workers' councils has come into use. Every collaborating group or personnel designates the members who in the council assemblies have to express its opinion and its wishes. These took an active part themselves in the deliberations of this group, they came to the front as able defenders of the views that carried the majority. Now they are sent as the spokesmen of the group to confront the views with those of other groups in order to come to a collective decision. Though their personal abilities play a role in persuading the colleagues and in clearing problems, their weight does not lay in their individual strength, but in the strength of the community that delegated them. What carries weight are not simple opinions but still more the will and the readiness of the group to act accordingly. Different persons will act as delegates according to the different questions raised and the forthcoming problems.

The chief problem, the basis of all the rest, is the production itself. Its organization has two sides, the establishment of general rules and norms and the practical work itself. Norms and rules must be established for the mutual relations in the work, for the rights and duties. Under capitalism the norm consisted in the command of the master, the director. Under State-capitalism it consisted in the mightier command of the Leader, the central government. Now, however, all producers are free and equal. Now in the economic field of labor the same change takes place as occur in former centuries in the political field, with the rise of the middle class. When the rule of the citizens came in place of the rule of the absolute monarch, this could not mean that for his arbitrary will the arbitrary will of everybody was substituted. It meant that, henceforward, laws established by the common will should regulate the public rights and duties. So now, in the realm of labor, the command of the master gives way to rules fixed in common, to regulate the social rights and duties, in production and consumption. To formulate them will be the first task of the workers' coun-

cils. This is not a difficult task, not a matter of profound study or serious dis-
cordance. For every worker these rules will immediately spring up in his consciousness as the natural basis of the new society: everyone's duty to take part
in the production in accordance with his forces and capacities, everyone's right
to enjoy his adequate part of the collective product.

How will the quantities of labor spent and the quantities of product to
which he is entitled be measured? In a society where the goods are produced
directly for consumption there is no market to exchange them; and no value,
as expression of the labor contained in them establishes itself automatically out
of the processes of buying and selling. Here the labor spent must be expressed
in a direct way by the number of hours. The administration keeps book
[records] of the hours of labor contained in every piece or unit quantity of
product, as well as of the hours spent by each of the workers. In the averages
over all the workers of a factory, and finally, over all the factories of the same
category, the personal differences are smoothed out and the personal results are
intercompared.

In the first times of transition when there is much devastation to be
repaired, the first problem is to build up the production apparatus and to keep
people alive. It is quite possible that the habit, imposed by war and famine, of
having the indispensable foodstuffs distributed without distinction is simply
continued. It is most probable that, in those times of reconstruction, when all
the forces must be exerted to the utmost, when, moreover, the new moral prin-
cipals of common labor are only gradually forming, the right of consumption
will be coupled to the performance of work. The old popular saying that whoever does not work shall not eat, expresses an instinctive feeling of justice. Here
it is not only the recognition that labor is the basis of all human life, but also
the proclaiming that now there is an end to capitalist exploitation and to appropriating the fruits of foreign labor by property titles of an idle class.

This does not mean, of course, that now the total produce is distributed
among the producers, according to the time given by each. Or, expressed in
another way, that every worker receives, in the form of products, just the quantity of hours of labor spent in working. A considerable part of the work must
be spent on the common property, on the perfection and enlargement of the
productive apparatus. Under capitalism part of the surplus-value served this
purpose; the capitalist had to use part of his profit, accumulated into new capital, to innovate, expand and modernize his technical equipment, in his case
driven by the necessity not to be outflanked by his competitors. So the progress
in technics took place in forms of exploitation. Now, in the new form of production, this progress is the common concern of the workers. Keeping themselves alive is the most immediate, but building the basis of future production
is the most glorious part of their task. They will have to settle what part of their
total labor shall be spent on the making of better machines and more efficient

tools, on research and experiment, for facilitating the work and improving the production.

Moreover, part of the total time and labor of society must be spent on non-productive, though necessary activities, on general administration, on education, on medical service. Children and old people will receive their share of the produce without corresponding achievements. People incapable of work must be sustained; and especially in the first time there will be a large number of human wrecks left by the former capitalist world. Probably the rule will prevail that the productive work is the task of the younger part of the adults; or, in other words, is the task of everybody during that period of his life when both the tendency and the capacity for vigorous activity are greatest. By the rapid increase of the productivity of labor this part, the time needed to produce all the life necessities, will continually decrease, and an increasing part of life will be available for other purposes and activities.

The basis of the social organization of production consists in a careful administration, in the form of statistics and bookkeeping. Statistics of the consumption of all the different goods, statistics of the capacity of the industrial plants, of the machines, of the soil, of the mines, of the means of transport, statistics of the population and the resources of towns, districts and countries, all these present the foundation of the entire economic process in well ordered rows of numerical data. Statistics of economic processes were already known under capitalism; but they remained imperfect because the independence and the limited view of the private business men and they found only a limited application. Now they are the starting point in the organization of production; to produce the right quantity of goods, the quantity used or wanted must be known. At the same time statistics as the compressed result of the numerical registration of the process of production, the comprehensive summary of the bookkeeping, expresses the course of development.

The general bookkeeping, comprehending and encompassing the administrations of the separate enterprises, combines them all into a representation of the economic process of society. In different degrees of range it registers the entire process of transformation of matter, following it from the raw materials at their origin, through all the factories, through all the hands, down to the goods ready for consumption. In uniting the results of co-operating enterprises of a sort into one whole it compares their efficiency, it averages the hours of labor needed and directs the attention to the ways open for progress. Once the organization of production has been carried out the administration is the comparatively simple task of a network of interconnected computing offices. Every enterprise, every contingent group of enterprises, every branch of production, every township or district, for production and for consumption, has its office, to take care of the administration, to collect, to treat and to discuss the figures and to put them into a perspicuous form easy to survey. Their combined work makes the material basis of life a mentally dominated process. As a plain and intelligible numerical image the process of production is laid open to everybody's views. Here mankind views and controls its own life. What the workers and their councils devise and plan in organized collaboration is shown in character and results in the figures of bookkeeping. Only because they are perpetually before the eyes of every worker the direction of social production by the producers themselves is rendered possible.

This organization of economic life is entirely different from the forms of organization developed under capitalism; it is more perfect and more simple. The intricacies and difficulties in capitalist organization, for which the much glorified genius of big business men was needed, always dealt with their mutual struggle, with the arts and tricks of capitalist warfare to subdue or annihilate the competitors. All this has disappeared now. The plain aim, the providing for the life necessities of mankind, makes the entire structure plain and direct. Administration of large quantities, fundamentally, is hardly more difficult or more complicated than that of small quantities; only a couple of ciphers has to be put behind the figures. The rich and multiform diversity of wants and wishes that in small groups of people is hardly less than in large masses, now, by their massal character, can be secured more easily and more completely.

The function and the place numerical administration occupies in society depends on the character of this society. Financial administration of States was always necessary as part of the central government, and the computing officials were subordinate servants of the kings or other rulers. Where in modern capitalism production subjected to an encompassing central organization, those who have the central administration in their hands will be the leading directors of economy and develop into a ruling bureaucracy. When in Russia the revolution of 1917 led to a rapid expansion of industry and hosts of workers still permeated by the barbarous ignorance of the villages crowded into the new factories they lacked the power to check the rising dominance of the bureaucracy then organizing into a new ruling class. When in Germany, 1933, a sternly organized party conquered the State power, as organ of its central administration it took in hand the organization of all the forces of capitalism.

Conditions are entirely different when the workers as masters of their labor and as free producers organize production. The administration by means of bookkeeping and computing is a special task of certain persons, just as hammering steel or baking bread is a special task of other persons, all equally useful and necessary. The workers in the computing offices are neither servants nor rulers. They are not officials in the service of the workers' councils, obediently having to perform their orders. They are groups of workers, like other groups collectively regulating their work themselves, disposing of their implements, performing their duties, as does every group, in continual connection with the needs of the whole. They are the experts who have to provide the basical data of the discussions and decisions in the assemblies of workers and of councils. They have to collect the data, to present them in an easily intelligible form of tables, of graphs, of pictures, so that every worker at every moment has a clear image of the state of things. Their knowledge is not a private property giving them power; they are not a body with exclusive administrative knowledge that thereby somehow could exert a deciding influence. The product of their labor, the numerical insight needed for the work's progress, is available to all. This general knowledge is the foundation of all the discussions and decisions of the workers and their councils by which the organization of labor is performed.

For the first time in history the economic life, in general and in detail, lies as an open book before the eyes of mankind. The foundations of society, under capitalism a huge mass hidden in the dark depths, dimly lighted here and there by statistics on commerce production, now has entered in to the full daylight and shows its detailed structure. Here we dispose of a science of society consisting of a well-ordered knowledge of facts, out of which leading causal relations are readily grasped. It forms the basis of the social organization of labor just as the knowledge of the facts of nature, condensed they too into causal relations, forms the basis of the technical organization of labor. As a knowledge of the common simple facts of daily life it is available to everyone and enables him to survey and grasp the necessities of the whole as well as his own part in it. It forms the spiritual equipment through which the producers are able to direct the production and to control their world.

5. OBJECTIONS

The principles of the new structure of society appear so natural and self-evident, that there may seem to be little room for doubts or objections. The doubts come from the old traditions that fill the minds with cobwebs, so long as the fresh storm wind of social activity does not blow through them. The objections are raised by the other classes that, up till now are leading society. So first we have to consider the objections of the bourgeoisie, the ruling class of capitalists.

One might say that the objections of the members of the capitalist class do not matter. We cannot convince them, nor is this necessary. Their ideas and convictions, as well as our own, are class ideas, determined by class conditions different from ours by the difference in life conditions and in social function. We have not to convince them by reasoning, but to beat them by power.

But, we should not forget that capitalist power to a great extent is spiritual power, power over the minds of the workers. The ideas of the ruling class dominate society and permeate the minds of the exploited classes. They are fixed there, fundamentally, by the inner strength and necessity of the system of production; they are actually implanted there by education and propaganda, by the influence of school, church, press, literature, broadcasting and film. As long as this holds, the working class, lacking consciousness of its class position, acquiescing in exploitation as the normal condition of life does not think of revolt and cannot fight. Minds submissive to the doctrines of the masters cannot hope to win freedom. They must overcome the spiritual sway of capitalism over their minds before they actually can throw off its yoke. Capitalism must be beaten theoretically before it can be beaten materially. Because then only the absolute certainty of the truth of their opinions as well as of the justice of their aims can give such confidence to the workers as is needed for victory. Because then only hesitation and misgivings will lame the forces of the foe. Because then only the wavering middle groups, instead of fighting for capitalism, may to a certain degree conceive the necessity of social transformation and the benefit of the new order.

So we have to face the objections raised from the side of the capitalist class. They proceed directly from its view of the world. For the bourgeoisie capitalism is the only possible and natural system of society, or at least, since more primitive forms preceded its most developed final form. Hence all the phenomena presented by capitalism are not considered as temporary but as natural phenomena, founded on the eternal nature of man. The capitalist class sees the deep aversion of the workers against their daily labor; and how they only resign themselves to it by dire necessity. It concludes that man in the great mass is naturally averse to regular productive work, and for that reason is bound to remain poor—with the exception of the energetic, industrious and capable minority, who love work and so become leaders, directors and capitalists. Then it follows that, if the workers should be collectively masters of the production, without the competitive principle of personal reward for personal exertion, the lazy majority will do as little as possible, trying to live upon what a more industrious minority performs; and universal poverty would inevitably be the result. All the wonderful progress, all the abundance capitalism has brought in the last century will then be lost, when the stimulus of personal interest is removed; and mankind will sink back into barbarism.

To refute such objections it is sufficient to point out that they form the natural viewpoint from the other side of society, from the side of the exploiting class. Never in history were the old rulers able to acknowledge the capability of a new rising class; they expected an inevitable failure as soon as it should try to manage the affairs; and the new class, conscious of its forces, could show these only in conquering and after having conquered power. Thus now the workers grow conscious of the inner strength of their class; their superior knowledge of the structure of society, of the character of productive labor shows them the futility of the capitalist point of view. They will have to prove their capacities, certainly. But not in the form of standing a test beforehand. Their test will be their fight and victory.

This argument is not directed to the capitalist class, but to my fellow workers. The middle class ideas still permeating large masses of them consist chiefly in doubt and disbelief in their own forces. As long as a class does not believe in themselves, they cannot expect that other groups should believe in them. This lack of self-confidence, the chief weakness now, cannot be entirely removed under capitalism with its many degrading and exhausting influences. In times of emergency, however, world crisis and impending ruin, compelling the working class to revolt and fight, will also, once it has won, compel it to take control of production. Then the command of dire need treads under foot the implanted timorous diffidence of their own forces and the imposed task rouses unexpected energies. Whatever hesitation or doubt may be in their minds this one thing the workers know for certain: that they, better than the idle people of property, know what is work, that they can work, and that they will work. The futile objections of the capitalist class will collapse with this class itself.

More serious objections are raised from other sides. From such as consider themselves and are considered as friends, as allies or spokesmen of the working class. In later capitalism there is a widespread opinion, among intellectuals and social reformers, among trade union leaders and social democrats, that capitalist production for profit is bad and has to disappear, and that it has to make place for some kind of socialist system of production. Organization of production, they say, is the means of producing abundance for all. The capitalist anarchy of the totality of production must be abolished by imitating the organized order within the factory. Just as in a well-directed enterprise the perfect running of every detail and the highest efficiency of the whole is secured by the central authority of the director and the staff, so in the still more complicated social structure the right interaction and connection of all its parts can only be secured by a central leading power.

The lack of such a ruling power, they say, is what must be objected to the system of organization by means of workers' councils. They argue that nowadays production is not the handling of simple tools, easily to survey by everybody, as in the bygone days of our ancestors, but the application of the most abstract sciences, accessible only to capable and well instructed minds. They say that a clear-sighted view on an intricate structure and its capable management demand talents that only few are gifted with; that it fails to see that the majority of people are dominated by narrow selfishness, and that they lack the capacities and even the interest to take up these large responsibilities. And should the workers in stupid presumption reject the leadership of the most capable, and try to direct production and society by their own masses, then, however industrious they may be, their failure would be inevitable; every factory would soon be a chaos, and decline would be the result. They must fail because they cannot muster a leading power of sufficient authority to impose obedience and thus to secure a smooth running of the complicated organization.

Where to find such a central power? They argue, we have it already in State government. Till now Government restricted its functions to political affairs; it will have to extend them to economic affairs—as already it is compelled to do in some minor cases—to the general management of production and distribution. For is not war against hunger and misery equally, and even more important than war against foreign enemies?

If the State directs the economic activities it acts as the central body of the community. The producers are master of the production, not in small groups separately, but in such a way that in their totality, as the entire class, as the whole people they are master. Public ownership of the means of production, for their most important part, means State ownership, the totality of the people being represented by the State. By the democratic State, of course, where people choose their rulers. A social and political organization where the masses choose their leaders, everywhere, in the factories, in the unions, in the State, may be called universal democracy. Once chosen, these leaders of course must be strictly obeyed. For only in this way, by obedience to the commandment of able leaders of production, the organization can work smoothly and satisfactorily.

Such is the point of the spokesmen of State socialism. It is clear that this plan of social organization is entirely different from a true disposal by the producers over the production. Only in name are the workers masters of their labor, just as only in name are the people masters of the State. In the so-called democracies, so-called because parliaments are chosen by universal suffrage, the governments are not at all delegates designated by the population as executors of its will. Everybody knows that in every country the government is in the hands of small, often hereditary or aristocratic groups of politicians and high officials. The parliamentarians, their body of supporters, are not selected by the constituents as mandataries to perform their will. The voters, practically, have only to choose between two sets of politicians, selected, presented and advertised to them by the two main political parties, whose leaders, according to the result, either form the ruling cabinet, or as "loyal opposition" stand in abeyance for their turn. The State officials, who manage the affairs, are not selected by the people either; they are appointed from above, by the government. Even if shrewd advertising calls them servants of the people, in reality they are its rulers, its masters. In the system of State socialism it is this bureaucracy of officials that, considerably enlarged, directs production. They dispose of the means of production, they have the upper command of labor. They have to take care that everything runs well, they administrate the process of production and determine the partition of the produce. Thus the workers have got new masters, who assign to them their wages and keep at their own disposal the remainder of the produce. This means that the workers are still exploited; State socialism may quite as well be called State capitalism, according to the emphasis laid on its different sides, and to the greater or smaller share of influence of the workers.

State socialism is a design for reconstructing society on the basis of a working class such as the middle class sees it and knows it under capitalism. In what is called a socialistic system of production the basic fabric of capitalism is preserved, the workers running the machines at the command of the leaders; but it is provided with a new improved upper story, a ruling class of humane reformers instead of profit-hungry capitalists. Reformers, who as true benefactors of mankind apply their capacities to the ideal task of liberating the working masses from want and misery.

It is easily understood that during the 19th century, when the workers only began to resist and to fight, but were not yet able to win power over society, this socialist ideal found many adherents. Not only among socially minded of the middle class who sympathized with the suffering masses, but also among the workers themselves. For here loomed up before them a vision of liberation from their yoke by the simple expression of their opinion in voting, by the use of the political power of their ballot to put into government their redeemers instead of their oppressors. And certainly, if it were only a matter of placid discussion and free choice between capitalism and socialism on the part of the masses, then socialism would have a good chance.

But reality is different. Capitalism is in power and it defends its power. Can anybody have the illusion that the capitalist class would give up its rule, its domination, its profit, the very basis of its existence, hence its existence itself, at the result of a vote? Or still more, to a campaign of publicity arguments, of public opinion demonstrated in mass meetings or street processions? Of course will fight, convinced of its right. We know that even for reforms, for every reform in capitalism there had to be fighting. Not to the utmost, to be sure; not or seldom by civil war and bloodshed. Because public opinion, in the bulk of the middle class, aroused by the determined resistance of the workers, saw that in their demands capitalism itself, in its essence, was not engaged, that profit as such was not endangered. Because it was felt that, on the contrary, capitalism would be consolidated rather, reform appeasing the workers and attaching them more firmly to the existing system.

If, however, the existence of the capitalist class itself, as a ruling and exploiting class is at stake, the entire middle class stands behind it. If its mastery, its exploitation, its profit is threatened, not by a sham revolution of outward appearances, but by a real revolution of the foundations of society, then we may be sure that it will resist with all its powers. Where, then, is the power to defeat it? The irrefutable arguments and the good intentions of noble-minder reformers, all these are not able to curb, still less to destroy its solid force. There is only one power in the world capable of vanquishing capitalism: the power of the working class. The working class can not be freed by others; it can only be freed by itself.

But the fight will be long and difficult. For the power of the capitalist class is enormous. It is firmly entrenched in the fabric of State and government, having all their institutes and resources at its disposal, their moral authority as well as their physical means of suppression. It disposes of all the treasures of the earth, and can spend unlimited amounts of money to recruit, pay and organize defenders, and to carry away public opinion. Its ideas and opinions pervade the entire society, fill up books and papers and dominate the minds of even the workers. Here lies the chief weakness of the masses. Against it the working class, certainly, has its numbers, already forming the majority of the population in capitalist countries. It has its momentous economic function, its direct hold over the machines, its power to run or stop them. But they are of no avail as long as their minds are dependent on and filled by the masters' ideas, as long as the workers are separate, selfish, narrow-minded, competing individuals. Number and economic importance alone are as the powers of a sleeping giant; they must first be awakened and activated by practical fight. Knowledge and unity must make them active power. Through the fight for existence, against exploitation and misery, against the power of the capitalist class and the State, through the fight for mastery over the means of production, the workers must acquire the consciousness of their position, the independence of thought, the knowledge of society, the solidarity and devotion to their community, the strong unity of class that will enable them to defeat capitalist power.

We cannot foresee what whirls of world politics will arouse them. But we can be sure that it is not a matter of years only, of a short revolutionary fight. It is a historical process that requires an entire epoch of ups and downs, of fights and lulls, but yet of unceasing progress. It is an intrinsic transformation of society, not only because the power relations of the classes are reversed, because property relations are changed, because production is re-organized on a new basis, but chiefly—decisive basis of all these things—because the working class itself in its deepest character is transformed. From obedient subjects they are changed into free and self-reliant masters of their fate, capable to build and manage their new world.

It was the great socialist humanitarian Robert Owen who has taught us that for a true socialist society the character of man must change; and that it is changed by environment and education. It was the great communist scientist Karl Marx who, completing the theory of his predecessor, has taught us that mankind itself has to change its environment and has to educate itself, by fighting, by the class-fight against exploitation and oppression. The theory of State socialism by reform is an arid mechanical doctrine in its belief that for a social revolution a change of political institutions, of outer conditions of life is sufficient, without the inner transformation of man that turns submissive slaves into proud and spirited fighters. State socialism was the political program of social-democracy, utopian, because it pretended to bring about a new system of production by simply converting people through propaganda to new political opinions. Social-democracy was not able, nor was it willing to lead the working class into a real revolutionary fight. So it went down when the modern development of big capitalism made socialism won by the ballot an obsolete illusion.

Yet socialist ideas still have their importance, though in a different way now. They are widespread all over society, among socially feeling middle class people as well as among the masses of the workers. They express the longing for a world without exploitation, combined, in the workers, with the lack of confidence in their own power. This state of mind will not disappear at once after the first successes have been won; for it is then that the workers will perceive the immensity of their task, the still formidable powers of capital, and how all the traditions and institutions of the old world are barring their way. When thus they stand hesitating, socialism will point to what appears to be an easier road, not beset with such insurmountable difficulties and endless sacrifices. For just then, in consequence of their success, numbers of socially-minded reformers will join their ranks as capable allies and friends, putting their capacities in the service of the rising class, claiming, of course, important positions, to act and to lead the movement after their ideas. If the workers put them in office, if they install or support a socialist government, then the powerful existing machinery of the State is available for the new purpose and can be used to abolish capitalist exploitation and establish freedom by law. How far more attractive this mode of action than implacable class war! Yes, indeed; with the same result as what happened in revolutionary movements in the 19th century, when the masses who fought down the old regime in the streets, were thereupon invited to go home, to return to their work and put their trust in the self-appointed "provisional government" of politicians that was prepared to take matters in hand.

The propaganda of the socialist doctrine has the tendency to throw doubts into the minds of the workers, to raise or to strengthen distrust in their own powers, and to dim the consciousness of their task and their potentialities. That is the social function of socialism now, and at every moment of workers' success in the coming struggles. From the hard fight for freedom brilliant ahead, the workers are to be lured by the soft shine of a mild new servitude. Especially when capitalism should receive a severe blow, all who distrust and fear the unrestricted freedom of the masses, all who wish to preserve the distinction of masters and servants, of higher and lower, will rally round this banner. The appropriate catchwords will readily be framed: "order" and "authority" against "chaos," "socialism" and "organization" against "anarchy." Indeed, an economic system where the workers are themselves masters and leaders of their work, to middle-class thinking is identical with anarchy and chaos. Thus the only role socialism can play in future will be to act as an impediment standing in the way of the workers' fight for freedom.

To summarize: the socialist plan of reconstruction, brought forward by reformers, must fail, first because they have no means to produce the forces to vanquish the power of capitalism. Second, because only the workers themselves can do that. Exclusively by their own fight they can develop into the mighty power needed for such a task. It is this fight that socialism tries to forestall. And once the workers have beaten down capitalist power and won freedom, why should they give it up and submit to new masters?

There is a theory to explain why indeed they should and they must. The theory of actual inequality of men. It points out that nature itself makes them different: a capable, talented and energetic minority rises out of an incapable, stupid and slow majority. Notwithstanding all theories and decrees instituting formal and legal equality, the talented energetic minority takes the lead and the incapable majority follows and obeys.

It is not for the first time that a ruling class tries to explain, and so to perpetuate, its rule as the consequences of an inborn difference between two kinds of people, one destined by nature to ride, the other to be ridden. The landowning aristocracy of former centuries defended their privileged position by boasting their extraction from a nobler race of conquerors that had subdued the lower race of common people. Big capitalists explain their dominating place by the assertion that they have brains and other people have none. In the same way now especially the intellectuals, considering themselves the rightful rulers of tomorrow, claim their spiritual superiority. They form the rapidly increasing class of university-trained officials and free professions, specialized in mental work, in study of books and of science, and they consider themselves as the people most gifted with intellect. Hence they are destined to be leaders of the production, whereas the ungifted mass shall execute the manual work, for which no brains are needed. They are no defenders of capitalism; not capital, but intellect should direct labor. The more so, since now society is such a complicated structure, based on abstract and difficult science, that only the highest intellectual acumen is capable of embracing, grasping and handling it. Should the working masses, from lack of insight, fail to acknowledge this need of superior intellectual lead, should they stupidly try to take the direction into their own hands, chaos and ruin will be the inevitable consequence.

Now it must be remarked that the term intellectual here does not mean possessor of intellect. Intellectuals is the name for a class with special functions in social and economic life, for which mostly university training is needed.

Intellect, good understanding, is found in people of all classes, among capitalists and artisans, among farmers and workers. What is found in the "intellectuals" is not a superior intelligence, but a special capacity of dealing with scientific abstractions and formulas, often merely of memorizing them, and combined, usually, with a limited notion of other realms of life. In their self-com-
placency appears a narrow intellectualism ignorant of the many other qualities
that play an important role in all human activities. A rich and varied multitude
of dispositions, different in character and in degree, is in man: here theoretical
power of abstraction, there practical skill, here acute understanding, there rich
fantasy, here rapidity of grasping, there deep brooding, here patient perseverance of purpose, there rash spontaneity, here indomitable courage in action and
fight, there all-embracing ethical philanthropy. All of them are necessary in
social life; in turns, according to circumstances, they occupy the foremost place
in the exigencies of practice and labor. It were silly to distinguish some of them
as superior, others as inferior. Their difference implies the predilection and
qualification of people for the most varied kinds of activity. Among them the
capacity for abstract or scientific studies, under capitalism often degenerated to
a limited training, takes its important place in attending to and directing the
technical processes: but only as one among many other capacities. Certainly
for these people there is no reason to look down upon the non-intellectual
masses. Has not the historian Trevalyan, treating the times of nearly three centuries ago, spoken as "the wealth of imagination, the depth of emotion, the
vigour and variety of intellect that were to be found among the poor ... once
awakened to the use of their minds"?

Of course in all of these qualities some people are more gifted than others;
men and women of talent or genius excel their fellow beings. Probably they are
even more numerous than it appears now under capitalism, with its neglect,
misuse and exploitation of human qualities. Free humanity will employ their
talents to the best use; and the consciousness to promote with their greater
force the common cause, will give them a greater satisfaction than any material privilege in a world of exploitation could do.

Let us consider the claim of the intellectual class, the domination of spiritual over manual work. Must not the mind rule over the body, the bodily activities? Certainly. Human mind is the highest product of nature; his spiritual
capacities elevate man above the animals. Mind is the most valuable asset of
man; it makes him lord of the world. What distinguishes human work from the
activities of the animals is this very rule of the mind, the thinking out, the med-
itating and planning before the performing. This domination of theory, of the
powers of the mind over practical work grows ever stronger, through the
increasing complication of the process of production and its increasing dependence on science.

This does not mean, however, that spiritual workers should hold sway over manual workers. The contradistinction between spiritual and manual work is not founded in nature, but in society: it is an artificial class-distinction. All work, even the most simple, is spiritual as well as manual. For all kinds of work, till by repetition it has become automatic, thinking is necessary; this combination of thinking and acting is the charm of all human activity. Also under the natural division of labor, as a consequence of differences in predilection and capacity, this charm remains. Capitalism, however, has vitiated these natural conditions. To increase profit it has exaggerated the division of labor to the extreme of one-sided specializing. Three centuries ago already, in the beginning of the manufactury-system, the endless repetition of always the same limited manipulations turned labor into a monotonous routine where, through undue training of some limbs and faculties at the cost of others, body and mind were crippled. In the same way capitalism now, in order to increase productivity and profit, has separated the mental and the manual part of work and made each of the object of specialized training at the cost of other capacities. It made the two sides that together constitute natural labor, the exclusive task of separate trades and different social classes. The manual workers, fatigued by long hours of spiritless work in dirty surroundings, are not able to develop the capacities of their minds. The intellectuals, on the other hand, through their theoretical training, kept aloof from the practical work and the natural activity of the body, must resort to artificial substitutes. In both groups full human endowment is crippled. Assuming this capitalistic degeneration to be permanent human nature, one of these classes now claims superiority and domination over the other.

By yet another line of argument the claim of the intellectual class for spiritual and, hence, social leadership is supported. Learned writers have pointed out that the entire progress of humanity is due to some few geniuses. It was this limited number of discoverers, of inventors, of thinkers, that built up science, that improved technics, that conceived new ideas and opened new ways, where then the masses of their fellow-men followed and imitated them. All civilization is founded upon this small number of eminent brains. So the future of mankind, the further progress of culture depends on the breeding and selection of such superior people and would be endangered by a general levelling.

Suppose the assertion to be true, the retort, with becoming irony, could be that the result of these superior brains, this pitiful world of ours, is indeed in keeping with such a narrow basis, and nothing to boast of. Could those great precursors witness what has been made of their discoveries they would not be very proud. Were we not able to do better, we should despair of humanity.

But the assertion is not true. Whoever makes a detailed study of any of the great discoveries in science, technics or what else is surprised by the great number of names associated with it. In the later popular and abridged historical text books, however, the source of so many superficial misconceptions, only a few prominent names are preserved and exalted, as if theirs was the sole credit. So these were coined exceptional geniuses. In reality every great progress proceeded from a social surrounding pregnant with it, where from all sides the new ideas, the suggestions, the glimpses of insight sprang up. None of the great men, extolled in history, because they took the decisive and salient steps, could have done so but for the work of a large number of precursors on whose achievements his are based. And besides, these most talented thinkers, praised in later centuries as the authors of the world's progress, were not at all the spiritual leaders of their time. They were often unknown to their contemporaries, quietly working in retirement; they mostly belonged to the subjected class, sometimes even they were persecuted by the rulers. Their present-day equivalents are not those noisy claimants for intellectual leadership, but silent workers again, hardly known, derided perhaps or persecuted. Only in a society of free producers, who are able to appreciate the importance of spiritual achievements and eager to apply them to the well-being of all, the creative genius will be recognized and estimated by his fellow-men at the full value.

Why is it that from the life work of all these men of genius in the past nothing better than present capitalism could result? What they were able to do was to lay the scientific and technical foundations of high productivity of labor. By causes beyond them it became the source of immense power and riches for the ruling minority that succeeded in monopolizing the fruits of this progress. A society of freedom and abundance for all, however, cannot be brought about by any superiority of some few eminent individuals whatever. It does not depend on the brains of the few, but on the character of the many. As far as it depends on science and technics to create abundance, they are already sufficient. What is lacking are the social forces that bind the masses of the workers into a strong unity of organization. The basis of the new society is not what knowledge they can adopt and what technics they can imitate from others, but what community feeling and organized activity they can raise in themselves. This new character cannot be infused by others, it cannot proceed from obedience to any masters. It can only sprout from independent action, from the fight for freedom, from revolt against the masters. All the genius of superior individuals is of no avail here.

The great decisive step in the progress of mankind, the transformation of society now impending, is essentially a transformation of the working masses. It can be accomplished only by the action, by the revolt, by the effort of the masses themselves; its essential nature is self-liberation of mankind. From this viewpoint it is clear that here no able leadership of an intellectual elite can be helpful. Any attempt to impose it could only be obnoxious, retarding as it does the necessary progress, hence acting as a reactionary force. Objections from the side of the intellectuals, based on the present inadequateness of the working class, in practice will find their refutation when world conditions compel the masses to take up the fight for world revolution.

6. DIFFICULTIES

More essential difficulties in the reconstruction of society arise out of the differences in outlook that accompany differences in development and size of the enterprises.

Technically and economically society is dominated by big enterprise, by big capital. The big capitalists themselves, however, are only a small minority of the propertied class. They have behind them, to be sure, the entire class of rentiers and shareholders. But these, as mere parasites, cannot give a solid support in the struggle of the classes. So big capital would be in an awkward position were it not backed by the small bourgeoisie, by the entire class of smaller business men. In its domination of society it takes advantage of the ideas and the moods growing out of the world of small trade, occupying the minds alike of masters and workers in these trades. The working class has to give good consideration to these ideas. Because its task and its goal, conceived on the basis of the developments of big capitalism, are conceived and judged in these circles after the familiar conditions of small trade.

In small capitalistic business the boss as a rule is the owner, sometimes the sole owner; or if not, the shareholders are some few friends or relatives. He is his own director and usually the best technical expert. In his person the two functions of technical leader and profit-making capitalist are not separated and hardly to be distinguished even. His profit seems to proceed not from his capital, but from his labor, not from exploitation of the workers, but from the technical capacities of the employer. His workers, either engaged as a few skilled assistants or as unskilled hands, are quite well aware of the generally larger experience and expertness of the boss. What in large enterprise, with its technical leadership by salaried officials, is an obvious measure of practical efficiency—the exclusion of all property interests—would here take the retrogressive form of the removal of the best technical expert and of leaving the work to the less expert or incompetent.

It must be clear that here there is no question of a real difficulty impeding the technical organization of industry. It is hardly to be imagined that the workers in the small shop should want to expel the best expert, even the former boss, if he is honestly willing with all his skill to co-operate in their work, on the foot of equality. Is not this contrary to basis and doctrine of the new world, the exclusion of the capitalist? The working class, when reorganizing society on a new basis, is not bound to apply some theoretical doctrine; but, to direct its practical measures, it possesses a great leading principle. The principle, living touchstone of practicability to the clear-sighted minds, proclaims that those who do the work must regulate the work, and that all who collaborate practically in the production dispose of the means of production, with the exclusion of all property or capital interests. It is on the basis of this principle that the workers will face all problems and difficulties in the organization of production and will find a solution.

Surely the technically backward branches of production exercised in small trade will present special, but not essential difficulties. The problem of how to organize them by means of self-governing associations, and to connect them with the main body of social organization must be solved mainly by the workers engaged in these branches, though collaboration from other sides may come to their aid. Once the political and social power is firmly in the hands of the working class and its ideas of reconstruction dominate the minds, it seems obvious that everybody who is willing to co-operate in the community of labor will be welcome and will find the place and the task appropriate to his capacities. Besides, in consequence of the increasing community feeling and the desire for efficiency in work, the units of production will not remain the isolated dwarfish shops of former times.

The essential difficulties are situated in the spiritual disposition, the mode of thinking produced by the conditions of small trade in all who are engaged here, masters as well as artisans and workers. It prevents them to see the problem of big capitalism and big enterprise as the real and main issue. It is easily understood, however, that the conditions of small trade, the basis of their ideas, cannot determine a transformation of society that takes its origin and its driving force from big capitalism. But it is equally clear that such a disparity of general outlook may be an ample source of discord and strife, of misunderstandings and difficulties. Difficulties in the fight, and difficulties in the constructive work. In small-trade circumstances social and moral qualities develop in another way than in big enterprises; organization does not dominate the minds in the same degree. Whereas the workers may be more headstrong and less submissive, the impulses of fellowship and solidarity are less also. So propaganda has to play a greater role here; not in the sense of impressing a theoretical doctrine, but in its pure sense of exposing wider views on society in general, so that the ideas are determined not by the narrow experience of their own conditions but by the wider and essential conditions of capitalist labor at large.

This holds good still more for agriculture, with its larger number and greater importance of small enterprises. There is a material difference, besides, because here the limited amount of soil brought into being one more parasite. Its absolute necessity for living room and foodstuff production enables the owners of the soil to levy tribute from all who want to use it: what in political economy is called rent. So here we have from olden times an ownership not based on labor, and protected by State power and law; an ownership consisting only in certificates, in titles, assuring claims on an often big part of the produce of society. The farmer paying rent to the landowner or interest to the real-estate bank, the citizen, whether capitalist or worker, paying in his house-rent high prices for barren soil, they are all exploited by landed property. A century ago, in the time of small capitalism, the difference between the two forms of income, the idle income of the landowner as contrasted with the hard-won earnings of business man, worker and artisan, was so strongly felt as undue robbery, that repeatedly projects were proposed to abolish it, by nationalization of the soil. Later on, when capitalist property ever more took on the same form of certificates commanding income without labor, land reform became silent. The antagonism between capitalist and landowner, between profit and rent disappeared; landed property is now simply one of the many forms of capitalist property.

The farmer tilling his own soil combines the character of three social classes, and his earnings are indiscriminately composed of wages for his own labor, profit from directing his farm and exploiting the farm hands, and rent from his ownership. Under the original conditions partly still living as tradition of an idealized past, the farmer produced nearly all the necessaries for himself and his family on his own or on rented soil. In modern times agriculture has to provide foodstuffs for the industrial population also, which gradually everywhere, and increasingly in the capitalist countries, forms the majority. In return the rural classes receive the products of industry, which they need for ever more purposes. This is not entirely a home affair. The bulk of the world's need of grain is supplied by large enterprises, on virgin soil in the new continents, on capitalist lines; while it exhausted the untouched fertility of those vast plains, it depressed by its cheap competition the rent of European landed property, causing agrarian crises. But also in the old European lands agrarian production nowadays is production of commodities, for the market; the farmers sell the chief part of their products and buy what they need for living. So they are subject to the vicissitudes of capitalist competition, now pressed down by low prices, mortgaged or ruined, then profiteering by favorable conditions. Since every increase of rent tends to be petrified in higher land prices, rising product prices make the former owner a rentier, whereas the next owner, starting with heavier expenses, suffers ruin in the case of falling prices. So the economic position of the agricultural class in general is weakened. On the whole their condition and their outlook on modern society is similar in a way to that of small capitalists or independent business people in industry.

There are differences, however, due to the limited amount of soil. Whereas in industry or commerce whoever has a small capital can venture to start a business and fight against competitors, the farmer cannot enter the lists when others occupy the land he needs. To be able to produce he must first have the soil. In capitalist society free disposal of the soil is only possible as ownership; if he is not landowner he can only work and apply his knowledge and capacity by suffering himself to be exploited by the possessor of the soil. So owner-ship and labor are intimately connected in his mind; this lies at the root of the often criticized property-fanaticism of the farmers. Ownership enables him to gain his living during all his years by heavy toiling. By letting or selling his property, hence living on the idle landowner's rent, ownership also enables him in his old age to enjoy the sustenance which every worker should be entitled to after a life of toil. The continuous struggle against the variable forces of nature and climate, with technics only slightly beginning to be directed by modern sci-ence, hence strongly dependent on traditional methods and personal capacity, is aggravated by the pressure from capitalist conditions. This struggle has cre-ated a strong stubborn individualism, that makes the farmers a special class with a special mentality and outlook, foreign to the ideas and aims of the work-ing class.

Still, modern development has worked a considerable change here also. The tyrannical power of the great capitalist concerns, of landed estate banks and railway magnates on whom the farmers depend for credit and for trans-port, squeezed and ruined them, and sometimes brought them to the verge of rebellion. On the other hand, the necessity of securing some of the advantages of large enterprise for small-scale business did much to enforce co-operation, as well for the buying of fertilizers and materials as for procuring the necessary foodstuffs for the accumulated city population. Here the demand for a uniform standardized product, in dairy production for instance, exacts rigid prescripts and control, to which the individual farms have to submit. So the farmers are taught a bit of community feeling, and their rugged individualism has to make many concessions. But this inclusion of their work into a social entirety assumes the capitalist form of subjection to a foreign master-power, thus sting-ing their feelings of independence.

All these conditions determine the attitude of the rural class to the workers' reorganization of society. The farmers, though as independent managers of their own enterprises comparable to industrial capitalists, usually take part themselves in the productive work, which depends in a high degree on their professional skill and knowledge. Though pocketing rent as landowners, their existence is bound up with their strenuous productive activity. Their manage-ment and control over the soil in their character of producers, of workers, in common with the laborers, is entirely in accordance with the principles of the new order. Their control over the soil in their character of landowners is entire-ly contrary to these principles. They never learned, though, to distinguish between these totally different sides of their position. Moreover, the disposal over the soil as producers according to the new principle, is a social function, a mandate of society, a service to provide their fellow-people with foodstuffs and raw materials, whereas old tradition and capitalist egotism tend to consid-er it an an exclusive personal right.

Such differences in outlook may give rise to many dissensions and difficulties between the producing classes of industry and of agriculture. The workers must adhere with absolute strictness to the principle of exclusion of all the exploitation-interests of ownership; they admit only interests based on productive work. Moreover, for the industrial workers, the majority of the population, being cut off from the agrarian produce means starvation, which they cannot tolerate. For the highly industrial countries of Europe, certainly, the transoceanic traffic, the interchange with other food-producing continents, here plays an important role. But there is no doubt that in some way a common organization of the industrial and the agricultural production in each country must be established.

The point is that between the industrial workers and the farmers, between the city and the country, there are considerable differences in outlook and ideas, but no real differences or conflicts of interest. Hence there will be many difficulties and misunderstandings, sources of dissent and strife, but there will be no war to the knife as between working class and capital. Though so far mostly the farmers, led by traditional political and narrow social slogans, as defenders of property interests stood on the side of capital against the workers—and this may still be so in future—the logics of their own real interests must finally place them over against capital. This, however, is not sufficient. As small business men they may be satisfied to be freed from pressure and exploitation through a victory of the workers with or without their help. But then, according to their ideas, it will be a revolution that makes them absolute and free private possessors of the soil, similar to former middle-class revolutions. Against this tendency the workers in intensive propaganda have to oppose the new principles: production a social function, the community of all the producers master of their work; as well as their firm will to establish this community of industrial and agricultural production. Whereas the rural producers will be their own masters in regulating and directing their work on their own responsibility, its interlocking with the industrial part of production will be a common cause of all the workers and their central councils. Their continual mutual intercourse will provide agriculture with all technical and scientific means and methods of organization available, to increase the efficiency and productivity of the work.

The problems met with in the organization of agricultural production are partly of the same kind as in industry. In big enterprises, such as the large estates for corn, wheat, and other mass production with the aid of motorized machines, the regulation of the work is made by the community of the workers and their councils. Where for careful treatment in detail small production units are necessary, co-operation will play an important role. The number and diversity of small-scale farms will offer the same kind of problems as small-scale industry, and their managing will be the task of their self-governing associations. Such local communities of similar and yet individually different farms will probably be necessary to relieve social management as a whole from dealing and reckoning with every small unit separately. All these forms of organization cannot be imagined before hand; they will be devised and built by the producers when they stand before the necessities of practice.

7. COUNCIL ORGANIZATION

The social system considered here might be called a form of communism, only that name, by the world-wide propaganda of the "Communist Party" is used for its system of State socialism under party dictatorship. But what is a name? Names are ever misused to fool the masses, the familiar sounds preventing them from critically using their brains and clearly recognizing reality. More expedient, therefore, than looking for the right name will it be to examine more closely the chief characteristic of the system, the council organization.

The workers' councils are the form of self-government which in the times to come will replace the forms of government of the old world. Of course not for all future; none such form is for eternity. When life and work in community are natural habit, when mankind entirely controls its own life, necessity gives way to freedom and the strict rules of justice established before dissolve into spontaneous behavior. Workers' Councils are the form of organization during the transition period it which the working classes fighting for dominance, is destroying capitalism and is organizing social production. In order to know their true character it will be expedient to compare them with the existing forms of organization and government as fixed by custom as self-evident in the minds of the people.

Communities too large to assemble in one meeting always regulate their affairs by means of representatives, of delegates. So the burgesses of free medieval towns governed themselves by town councils, and the middle class of all modern countries, following the example of England, have their Parliaments. When speaking of management of affairs by chosen delegates we always think of parliaments; so it is with parliaments especially that we have to compare the workers' councils in order to discern their predominant features. It stands to reason that with the large differences between the classes and between their aims, also their representative bodies must be essentially different.

At once this difference strikes the eye: workers' councils deal with labor, have to regulate production, whereas parliaments are political bodies, discussing and deciding laws and State affairs. Politics and economy, however, are not entirely unrelated fields. Under capitalism State and Parliament took the measures and enacted the laws needed for the smooth course of production; such as the providing for safety in traffic and dealings, for protection of com-

merce and industry, of business and travel at home and abroad, for administration of justice, for coinage and uniform weights and measures. And its political work, too, not at first sight connected with economic activity, dealt with
general conditions in society, with the relations between the different classes,
constituting the foundation of the system of production. So politics, the activity of Parliaments may, in a wider sense, be called an auxiliary for production.

What, then, under capitalism, is the distinction between politics and economy? They compare together as the general regulation compares with the
actual practice. The task of politics is to establish the social and legal conditions
under which productive work may run smoothly; the productive work itself is
the task of the citizens. Thus there is a division of labor. The general regulations, though necessary foundations, constitute only a minor part of social
activity, accessory to the work proper, and can be left to a minority of ruling
politicians. The productive work itself, basis and contents of social life, consists
in the separate activities of numerous producers, completely filling their lives.
The essential part of social activity is the personal task. If everybody takes care
of his own business and performs his task well, society as a whole runs well.
Now and then, at regular intervals, on the days of parliamentary election, the
citizens have to pay attention to the general regulations. Only in times of social
crisis, of fundamental decisions and severe contests, of civil strife and revolution, the mass of the citizens had to devote their entire time and forces to these
general regulations. Once the fundamentals decided, they could return to their
private business and once more leave these general affairs to the minority of
experts, to lawyers and politicians, to Parliament and Government.

Entirely different is the organization of common production by means of
workers' councils. Social production. is not divided up into a number of separate enterprises each the restricted life-task of one person or group; now it
forms one connected entirety, object of care for the entirety of workers, occupying their minds as the common task of all. The general regulation is not an
accessory matter, left to a small group of specialists; it is the principal matter,
demanding the attention of all in conjunction. There is no separation between
politics and economy as life activities of a body of specialists and of the bulk of
producers. For the one community of producers politics and economy have
now coalesced into the unity of general regulation and practical productive
labor. Their entirety is the essential object for all.

This character is reflected in the practice of all proceedings. The councils
are no politicians, no government. They are messengers, carrying and interchanging the opinions, the intentions, the will of the groups of workers. Not,
indeed, as indifferent messenger boys passively carrying letters or messages of
which they themselves know nothing. They took part in the discussions, they
stood out as spirited spokesmen of the prevailing opinions. So now, as delegates of the group, they are not only able to defend them in the council meet-

ing, but at the same time they are sufficiently unbiased to be accessible to other arguments and to report to their group opinions more largely adhered to. Thus they are the organs of social intercourse and discussion.

The practice of parliaments is exactly the contrary. Here the delegates have to decide without asking instructions from their voters, without binding mandate. Though the M.P., to keep their allegiance, may deign to speak to them and to expound his line of conduct, he does so as the master of his own deeds. He votes as honor and conscience dictate him, according to his own opinions. Of course; for he is the expert in politics, the specialist in legislative matters and cannot let himself be directed by instructions from ignorant people. Their task is production, private business, his task is politics, the general regulations. He has to be guided by high political principles and must not be influenced by the narrow selfishness of their private interests. In this way it is made possible that in democratic capitalism politicians, elected by a majority of workers, can serve the interests of the capitalist class.

In the labor movement also the principles of parliamentarism took a footing. In the mass organizations of the unions, or in such gigantic political organizations as the German Social-Democratic Party, the officials on the boards as a kind of government got power over the members, and their annual congresses assumed the character of parliaments. The leaders proudly called them so, parliaments of labor, to emphasize their importance; and critical observers pointed to the strife of factions, to the leaders, to the intrigue behind the scenes as indications of the same degeneration as appeared in the real parliaments. Indeed, they were parliaments in their fundamental character. Not in the beginning, when the unions were small, and devoted members did all the work themselves, mostly gratuitously. But with the increase of membership there came the same division of labor as in society at large. The working masses had to give all their attention to their separate personal interests, how to find and to keep their job, the chief contents of their life and their mind; only in a most general way they had, moreover, to decide by vote over their common class and group interests. It was to the experts, the union officials and party leaders, who knew how to deal with capitalist bosses and State tribunals, that the detailed practice was left. And only a minority of local leaders was sufficiently acquainted with these general interests to be sent as delegates to the congresses, where notwithstanding the often binding mandates, they actually had to vote after their own judgment.

In the council organization the dominance of delegates over the constituents has disappeared because its basis, the division of task, has disappeared. Now the social organization of labor compels every worker to give his entire attention to the common cause the totality of production. The production of the necessaries for-life as, the basis of life, as before entirely occupies the mind. Not in the form, now, as care for the own enterprise, the own job, in competition with others. Life and production now can be secured only by col- laboration, by collective work with the companions. So this collective work is uppermost in the thoughts of everybody. Consciousness of community is the background, the basis of all feeling and thinking.

This means a total revolution in the spiritual life of man. He has now learned to see society, to know community. In former times, under capitalism, his view was concentrated on the small part related with his business, his job, himself and his family. This was imperative, for his life, his existence. As a dim, unknown background society hovered behind his small visible world. To be sure, he experienced its mighty forces that determined luck or failure as the outcome of his labor; but guided by religion he saw them as the working of supernatural Supreme Powers. Now, on the contrary, society comes into the full light, transparent and knowable; now the structure of the social process of labor lies open before man's eyes. Now his view is directed to the entirety of production; this is imperative, for his life, his existence. Social production is now the object of conscious regulation. Society is now a thing handled, manip- ulated by man, hence understood in its essential character. Thus the world of the workers' councils transforms the mind.

To parliamentarism, the political system of the separate business, the peo- ple were a multitude of separate persons, at the best, in democratic theory, each proclaimed to be endowed with the same natural rights. For the election of del- egates they were grouped according to residence in constituencies. In the times of petty-capitalism a certain community of interests might be assumed for neighbors living in the same town or village. In later capitalism this assumption ever more became a senseless fiction. Artisans, shopkeepers, capitalists, work- ers living in the same quarter of a town have different and opposed interests; they usually give their vote to different parties, and chance majorities win. Though parliamentary theory considers the man elected as the representative of the constituency, it is clear that all these voters do not belong together as a group that sends him as its delegate to represent its wishes.

Council organization, in this respect, is quite the contrary of parliamen- tarism. Here the natural groups, the collaborating workers, the personnels of the factories act as unities and designate their delegates. Because they have common interests and belong together in the praxis of daily life, they can send some of them as real representatives and spokesmen. Complete democracy is realized here by the equal rights of everyone who takes part in the work. Of course, whoever stands outside the work does not have a voice in its regula- tion. It cannot be deemed a lack of democracy that in this world of self-rule of the collaborating groups all that have no concern with the work—such as remained in plenty from capitalism: exploiters, parasites, rentiers – do not take part in the decisions.

Seventy years ago Marx pointed out that between the rule of capitalism and the final organization of a free humanity there will be a time of transition in which the working class is master of society but in which the bourgeoisie has not yet disappeared. He called this state of things the dictatorship of the proletariat. At that time this word had not yet the ominous sound of modern systems of despotism, nor could it be misused for the dictatorship of a ruling party, as in later Russia. It meant simply that the dominant power over society was transferred from the capitalist to the working class. Afterwards people, entirely confined within the ideas of parliamentarism, tried to materialize this conception by taking away the franchise for political bodies from the propertied classes. It is clear that, violating as it did the instinctive feeling of equal rights, it was in contrast to democracy. We see now that council organization puts into practice what Marx theoretically anticipated but for what at that time the practical form could not yet be imagined. When production is regulated by the producers themselves the formerly exploiting class automatically is excluded from taking part in the decisions, without any artificial stipulation. Marx's conception of the dictatorship of the proletariat now appears to be identical with the labor democracy of the council organization.

This labor democracy is entirely different from political democracy of the former social system. The so-called political democracy under capitalism was a mock democracy, an artful system conceived to mask the real domination of the people by a ruling minority. Council organization is a real democracy, the democracy of labor, making the working people master of their work. Under council organization political democracy has disappeared, because politics itself disappeared and gave way to social economy. The activity of the councils, put in action by the workers as the organs of collaboration, guided by perpetual study and strained attention to circumstances and needs, covers the entire field of society. All measures are taken in constant intercourse, by deliberation in the councils and discussion in the groups and the shops, by actions in the shops and decisions in the councils. What is done under such conditions could never be commanded from above and proclaimed by the will of a government. It proceeds from the common will of all concerned; because it is founded on the labor experience and knowledge of all, and because it deeply influences the life of all. Measures can be executed only in such a way that the masses put them into practice as their own resolve and will; foreign constraint cannot enforce them, simply because such a force is lacking. The councils are no government; not even the most central councils bear a governmental character. For they have no means to impose their will upon the masses; they have no organs of power. All social power is vested in the hands of the workers themselves. Wherever the use of power is needed against disturbances or attacks upon the existing order it proceeds from the collectivities of the workers in the shops and stands under their control.

Governments were necessary, during the entire period of civilization up to now, as instruments of the ruling class to keep down the exploited masses. They also assumed administrative functions in increasing measure; but their chief character as power structures was determined by the necessity of upholding class domination. Now that the necessity has vanished, the instrument, too, has disappeared. What remains is administration, one of the many kinds of work, the task of special kinds of workers; what comes in its stead, the life spirit of organization, is the constant deliberation of the workers, in common thinking attending to their common cause. What enforces the accomplishment of the decisions of the councils is their moral authority. But moral authority in such a society has a more stringent power than any command or constraint from a government.

When in the preceding time of governments over the people political power had to be conceded to the people and their parliaments a separation was made between the legislative and the executive part of government, sometimes completed by the judicial as a third independent power. Law-making was the task of parliaments, but the application, the execution, the daily governing was reserved to a small privileged group of rulers. In the labor community of the new society this distinction has disappeared. Deciding and performing are intimately connected; those who have to do the work have to decide, and what they decide in common they themselves have to execute in common. In the case of great masses, the councils are their organs of deciding. Where the executive task was entrusted to central bodies these must have the power of command, they must be governments; where the executive task falls to the masses themselves this character is lacking in the councils. Moreover, according to the varied problems and objects of regulation and decision, different persons in different combinations will be sent out and gather. In the field of production itself every plant has not only to organize carefully its own extensive range of activities, it has also to connect itself horizontally with similar enterprises, vertically with those who provide them with materials or use their products. In the mutual dependence and interconnection of enterprises, in their conjunction to branches of production, discussing and deciding councils will cover ever wider realms, up to the central organization of the entire production. On the other hand the organization of consumption, the distribution of all necessaries to the consumer, will need its own councils of delegates of all involved, and will have a more local or regional character.

Besides this organization of the material life of mankind there is the wide realm of cultural activities, and of those not directly productive which are of primary necessity for society, such as education of the children, or care for the health of all. Here the same principle holds, the principle of self-regulation of these fields of work by those who do the work. It seems altogether natural that in the care for universal health, as well as in the organization of education, all who take part actively, here the physicians, there the teachers, by means of their associations regulate and organize the entire service. Under capitalism, where they had to make a job and a living out of the human disease or out of drilling children, their connection with society at large had the form either of competitive business or of regulation and command by Government. In the new society, in consequence of the much more intimate connection of health with labor, and of education with labor, they will regulate their tasks in close touch and steady collaboration of their organs of intercourse, their councils, with the other workers' councils.

It must be remarked here that cultural life, the domain of arts and sciences, by its very nature is so intimately bound up with individual inclination and effort, that only the free initiative of people not pressed down by the weight of incessant toil can secure its flowering. This truth is not refuted by the fact that during the past centuries of class society princes and governments protected and directed arts and sciences, aiming of course to use them as utensils for their glory and the preservation of their domination. Generally speaking, there is a fundamental disparity for the cultural as well as for all the non-productive activities, between organization imposed from above by a ruling body and organization by the free collaboration of colleagues and comrades. Centrally directed organization consists in regulation as much as possible uniform all over the realm; else it could not be surveyed and conducted from one centre. In the self-regulation by all concerned the initiative of numerous experts, all poring over their work, perfecting it by emulating, imitating, consulting each other in constant intercourse, must result in a rich diversity of ways and means. Dependent on the central command of a government, spiritual life must fall into dull monotony; inspired by the free spontaneity of massal human impulse it must unfold into brilliant variety. The council principle affords the possibility of finding the appropriate forms of organization.

Thus council organization weaves a variegated net of collaborating bodies through society, regulating its life and progress according to their own free initiative. And all that in the councils is discussed and decided draws its actual power from the understanding, the will, the action of working mankind itself.

8. GROWTH

When in the difficult fight against capital, in which the workers' councils came up and developed, victory is won by the working class, it takes up its task, the organization of production.

We know, of course, that victory will not be one event, finishing the fight and introducing a then following period of reconstruction. We know that social fight and economic construction will not be separated, but will be associated as a series of successes in fight and starts of new organization, interrupted perhaps by periods of stagnation or social reaction. The workers' councils growing up as organs of fight will at the same time be organs of reconstruction. For clear understanding, however, we will distinguish these two tasks, as if they were separate things, coming one after another. In order to see the true character of the transformation of society we must treat it in a schematical way, as a uniform, continuous process starting "the day after the victory."

As soon as the workers are master of the factories, master of society, they will set the machines running. They know that this cannot wait; to live is the first necessity, and their own life, the life of society depends on their labor. Out of the chaos of crumbling capitalism the first working order must be created by means of the councils. Endless difficulties will stand in their way; resistance of all kinds must be overcome, resistance by hostility, by misunderstanding. by ignorance. But new unsuspected forces have come into being, the forces of enthusiasm, of devotion, of insight. Hostility must be beaten down by resolute action, misunderstanding must be taken away by patient persuading, ignorance must be overcome by incessant propaganda and teaching. By making the connection of the shops ever stronger, by including ever wider realms of production, by making ever more precise accounts and estimates in the plannings, the regulation of the process of production continually progresses. In this way step by step social economy is growing into a consciously dominated organization able to secure life necessities to all.

With the realization of this program the task of the workers' councils is not finished. On the contrary, this is only the introduction to their real, more extensive and important work. A period of rapid development now sets in. As soon as the workers feel themselves master of their labor, free to unfold their forces, their first impulse will be the determinate will to do away with all the misery and ugliness, to finish with the shortcomings and abuses, to destroy all poverty and barbarism that as inheritances of capitalism disgrace the earth. An enormous backwardness must be made up for; what the masses got lagged far behind what they might and should get under existing conditions. With the possibility of fulfilling them, their wants will be raised to higher standards; the height of culture of a people is measured by the extent and the quality of its life exigencies. By simply using the available means and methods of working, quantity and quality of homes, of food, of clothing for all can be raised to a level corresponding to the existing productivity of labor. All productive force that in the former society was wasted or used for luxury of the rulers can now be used to satisfy the higher wants of the masses. Thus, first innovation of society, a general prosperity will arise.

But also the backwardness in the methods of production will from the beginning have the attention of the workers. They will refuse to be harrowed and fatigued with primitive tools and obsolete working methods. If the technical methods and the machines are improved by the systematic application of all known inventions of technics and discoveries of science, the productivity of labor can be increased considerably. This better technics will be made accessible to all; the including in productive work of the many who before had to waste their forces in the bungling of petty trade, because capitalism had no use for them, or in personal service of the propertied class, now helps to lower the necessary hours of labor for all. So this will be a time of supreme creative activity. It has to proceed from the initiative of the expert producers in the enterprises; but it can take place only by continual deliberation, by collaboration, by mutual inspiration and emulation. So the organs of collaboration, the councils, are put into (unceasing) action. In this new construction and organization of an ever more excellent productive apparatus the workers' councils, as the connecting nerve strings of society, will rise to the full height of their faculties. Whereas the abundance of life necessities, the universal prosperity represents the passive side of the new life, the innovation of labor itself as its active side makes life a delight of glorious creative experience.

The entire aspect of social life changes. Also in its outer appearance, in surroundings and utensils, showing in their increasing harmony and beauty the nobleness of the work that shaped them new. What William Morris said, speaking of the crafts of olden times with their simple tools: that the beauty of their products was due to work being a joy for man—hence it was extinguished in the ugliness of capitalism—again asserts itself; but now on the higher stage of mastery over the most perfect technics. William Morris loved the tool of the craftsman and hated the machine of the capitalist. For the free worker of the future the handling of the perfectly constructed machine, providing a tension of acuteness, will be a source of mental exaltation, of spiritual rejoicing, of intellectual beauty.

Technics make man a free master of his own life and destiny. Technics, in a painful process of growth during many thousands of years of labor and fight developed to the present height, put an end to all hunger and poverty, to all toiling and slavery. Technics put all the forces of nature at the service of mankind and its needs. The growth of the science of nature opens to man new forms and new possibilities of life so rich and manifold that they far surpass what we can imagine today. But technics alone cannot perform that. Only technics in the hands of a humanity that has bound itself consciously by strong ties of brotherhood into a working community controlling its own life. Together, indissolvably connected, technics as material basis and visible power, the community as ethical basis and consciousness, they determine the entire renovation of labor.

And now, with his work, man himself is changing. A new feeling is taking hold of him, the feeling of security. Now at last the gnawing solicitudes for life falls off from mankind. During all the past centuries, from original savageness till during modern civilization, life was not secure. Man was not master over his subsistence. Always, also in times of prosperity, and for the wealthiest even, behind the illusion of perpetual welfare, in the subconsciousness lurked a silent solicitude for the future. As a permanent oppression this anxiety was sunk in the hearts, weighed heavily upon the brain and hampered the unfolding of free thinking. For us, who ourselves live under this pressure, it is impossible to imagine what a deep change in outlook, in world vision, in character, the disappearance of all anxiety about life will bring about. Old delusions and superstitions that in past times had to uphold mankind in its spiritual helplessness, now are dropped. Now that man feels certain that he truly is master of his life, their place is taken by knowledge accessible to all, by the intellectual beauty of an all-encompassing scientific world view.

Even more than in labor itself, the innovation of life will appear in the preparing of future labor, in the education and training of the next generation. It is clear that, since every organization of society has its special system of education adapted to its needs, this fundamental change in the system of production must be accompanied immediately by a fundamental change in education. In the original small-trade economy, in the farmer and artisan world, the family with its natural division of labor was the basic element of society and of production. Here the children grew up and learned the methods of working by gradually taking their part in the work. Afterwards, under capitalism, the family lost its economic basis, because productive labor ever more was transferred to the factories. Labor became a social process with broader theoretical basis; so a broader knowledge and a more intellectual education was necessary for all. Hence schools were founded, as we know them: masses of children, educated in the isolated small homes without any organic connection with labor, flocking into the schools to learn such abstract knowledge as is needed for society, here again without direct connection with living labor. And different of course according to social classes. For the children of the bourgeoisie, for the future officials and intellectuals a good theoretical and scientific training, enabling them to direct and rule society. For the children of the farmers and the working class an indispensible minimum: reading, writing, computing, needed for their work, completed by history and religion, to keep them obedient and respectful towards their masters and rulers. Learned writers of pedagogy text books, unacquainted with the capitalistic basis of these conditions which they assume to be lasting, vainly try to explain and to smooth out the conflicts proceeding from this separation of productive labor and education, from the contradiction between narrow family isolation and the social character of production.

In the new world of collaborate production these contradictions have disappeared, and harmony between life and labor is restored, now on the wide base of society at large. Now again education of the youth consists in learning the working methods and their foundation by gradually taking part in the productive process. Not in family isolation; now that the material provision of life necessities has been taken over by the community, besides its function as productive, the family loses that of consumption unit. Community life, corresponding to the strongest impulses within the children themselves, will take much larger place; out of the small homes they enter into the wide air of society. The hybridical combination of home and school gives way to communities of children, for a large part regulating their own life under careful guidance of adult educators. Education, instead of passively imbibing teachings from above, is chiefly personal activity, directed towards and connected with social labor. Now the social feelings, as an inheritance of primeval times living in all, but extremely strong in children, can develop without being suppressed by the need of egotism of the capitalist struggle for life.

Whereas the forms of education are determined by community end self-activity, its contents are given by the character of the production system, towards which it prepares. This production system was ever more, especially in the last century, based upon the application of science to technics. Science gave man mastery over the forces of nature; this mastery has made possible the social revolution and affords the basis of the new society. The producers can be master of their labor, of production, only if they master these sciences. Hence the growing generation must be instructed in the first place in the science of nature and its application. No longer, as under capitalism, will science be a monopoly of a small minority of intellectuals, and the uninstructed masses be restricted to subordinate activities. Science in its full extent will be open to all. Instead of the division between one-sided manual and one-sided mental work as specialities of two classes, now comes the harmonious combination of manual and mental work for everybody. This will be necessary also for the further development of the productivity of labor, depending as it does on the further progress of its foundations, science and technics. Now it is not merely a minority of trained intellectuals, but it is all the good brains of the entire people, all prepared by the most careful education, that occupy themselves with the creation of knowledge and its application in labor. Then may be expected a tempo of progress in the development of science and technics, compared to which the much praised progress under capitalism is only a poor commencement.

Under capitalism there is a distinctive difference between the tasks of the young and of the adults. Youth has to learn, the adults have to work. It is clear that as long as labor is toiling in exploitative service [for a purpose in opposition to the well-being and comfort of the workers] to produce the highest profit for capital, every capacity, once acquired, must be used up to the limits of time and force. No time of a worker could be wasted for learning ever new things. Only an exceptional adult had the possibility, and still less had the duty regularly to instruct himself during his further life. In the new society this difference disappears. Now in youth the learning consists in taking part, in increasing rate with the years, in the productive work. And now with the increase of productivity and the absence of exploitation ever more leisure is available to the adults for spiritual activities. It enables them to keep apace with the rapid development of the methods of work. This indeed is necessary for them. To take part in the discussions and decisions is only possible if they can study the problems of technics that continually incite and stimulate their attention. The grand development of society through the unfolding of technics and science, of security and abundance, of power over nature and life, can only be ascertained by the growth of capability and knowledge of all the partners. It gives new contents of thrilling activity to their life; it elevates existence and makes it a conscious delight of eager participation in the spiritual and practical progress of the new world.

Added to these sciences of nature are now the new sciences of society that were lacking under capitalism. The special feature of the new system of production is that man now dominates the social forces which determine his ideas and impulses. Practical domination must find its expression in theoretical domination, in knowledge of the phenomena and the determining forces of human action and life, of thinking and feeling. In former times, when through ignorance about society their social origin was unknown, their power was ascribed to the supernatural character of spirit, to a mysterious power of the mind, and the disciplines dealing with them were labeled spiritual sciences: psychology, philosophy, ethics, history, sociology, aesthetics. As with all science their beginnings were full of primitive mysticism and tradition; but contrary to the sciences of nature their rise to real scientific height was obstructed by capitalism. They could not find a solid footing because under capitalism they proceeded from the isolated human being with its individual mind, because in those times of individualism, it was not known that man is essentially a social being, that all his faculties emanate from society and are determined by society. Now, however, that society lies open to the view of man, as an organism of mutually connected human beings, and that the human mind is understood as their main organ of interconnection, now they can develop into real sciences.

And the practical importance of these sciences for the new community is no less than that of the sciences of nature. They deal with the forces lying in man, determining his relations to his fellow men and to the world, instigating his actions in social life, appearing in the events of history past and present. As mighty passions and blind impulses they worked in the great social fights of mankind, now elating man to powerful deeds, then by equally blind traditions keeping him in apathetic submissivity, always spontaneous, ungoverned, unknown. The new science of man and society discloses these forces and so enables man to control them by conscious knowledge. From masters driving him through passive instincts they become servants, ruled by self-restraint, directed by him towards his well-conceived purposes.

The instruction of the growing generation in the knowledge of these social and spiritual forces, and its training in consciously directing them will be one of the chief educational tasks of the new society. Thus the young will be enabled to develop all endowments of passion and will-power, of intelligence and enthusiasm, and to apply them in efficient activity. It is an education of character as well as of knowledge. This careful education of the new generation, theoretical and practical, in natural science and in social consciousness, will form a most essential element in the new system of production. Only in this way an unhampered progression of social life will be secured. And in this way, too, the system of production will develop to ever higher forms. Thus by theoretical mastery of the sciences of nature and society, and by their practical application in labor and life, the workers will make the earth into a happy abode of free mankind.

II. The Fight

1. TRADE UNIONISM

The task of the working class to take production in its own hand and to organize it first has to be dealt with. In order to carry on the fight it is necessary to see the goal in clear and distinct lines before us. But the fight, the conquest of power over production is the chief and most difficult part of the work. It is in this fight that the workers' councils will be created.

We cannot exactly foresee the future forms of the workers' fight for freedom. They depend on social conditions and must change along with the increasing power of the working class. It will be necessary, therefore, to survey how so far it has fought its way upward, adapting its modes of action to the varying circumstances. Only by learning from the experience of our predecessors and by considering it critically will we be able in our turn to meet the demands of the hour.

In every society depending on the exploitation of a working class by a ruling class there is a continuous struggle over the division of the total produce of labor, or in other words: over the degree of exploitation. Thus medieval times, as well as later centuries, are full of incessant struggles and furious fights between the landowners and the farmers. At the same time we see the fight of the rising burgher class against nobility and monarchy, for power over society. This is a different kind of class struggle, associated with the rise of a new system of production, proceeding from the development of technics, industry and commerce. It was waged between the masters of the land and the masters of capital, between the declining feudal and the rising capitalist system. In a series of social convulsions, of political revolutions and wars, in England, in France and in other countries consecutively, the capitalist class has gained complete mastery over society.

The working class under capitalism has to carry on both kinds of fight against capital. It has to keep up a continual struggle to mitigate the heavy pressure of exploitation, to increase wages, to enlarge or keep up its share in the total produce. Besides, with the growth of its strength, it has to gain mastery over society in order to overthrow capitalism and bring about a new system of production.

When for the first time, in the beginning of the Industrial Revolution in England, spinning and then weaving machines were introduced, we hear of revolting workers destroying the machines. They were not workers in the modern sense, not wage earners. They were small artisans, independent before, now starved by the competition of cheaply producing machines, and trying in vain to remove the cause of their misery. Afterwards, when they or their children became wage workers, themselves handling the machines, their position was different. It was the same for the hosts from the countryside, who, during the entire 19th century of growing industry, flocked into the towns, lured by what to them appeared good wages. In modern times it is ever more the offspring of the workers themselves that fill the factories.

For all of them the struggle for better working conditions is of immediate necessity. The employers, under the pressure of competition, to enlarge their profits, try to lower the wages and to increase the hours as much as possible. At first the workers, powerless by the constraint of hunger, have to submit in silence. Then resistance bursts forth, in the only possible form, in the refusal to work, in the strike. In the strike for the first time the workers discover their strength, in the strike arises their fighting power. From the strike springs up the association of all the workers of the factory, of the branch, of the country. Out of the strike sprouts the solidarity, the feeling of fraternity with the comrades in work, of unity with the entire class: the first dawn of what some day will be the lifespending sun of the new society. The mutual help, at first appearing in spontaneous and casual money collections, soon takes the lasting form of the trade union.

For a sound development of trade-unionism certain conditions are necessary. The rough ground of lawlessness, of police arbitrarity and prohibitions, mostly inherited from pre-capitalistic times, must be smoothed before solid buildings may be erected. Usually the workers themselves had to secure these conditions. In England it was the revolutionary campaign of Chartism; in Germany, half a century later, it was the fight of Social Democracy that, by enforcing social acknowledgment for the workers, laid the foundations for the growth of the unions.

Now strong organizations are built up, comprising the workers of the same trade all over the country, forming connections with other trades, and internationally with unions all over the world. The regular paying of high dues provides the considerable funds from which strikers are supported, when unwilling capitalists must be forced to grant decent working conditions. The ablest among the colleagues, sometimes victims of the foe's wrath from former fights, are appointed as salaried official, who, as independent and expert spokesmen of the workers, can negotiate with the capitalist employers. By strike at the right moment, supported by the entire power of the union, and by ensuing negotiations, agreements can be reached about better and more uniform wages and about fair working hours, in so far as the latter are not yet fixed by law.

So the workers are no longer powerless individuals, forced by hunger to sell their labor-power at any price. They are now protected by their union, protected by the power of their own solidarity and cooperation; for every member not only gives part of his earnings for the colleagues, but is ready also to risk his job in defending the organization, their community. Thus a certain equilibrium is reached between the power of the employers and the power of the workers. The working conditions are no longer dictated by all-powerful capitalist interests. The unions are recognized gradually as representatives of the workers' interests; though ever again fighting is necessary, they become a power that takes part in the decisions. Not in all trades surely, and not at once everywhere. Usually skilled craftsmen are the first in building their unions. The unskilled masses in the great factories, standing against more powerful employers, mostly come later; their unions often started from sudden outbursts of great fights. And against the monopolistic owners of giant enterprises the unions have little chance; these all powerful capitalists wish to be absolute master, and in their haughtiness they hardly allow even servile yellow shop unions.

Apart from this restriction, and even assuming trade unionism to be fully developed and in control of all industry, this does not mean that exploitation is abolished, that capitalism is repressed. What is repressed is the arbitrariness of the single capitalist; abolished are the worst abuses of exploitation. And this is in the interest of the fellow-capitalists, too—to guard them against unfair competition—and in the interest of capitalism at large. By the power of the unions capitalism is normalized; a certain norm of exploitation is universally established. A norm of wages, allowing for the most modest life exigencies, so that the workers are not driven again and again into hunger revolts, is necessary for uninterrupted production. A norm of working hours, not quite exhausting the vitality of the working class—though reduction of hours is largely neutralized by acceleration of tempo and more intense exertion—is necessary for capitalism itself, to preserve a usable working class as the basis of future exploitation. It was the working class that by its fight against the narrowness of capitalist greed had to establish the conditions of normal capitalism. And ever again it has to fight, to preserve the uncertain equilibrium. In this fight the trade unions are the instruments; thus the unions perform an indispensable function in capitalism. Narrow-minded employers do not see this, but their broader-minded political leaders know quite well that trade unions are an essential element of capitalism, that without the workers' unions as normalizing power capitalism is not complete. Though products of the workers' fight, kept up by their pains and efforts, trade unions are at the same time organs of capitalist society.

With the development of capitalism, however, conditions gradually grow more unfavorable for the workers. Big capital grows, feels its power, and wishes to be master at home. Capitalists also have learned to understand the power of association; they organize into employers' unions. So instead of the equality of forces arises a new ascendancy of capital. Strikes are countered by lock-outs that drain the funds of the trade unions. The money of the workers cannot compete with the money of the capitalists. In the bargaining about wages and working conditions the unions are more than ever the weaker party, because they have to fear, and hence must try to avoid great fights that exhaust the reserves and thereby endanger the secured existence of the organization and its officials. In the negotiations the union officials often have to accept a lowering of conditions in order to avoid fighting. To them this is unavoidable and self-evident, because they realize that by the changed conditions the relative fighting power of their organization has diminished.

For the workers, however, it is not self-evident that they are silently to accept harder working and living conditions. They want to fight. So a contradiction of viewpoints arises. The officials seem to have common sense on their side; they know that the unions are at a disadvantage and that fight must result in defeat. But the workers feel by instinct that great fighting powers still lie hidden in their masses; if only they knew how to use them. They rightly realize that by yielding, again and again, their position must grow worse, and that this can be prevented only by fighting. So conflicts must arise in the unions between the officials and the members. The members protest against the new tariffs [awards] favorable to the employers; the officials defend the agreements reached by long and difficult negotiations and try to have them ratified. So they often have to act as spokesmen of capital interests against workers' interests. And because they are the influential rulers of the unions throwing all the weight of power and authority on this side, the unions in other hands may be said to develop into organs of capital.

The growth of capitalism, the increase of the number of workers, the urgent necessity of association, make the trade unions giant organizations, needing an ever increasing staff of officials and leaders. These develop into a bureaucracy administering all business, a ruling power over the members, because all the power factors are in their hands. As the experts they prepare and manage all affairs; they administrate the finances and the spending of money for different purposes; they are editors of the union papers, by which they can force their own ideas and points of view upon the members. Formal democracy prevails; the members in their assemblies, the chosen delegates in the congresses have to decide, just as the people decide politics in Parliament and State. But the same influences that render Parliament and Government lords over the people are operative in these Parliaments of Labor. They turn the alert bureaucracy of expert officials into a kind of union government, over the members absorbed by their daily work and cares. Not solidarity, the proletarian virtue, but discipline, obedience to the decisions is asked from them. Thus there arises a difference in viewpoint, a contrast in opinions on the various questions. It is enhanced by the difference in life conditions: the insecurity of the workers' job, always threatened by depression forces and unemployment, as contrasted to the security that is necessary for officials to well-manage the union affairs.

It was the task and the function of trade unionism, by their joint united fight to raise the workers out of their helpless misery, and to gain for them an acknowledged place in capitalist society. It had to defend the workers against the ever increasing exploitation of capital. Now that big capital consolidates more than ever into a monopolistic power of banks and industrial concerns, this former function of trade unionism is finished. Its power falls short compared to the formidable power of capital. The unions are now giant organizations, with their acknowledged place in society; their position is regulated by law, and their tariff [Court Award] agreements are given legally binding force for the entire industry. Their leaders aspire at forming part of the power ruling industrial conditions. They are the apparatus by means of which monopolistic capital imposes its conditions upon the entire working class. To this now all-powerful capital it is, normally, far more preferable to disguise its rule in democratic and constitutional forms than to show it in the naked brutality of dictatorship. The working conditions which it thinks suitable to the workers will be accepted and obeyed much more easily in the form of agreements concluded by the unions than in the form of dictates arrogantly imposed. Firstly, because to the workers the illusion is left that they are masters of their own interests. Secondly, because all the bonds of attachment, which as their own creation, the creation of their sacrifices, their fight, their elation, render the unions dear to the workers, now are subservient to the masters. Thus under modern conditions trade unions more than ever are turned into organs of the domination of monopolist capital over the working class.

2. DIRECT ACTION

As an instrument of fight for the working class against capital the trade unions are losing their importance. But the fight itself cannot cease. The depressing tendencies grow stronger under big capitalism and so the resistance of the workers must grow stronger, too. Economic crises grow more and more destructive and undermine apparently secured progress. The exploitation is intensified to retard the lowering of the profit rate for rapidly increasing capital. So again and again the workers are provoked to resistance. But against the strongly increased power of capital the old methods of fight no longer can serve. New methods are needed, and before long their beginnings present themselves. They spring up spontaneously in the wild [outlaw] strike, in the direct action.

Direct action means action of the workers themselves without the intermediary of trade union officials. A strike is called wild [outlaw or unofficial] as contrasted to the strike proclaimed by the union according to the rules and regulations. The workers know that the latter is without effect, where the officials against their own will and insight are made to proclaim it, perhaps thinking a defeat a healthy lesson for the foolish workers, and in every case trying to finish it as soon as possible. Thus, when the pressure is too heavy, when negotiations with the directors drag along without effect, at last in smaller or larger groups the exasperation breaks loose in a wild strike.

Fight of the workers against capital is not possible without organization. And organization springs up spontaneously, immediately. Not of course in such form that a new union is founded, with a board chosen and regulations formulated in ordered paragraphs. Sometimes, to be sure, it was done in this way; attributing the inefficiency to personal shortcomings of the old leaders, and embittered against the old trade union, they founded a new one, with their most able and energetic men at the head. Then indeed in the beginning all was energy and strong action; but in the long run the new union, if it remains small, lacks power notwithstanding its activity, and if it grows large, of necessity develops the same characteristics as the old one. After such experiences the workers at last will follow the other way, of keeping the direction of their fight entirely in their own hands.

Direction in their own hands, also called their own leadership, means that all initiative and all decisions proceed from the workers themselves. Though there is a strike committee, because all cannot be always together, everything is done by the strikers; continually in touch with one another they distribute the work, they devise all measures and decide on all actions directly. Decision and action, both collective, are one.

The first and most important task is the propaganda to expand the strike. The pressure upon capital must be intensified. Against the enormous power of capital not only the individual workers, but also the separate groups are powerless. The sole power that is a match for capital is the firm unity of the entire working class. Capitalists know or feel this quite well, and so the only inducement to concessions is the fear the strike might spread universally. The more manifestly determinate the will of the strikers, the greater the numbers taking part in it, the more the chance of success.

Such an extension is possible because it is not the strike of a tardy group, in worse conditions than others, trying to raise itself to the general level. Under the new circumstances discontent is universal; all the workers feel depressed under capitalist superiority; fuel for explosions has accumulated everywhere. It is not for others, it is for themselves if they join the fight. As long as they feel isolated, afraid to lose their job, uncertain what the comrades will do, without firm unity, they shrink from action. Once, however, they take up the fight, they are changed into new personalities; selfish fear recedes to the background and forth spring the forces of community, solidarity and devotion, rousing courage and perseverance. These are contagious; the example of fighting activity rouses in others, who feel in themselves the same forces awakening, the spirit of mutual and of self-confidence. Thus the wild strike as a prairie fire may spring over to other enterprises and involve ever greater masses.

Such cannot be the work of a small number of leaders, either union officials or self-imposed new spokesmen, though, of course, the push of some few intrepid comrades may give strong impulses. It must be the will and the work of all, in common initiative. The workers have not only to do, but also to contrive, to think out, to decide everything themselves. They cannot shift decision and responsibility to a body, a union, that takes care of them. They are entirely responsible for their fight, success or failure depends on themselves. From passive they have turned into active beings, determinedly taking their destiny into their own hands. From separate individuals each caring for himself, they have become a solid, firmly cemented unity.

Such spontaneous strikes present yet another important side; the division of the workers into different separate unions is effaced. In the trade union world traditions from former petty-capitalist times play an important role in separating the workers in often competing, jealous and bickering corporations; in some countries religious and political differences act as partition fences in establishing separate liberal, catholic, socialist and other unions. In the workshop the members of different unions stand beside one another. But even in strikes they often are kept asunder, so as not to have them infected with too much unity ideas, and the concordance in action and negotiation is solely kept up by the boards and officials. Now, however, in direct actions, these differences of union membership become unreal as outside labels. For such spontaneous fights unity is the first need; and unity there is, else there could be no fight. All who stand together in the shop, in the very same position, as direct associates, subject to the same exploitation, against the same master, stand together in common action. Their real community is the shop; personnel of the same enterprise, they form a natural union of common work, common lot and common interests. Like specters from the past the old distinctions of different membership fall back, almost forgotten in the new living reality of fellowship in common fight. The vivid consciousness of new unity enhances the enthusiasm and the feeling of power.

Thus in the wild strikes some characteristics of the coming forms of fight make their appearance: first the self-action, the self-initiative, keeping all activity and decision in their own hands; and then the unity, irrespective of old memberships, according to the natural grouping of the enterprises. These forms come up, not through shrewd planning, but spontaneously, irresistible, urged by the heavy superior power of capital against which the old organizations cannot fight seriously any more. Hence it does not mean that now the scales have turned, that now the workers win. Wild strikes mostly bring defeat; their extent is too narrow. Only in some favorable cases they have success in preventing a lowering in working conditions. Their importance is that they demonstrate a fresh fighting spirit that cannot be suppressed. One of the deepest instincts of self-preservation, of duty against family and comrades, the will to assent oneself ever again springs up. There is a gain of increasing self-reliance and class-feeling. They are the harbingers of future greater fights, when great social emergencies, with heavier pressure and deeper distress, drive the masses into stronger action.

When wild strikes break out on a larger scale, comprising great masses, entire branches of industry, towns or districts, the organization has to assume new forms. Deliberation in one assembly is impossible; but more than ever mutual understanding is necessary for common action. Strike committees are formed out of the delegates of all the personnels, for continual discussion of circumstances. Such strike committees are entirely different from union boards of officials; they show the characteristics already of workers' councils. They come up out of the fight, to give it unity of direction. But they are no leaders in the old sense, they have no direct power. The delegates, often different persons, come to express the opinion and the will of the personnels [groups] that sent them. For these personnel stand for the action in which the will manifests itself. Yet the delegates are no simple messengers of their mandatory groups; they took a foremost part in the discussion, they embody the prevalent convictions. In the committee assemblies the opinions are discussed and put to the test of momentary circumstances; the results and the resolutions are brought back by the delegates into the personnel [group] assemblies. Through these intermediaries the shop personnels themselves take part in the deliberations and decisions. Thus unity of action for great masses is secured.

Not, to be sure, in such a way that every group bows obediently to the decisions of the committee. There are no paragraphs to confer such power on it. Unity in collective fighting is not the outcome of judicious regulation of competencies but of spontaneous necessities in a sphere of passionate action. The workers themselves decide, not because such a right is given to them in accepted rules, but because they actually decide, by their actions. It may happen that a group cannot convince other groups by arguments, but then by its action and example it carries them away. The self-determination of the workers over their fighting action is not a demand put up by theory, by arguments of practicability, but the statement of a fact evolving from practice. Often in great social movements it occurred—and doubtless will occur again—that the actions did not comply with the decisions. Sometimes central committees made an appeal for universal strike, and only small groups here and there followed; elsewhere the committees weighed scrupulously, without venturing a decision, and the workers broke loose in massal fight. It may be possible even that the same workers who enthusiastically resolved to strike shrink back when standing before the deed. Or, conversely, that prudent hesitation governs the decisions and yet, driven by inner forces, a non-resolved strike irresistibly breaks out. Whereas in their conscious thinking old watchwords and theories play a role and determine arguments and opinions, at the moment of decision on which weal and woe depend, strong intuition of real conditions breaks forth, determining the actions. This does not mean that such intuition always guides right; people may be mistaken in their impression of outer conditions. But it decides; it cannot be replaced by foreign leadership, by guardians however clever, directing them. By their own experiences in fight, in success and adversity, by their own efforts the workers must acquire the capacities rightly to take care of their interests.

Thus the two forms of organization and fight stand in contrast, the old one of trade unions and regulated strike, the new one of spontaneous strike and workers' councils. This does not mean that the former at some time will be simply substituted by the latter as the only alternative. Intermediate forms may be conceived, attempts to correct the evils and weakness of trade unionism and preserve its right principles; to avoid the leadership of a bureaucracy of officials, to avoid the separation by narrow craft and trade interests, and to preserve and utilize the experiences of former fights. This might be done by keeping together, after a big strike, a core of the best fighters, in one general union. Wherever a strike breaks out spontaneously this union is present with its skilled propagandists and organizers to assist the inexperienced masses with their advice, to instruct, to organize, to defend them. In this way every fight means a progress of organization, not in the sense of fees-paying membership, but in the sense of growing class unity.

An example for such a union might be found in the great American union "Industrial Workers of the World" (I.W.W.). At the end of last century in contrast to the conservative trade unions of well-paid skilled labor, united in the "American Federation of Labor," it grew up out of special American conditions. Partly out of the fierce struggles of the miners and lumbermen, independent pioneers in the wilds of the Far West, against big capital that had monopolized and seized the riches of wood and soil. Partly out of the hunger strikes of the miserable masses of immigrants from Eastern and Southern Europe, accumulated and exploited in the factories of the Eastern towns and in the coal mines, despised and neglected by the old unions. The I.W.W. provided them with experienced strike leaders and organizers, who showed them how to stand against police terrorism, who defended them before public opinion and the courts, who taught them the practice of solidarity and unity and opened to them wider views on society, on capitalism and class fight. In such big fights ten thousands of new members joined the I.W.W., of whom only a small fraction remained. This "one big union" was adapted to the wild growth of American capitalism in the days when it built up its power by subjecting the masses of the independent pioneers.

Similar forms of fight and organization may be propagated and may come up elsewhere, when in big strikes the workers stand up, without as yet having the complete self-confidence of taking matters entirely in their own hands. But only as temporary transition forms. There is a fundamental difference between the conditions of future fight in big industry and those of America in the past. There it was the rise, now it will be the downfall of capitalism. There the rugged independence of pioneers or the primitive existence-seeking egoism of immigrants were the expression of a middle class individualism that had to be curbed under the yoke of capitalist exploitation. Now masses trained to discipline during a life time by machine and capital, connected by strong technical and spiritual ties to the productive apparatus, organize its utilization on the new basis of collaboration. These workers are thoroughly proletarian, all obstinacy of middle class individualism having been worn off long ago by the habit of collaborate work. The forces of solidarity and devotion hidden in them only wait for great fights to develop into a dominating life principle. Then even the most suppressed layers of the working class, who only hesitatingly join their comrades, wanting to lean upon their example, will soon feel the new forces of community growing also in themselves. Then they will perceive that the fight for freedom asks not only their adherence but the development of all their powers of self-activity and self-reliance. Thus overcoming all intermediate forms of partial self-determination the progress will definitely go the way of council organization.

3. SHOP OCCUPATION

Under the new conditions of capitalism a new form of fight for better working conditions came up, the shop occupation, mostly called sit-down strike, the workers ceasing to work but not leaving the factory. It was not invented by theory, it arose spontaneously out of practical needs; theory can do no more than afterwards explain its causes and consequences. In the great world crisis of 1930 unemployment was so universal and lasting that there arose a kind of class antagonism between the privileged number of employed and the unemployed masses. Any regular strike against wage cuttings was made impossible, because the shops after being left by the strikers, immediately would be flooded by the masses outside. So the refusal to work under worse conditions must needs be combined with sticking to the place of work by occupying the shop.

Having sprung up, however, in these special circumstances, the sit-down strike displays some characteristics that make it worth while to consider it more closely as the expression of a further developed fighting form. It manifests the formation of a more solid unity. In the old form of strike the working community of the personnel dissolved when leaving the shop. Dispersed over the streets and homes between other people they were separated into loose individuals. To discuss and decide as one body they had then to assemble in meeting halls, in streets and squares. However often police and authorities tried to hinder or even to forbid this, the workers held fast to their right of using them, through the consciousness that they fought with legitimate means for lawful aims. The legality of trade union practice was generally recognized by public opinion.

When, however, this legality is not recognized, when the increasing power of big capital over State authorities disputes the use of hall and square for assemblies, the workers, if they will fight, have to assert their rights by taking them. In America every great strike was as a rule accompanied by a continuous fight with the police over the use of the streets and rooms for meeting. The sit-down strike releases the workers from this necessity by their taking the right to assemble at the adequate place, in the shop. At the same time the strike is made truly efficient by the impossibility of strike-breakers to take their places.

Of course this entails new stiff fighting. The capitalists as owners of the shop consider occupation by the strikers as a violation of their ownership; and on this juridical argument they call for the police to turn the workers out. Indeed, from the strict puridical viewpoint, shop occupation is in conflict with formal law. Just as strike is in conflict with formal law. And in fact the employer regularly appealed to this formal law as a weapon in the fight, by stigmatizing the strikers as contract breakers, thus giving him the right to put new workers in their places. But against this juridical logic strikes have persisted and developed as a form of fight; because they were necessary.

Formal law, indeed, does not represent the inner reality of capitalism, but only its outer forms, to which middle class and juridical opinion cling. Capitalism in reality is not a world of equal and contracting individuals, but a world of fighting classes. When the power of the workers was too small the middle class opinion of formal law prevailed, the strikers as contract breakers were turned out and replaced by others. Where, however, trade union fight had won its place, a new and truer juridical conception asserted itself: a strike is not a break, not a cessation, but a temporary suspending of the labor contract, to settle the dispute over working terms. Lawyers may not accept theoretically this point of view, but society does, practically.

In the same way shop occupation asserted itself as a method in fight, where it was needed and where the workers were able to take a stand. Capitalists and lawyers might splutter over the violation of property rights. For the workers, however, it was an action that did not attack the property rights but only temporarily suspended their effects. Shop occupation is not shop-expropriation. It is only a momentary suspension of the disposal by the capitalist. After the contest has been settled, he is master and undisputed owner as before.

Yet, at the same time, it is more. In it, as in a light flash at the horizon, a glimpse of future development springs up. By shop occupation the workers, unwittingly, demonstrate that their fight has entered into a new phase. Here their firm interjunction as a shop organization appears, a natural unity not to be dissolved into single individuals. Here the workers become conscious of their intimate connection with the shop. To them it is not another man's building where only at his command they come to work for him till he sends them away. To them the shop with its machines is a productive apparatus they handle, an organ that only by their work is made a living part of society. It is nothing foreign to them; they are at home here, much more than the juridical owners, the shareholders who do not even know its whereabouts. In the factory the workers grow conscious of the contents of their life, their productive work their work-community as a collectivity that makes it a living organism, an element of the totality of society. Here, in shop occupation a vague feeling arises that they ought to be entirely master of production, that they ought to expel the unworthy outsiders, the commanding capitalists, who abuse it in wasting the riches of mankind and in devastating the earth. And in the heavy fight that will be necessary, the shops again will play a primary role, as the units of organization, of common action, perhaps as the supports and strongholds, pivots of force and objects of struggle. Compared with the natural connection of workers and shops the command of capital appears as an artificial outside domination, powerful as yet, but hanging in the air; whereas the growing hold of the workers is firmly rooted in the earth. Thus in shop occupation the future forecasts its light in the growing consciousness that the shops belong with the workers, that together they form a harmonious unity, and that the fight for freedom will be fought over, in, and by means of the shops.

4. POLITICAL STRIKES

Not all the great strikes of the workers in the last century were fought over wages and working conditions. Besides the so-called economic strikes, political strikes occurred. Their object was the promotion or the prevention of a political measure. They were not directed against the employers but against State government, to induce it to give to the workers more political rights, or to dissuade it from obnoxious acts. Thus it could happen that the employers agreed with the aims and promoted the strike.

A certain amount of social equality and political rights for the working class is necessary in capitalism. Modern industrial production is based upon intricate technics, product of highly developed knowledge, and demands careful personal collaboration and capability of the workers. The utmost exertion of forces cannot, as in the case of coolies or slaves, be enforced by rough physical compulsion, by whip or outrage; it would be revenged by equally rough-mis-handling of the tools. The constraint must come from inner motives, from moral means of pressure based upon individual responsibility. The workers must not feel powerless embittered slaves; they must have the means to go against inflicted wrongs. They have to feel themselves free sellers of their labor-power, exerting all their forces, because, formally and apparently, they are determining their own lot in the general competition. To maintain themselves as a working class they need not only the personal liberty and legal equality proclaimed by middle class laws: Special rights and liberties, too, are necessary to secure these possibilities; the right of association, the right of meeting in assembly, the right to form unions, freedom of speech, freedom of press. And all these political rights must be protected by universal suffrage, for the workers to assert their influence over Parliament and law.

Capitalism began by refusing these rights, assisted herein by the inherited despotism and backwardness of existing governments, and tried to make the workers powerless victims of its exploitation. Only gradually, in consequence of fierce struggle against inhuman oppression, some rights were won. Because in its first stage capitalism feared the hostility of the lower classes, the artisans impoverished by its competition, and the workers starved by low wages, the suffrage was kept restricted to the wealthy classes. Only in later times, when capitalism was firmly rooted, when its profits were large and its rule was secured, the restrictions on the ballot were gradually removed. But only under compulsion of strong pressure, often of hard fight from the side of the workers. Fight for democracy fills the history of home politics during the 19th century, first in England, and then in all countries where capitalism introduced itself.

In England universal suffrage was one of the main points of the charter of demands put up by the English workers in the Chartist movement, their first and most glorious period of fight. Their agitation had been a strong induce-ment to the ruling land owner class to yield to the pressure of the simultaneous Reform movement of the rising industrial capitalists. So through the Reform Act 1832 the industrial employers got their share in political power; but the workers had to go home empty-handed, and to continue their strenuous strug-gle. Then, at the climax of Chartism, a "holy month" was projected in 1839, when all the work had to rest till the demands were granted. Thus the English workers were the first to proclaim the political strike as a weapon in their fight. But it could not be put into effect; and at an outburst (1842) it had to be bro-ken off without success; it could not curb the greater power of the now com-bined ruling classes of landowners and factory owners. Not till a generation later, when after a period of unprecedented industrial prosperity and expansion the propaganda was once more taken up, now by the trade unions combined in the "International Workers' Association" (the "First International" of Marx and Engels), public opinion in the middle class was ready to extend, in consecutive steps, the suffrage to the working class.

In France universal suffrage since 1848 formed part of republican constitution, dependent as such government always was on the support of the workers. In Germany the foundation of the Empire, in the years 1866–70, product of a feverish capitalist development activating the entire population, entailed universal suffrage as a warrant of continued contact with the masses of the people. But in many other countries the propertied class, often only a privileged part of it, kept fast to its monopoly of political influence. Here the campaign for the ballot, obviously the gate to political power and freedom, roused ever larger parts of the working class to participation, to organization and to political activity. Conversely, the fear of the propertied classes for political domination of the proletariat stiffened their resistance. Formally the matter looked hopeless for the masses; universal suffrage had to be legally enacted by a Parliament chosen by the privileged minority, and thus invited to destroy its own foundations. This implies that only by extraordinary means, by pressure from outside, finally by political mass strikes the aim could be achieved. How it happens may be learned from the classical example of the Belgian suffrage strike in 1893.

In Belgium, through a limited census-suffrage, government was perpetually in the hands of a small clique of conservatives of the clerical party. Labor conditions in the coal mines and factories were notoriously among the worst in Europe and led to explosions in frequent strikes. Extension of suffrage as a way to social reform, frequently proposed by some few liberal parliamentarians, always again was defeated by the conservative majority. Then the Workers' Party, agitating, organizing and preparing for many years, decided upon a universal strike. Such a strike had to exert political pressure during the parliamentary discussion on a new suffrage proposal. It had to demonstrate the intense interest and the grim will of the masses, who abandoned their work to give all attention to this fundamental question. It had to arouse all the indifferent elements among the workers and the small business men to take part in what for all of them was a life interest. It had to show the narrow-minded rulers the social power of the working class, to impress upon them that it refused longer to be kept under tutelage. At first, of course, the parliamentary majority took a stand, refused to be coerced by pressure from outside, wishing to decide after their own will and conscience; so it took the suffrage bill from the rolls and ostensibly began to discuss other matters. But in the meantime the strike went on, extended more than before, and brought production to a standstill; traffic ceased, and even dutiful public services became restive. The governmental apparatus itself was hampered in its functions; and in the business world, with the growing feeling of uncertainty, opinion became loud that to grant the demands was less dangerous than to provoke a catastrophe. So the determination of the parliamentarians began to crumble; they felt that they had to choose between yielding or crushing the strike by military force.

But could the soldiers be trusted in such a case? Thus their resistance had to give way; will and conscience had to be revised, and at last they accepted and enacted the proposals. The workers, by means of a political strike, had reached their aim and won their fundamental political right.

After such a success many workers and their spokesmen supposed that this new powerful weapon could be used oftener to win important reforms. But therein they were disappointed; the history of labor movement knows of more failures than successes in political strikes. Such a strike tries to impose the will of the workers upon a government of the capitalist class. It is somewhat of a revolt, a revolution, and calls up in that class the instincts of self-defense and the impulses of suppression. These instincts were repressed when part of the bourgeoisie itself grew annoyed by the backwardness of political institutions and felt the need of fresh reforms. Then the mass action of the workers was an instrument to modernize capitalism. Because the workers were united and full of enthusiasm, whereas the propertied class in any case was divided, the strike succeeded. It could succeed not because of the weakness of the capitalist class, but because of the strength of capitalism. Capitalism is strengthened when its roots, by universal suffrage, securing at least political equality, are driven deeper into the working class. Workers' suffrage belongs to developed capitalism; because the workers need the ballot, as well as trade unions, to maintain themselves in their function in capitalism.

If now, however, in minor points they should suppose themselves able to impose their will against the real interests of the capitalists, they find this class as a solid unity against them. They feel it as by instinct; and not being carried away by a great inspiring aim that dispels all hesitations, they remain uncertain and divided. Every group, seeing that the strike is not universal, hesitates in its turn. Volunteers of the other classes offer themselves for the most needed services and traffic though they are not really able to uphold production, their activity at least discourages the strikers. Prohibition of assemblies, display of armed forces, martial law may still more demonstrate the power of government and the will to use it. So the strike begins to crumble and must be discontinued, often with considerable losses and disillusion for the defeated organizations. In experiences like these the workers discovered that by its inner strength capitalism is able to withstand even well organized and massal assaults. But at the same time they felt sure that in mass strikes, if only applied at the right time, they possess a powerful weapon.

This view was confirmed in the first Russian Revolution of 1905. It exhibited an entirely new character in mass-strikes. Russia at that time showed only the beginnings of capitalism: some few large factories in great towns, supported mostly by foreign capital with State subsidies, where starving peasants flocked to work as industrial hands. Trade unions and strikes were forbidden; government was primitive and despotic. The Socialist Party, consisting of intellectuals and workers, had to fight for what middle-class revolutions in Western Europe had already established: the destruction of absolutism and the introduction of constitutional rights and law. Hence the fight of the Russian workers was bound to be spontaneous and chaotic. First as wild strikes against miserable working conditions, severely suppressed by Cossacks and police, then acquiring a political character, in demonstrations and the unfolding of red flags in the streets, the struggle manifest itself. When the Japanese war of 1905 had weakened the Czarist government and shown up its inner rottenness, the revolution broke out as a series of wild-strike movements on a gigantic scale. Now they flamed up, springing like wildfire from one factory, one town to another, bringing the entire industry to a standstill; then they dissolved into minor local strikes, dying away after some concessions from the employers, or smoldered until new outbreaks came. Often there were street demonstrations and fights against police and soldiers. Days of victory came where the delegates of the factories assembled unmolested to discuss the situation, then, joined by deputations of other groups, of rebellious soldiers even, to express their sympathy, whilst the authorities stood passively by. Then again the Government made a move and arrested the entire body of delegates, and the strike ended in apathy. Till at last, in a series of barricade fights in the capital cities the movement was crushed by military force.

In Western Europe political strikes had been carefully premeditated actions for specially indicated aims, directed by the union or the Socialist Party leaders. In Russia the strike movement was the revulsion of heavily abused humanity, uncontrolled, as a storm or a flood forcing its way. It was not the fight of organized workers claiming along denied right; it was the rise of a down-trodden mass to human consciousness in the only form of fight then possible. Here there could be no question of success or defeat, the fact of an outbreak was already a victory, no more to be undone, the beginning of, a new epoch. In outward appearance the movement was crushed and Czarist government again was master. But in reality these strikes had struck a blow at Czarism from which it could not recover. Some reforms were introduced, political, industrial and agrarian. But the whole fabric of the State with its arbitrary despotism of incapable chinowniks could not be modernized, it had to disappear. This revolution prepared the next one, in which old barbarous Russia was to be destroyed.

The first Russian revolution has strongly influenced the ideas of the workers in Central and Western Europe. Here a new development of capitalism had set in that made felt the need of new and more powerful methods of fight, for defense and for attack. Economic prosperity, which began in the nineties and lasted till the first world war, brought an unprecedented increase of production and wealth. Industry expanded, especially iron and steel industry, new markets were opened, railways and factories were built in foreign countries and other continents; now for the first time capitalism spread all over the earth. America and Germany were the scenes of the most rapid industrial development. Wages increased, unemployment nearly disappeared, the trade unions grew into mass organizations. The workers were filled with hopes of continual progress in prosperity and influence, and visions loomed up of a coming age of industrial democracy.

But then, at the other side of society, they saw another image. Big capital concentrated production and finance, wealth and power, in a few hands and built up strong industrial concerns and capitalist associations. Its need for expansion, for the disposal over foreign markets and raw materials, inaugurated the policy of imperialism, a policy of stronger ties to old, and conquest of new colonies, a policy of growing antagonism between the capitalist classes of different countries, and of increasing armaments. The old peaceful freetrade ideals of the "little Englanders" were ridiculed and gave way to new ideals of national greatness and power. Wars broke out in all continents, in the Transvaal, in China, Cuba, and the Phillipines, in the Balkans; England consolidated its Empire, and Germany, claiming its share in world power, prepared for world war. Big capital in its growing power ever more determined the character and opinions of the entire bourgeoisie, filling it with its anti-democratic spirit of violence. Though sometimes it tried to lure the workers by the prospect of a share in the spoils, there was on the whole less inclination than in previous times to make concessions to labor. Every strike for better wages, engaged in order to catch up with rising prices, met with stiffer resistance. Reactionary and aristocratic tendencies got hold of the ruling class; it spoke not of extension but of restriction of popular rights, and threats were heard, especially in continental countries, of suppressing the workers' discontent by violent means.

Thus circumstances had changed and were changing ever more. The power of the working class had increased through its organization and its political action. But the power of the capitalist class had increased still more. This means that heavier clashes between the two classes might be expected. So the workers had to look for other and stronger methods of fight. What were they to do if regularly even the most justifiable strikes are met by big lock-outs, or if their parliamentary rights are reduced or circumvented, or if capitalist government will make war notwithstanding their urgent protests?

It is easily seen that under such conditions there was among the foremost elements of the working class much thought and discussion on mass action and the political strike, and that the general strike was propagated as a means against the outbreak of war. Studying the examples of such actions as the Belgian and the Russian strikes, they had to consider the conditions, the possibilities, and the consequences of mass-actions and political strikes in the most highly developed capitalist countries with strong governments and powerful capitalist classes. It was clear that strong odds were against them. What could not have happened in Belgium and Russia would be the immediate result here: the annihilation of their organizations. If the combined trade unions, Socialist or Labor Parties should proclaim a general strike, Government, sure of the support of the entire ruling and middle class, doubtless would be able to imprison the leaders, persecute the organizations as endangering the safety of the State, suppress their papers, by a state of siege prevent all mutual contact of the strikers, and by mobilizing military forces, assert its undisputed public power. Against this display of power the workers, isolated, exposed to the threats and calumnies, disheartened by distorted information from the press, would have no chance. Their organizations would be dissolved and break down. And the organizations lost, the fruits of years of devoted struggle, all is lost.

Thus the political and labor leaders asserted. Indeed, to them, with their outlook entirely limited within the confines of present forms of organization it must appear so. So they are fundamentally opposed to political strikes. This means that in this form, as premeditated and well decided actions of the existing organizations, directed by their leaders, such political strikes are not possible. As little as a thunderstorm in a placid atmosphere. It may be true that, for special aims entirely within the capitalist system, a political strike remains entirely within the bounds of legal order, so that after it is over capitalism resumes its ordinary course. But this truth does not prevent the ruling class from being angrily aroused against every display of workers' power, nor political strikes from having consequences far beyond their immediate aims. When social conditions become intolerable for the workers, when social or political crises are threatening them with ruin, it is inevitable that mass-actions and gigantic strikes break forth spontaneously, as the natural form of fight, notwithstanding all objections and resistance of the existing unions, irresistibly, like thunderstorms out of a heavy electric tension in the atmosphere. And again the workers face the question whether they have any chance against the power of State and capital.

It is not true that with a forcible suppression of their organizations all is lost. These are only the outer form of what in essence lives within. To think that by such Government measures the workers suddenly should change into the selfish, narrow-minded, isolated individuals of olden times! In their hearts all the powers of solidarity, of comradeship, of devotion to the class remain living, are growing even more intense through the adverse conditions; and they will assert themselves in other forms. If these powers are strong enough no force from above can break the unity of the strikers. Where they suffer defeat it is mainly due to discouragement No government power can compel them to work; it can only prohibit active deeds; it can do no more a than threaten and try to intimidate them, try by fear to dissolve their unity. It depends on the inner strength of the workers, on the spirit of organization within them, whether that can be successful. Certainly thus the highest demands are made on social and moral qualities; but just for this reason these qualities will be strained to the highest possible pitch and will be hardened as steel in the fire.

This is not the affair of one action, one strike. In every such contest the force of the workers is put to the test, whether their unity is strong enough to resist the attempts of the ruling powers to break it. Every contest arouses new strenuous efforts to strengthen it so as not to be broken. And when, actually, the workers remain steadfast, when notwithstanding all acts of intimidation, of suppression, of isolation, they hold out, when there is no yielding of any group, then it is on the other side that the effects of the strike become manifest. Society is paralyzed, production and traffic are stopped, or reduced to a minimum, the functioning of all public life is hampered, the middle classes are alarmed and may begin to advise concessions. The authority of Government, unable to restore the old order, is shaken. Its power always consisted in the solid organization of all officials and services, directed by unity of purpose embodied in one self-sure will, all of them accustomed by duty and conviction to follow the intentions and instructions of the central authorities. When, however, it stands against the mass of the people, it feels itself ever more what it really is, a ruling minority, inspiring awe only as long as it seemed all-powerful, powerful only as long as it was undisputed, as long as it was the only solidly organized body in an ocean of unorganized individuals. But now the majority also is solidly organized, not in outward forms but in inner unity. Standing before the impossible task of imposing its will upon a rebellious population, Government grows uncertain, divided, nervous, trying different ways. Moreover, the strike impedes the intercommunication of the authorities all over the country, isolates the local ones, and throws them back upon their own resources. Thus the organization of State power begins to lose its inner strength and solidity. Neither can the use of armed forces help otherwise than by more violent threats. Finally the army consists either of workers too, in different dress and under the menace of stricter law, but not intended to be used against their comrades; or it is a minority over against the entire people. If put to the strain of being commanded to fire at unarmed citizens and comrades, the imposed discipline in the long run must give way. And then State power, besides its moral authority, would have lost its strongest material weapon to keep the masses in obedience.

Such considerations of the important consequences of mass strikes, once that great social crises stir up the masses to a desperate fight, could mean of course no more than the view of a possible future. For the moment, under the mollifying effects of industrial prosperity, there were no forces strong enough to drive the workers into such actions. Against the threatening war their unions and parties restricted themselves to professing their pacifism and international feelings, without the will and the daring to call upon the masses for a desperate resistance. So the ruling class could force the workers into its capitalist mass-action, into world war. It was the collapse of the appearances and illusions of self-satisfied power of the working class at the time, now disclosed as inner weakness and insufficiency.

One of the elements of weakness was the lack of a distinct goal. There was not, and could not be, any clear idea of what had to come after successful mass-actions. The effects of mass strikes so far appeared destructive only, not constructive. This was not true, to be sure; decisive inner qualities, the basis of a new society, develop out of the fights. But the outer forms in which they had to take shape were unknown; nobody in the capitalist world at the time had heard of workers' councils. Political strikes can only be a temporary form of battle; after the strike constructive labor has to provide for permanency.

5. THE RUSSIAN REVOLUTION

The Russian revolution was an important episode in the development of the working class movement. Firstly, as already mentioned, by the display of new forms of political strike, instruments of revolution. Moreover, in a higher degree, by the first appearance of new forms of self-organization of the fighting workers, known as soviets, *i.e.*, councils. In 1705 they were hardly noticed as a special phenomenon and they disappeared with the revolutionary activity itself. In 1917 they reappeared with greater power; now their importance was grasped by the workers of Western Europe, and they played a role here in the class struggles after the first world war.

The soviets, essentially, were simply strike committees, such as always arise in wild strikes. Since the strikes in Russia broke out in large factories, and rapidly expanded over towns and districts, the workers had to keep in continual touch. In the shops the workers assembled and discussed regularly after the close of the work, or in times of tension even continually, the entire day. They sent their delegates to other factories and to the central committees, where information was interchanged, difficulties discussed, decisions taken, and new tasks considered.

But here the tasks proved more encompassing than in ordinary strikes. The workers had to throw off the heavy oppression of Czarism; they felt that by their action Russian society was changing in its foundations. They had to consider not only wages and labor conditions in their shops, but all questions related to society at large. They had to find their own way in these realms and to take decisions on political matters. When the strike flared up, extended over the entire country, stopped all industry and traffic and paralyzed the functions of government, the soviets were confronted with new problems. They had to regulate public life, they had to take care of public security and order, they had to provide for the indispensible public utilities and services. They had to perform governmental functions; what they decided was executed by the workers, whereas Government and police stood aloof, conscious of their impotence against the rebellious masses. Then the delegates of other groups, of intellectuals, of peasants, of soldiers, who came to join the central soviets, took part in the discussions and decisions. But all this power was like a flash of lightning, like a meteor passing. When at last the Czarist government mustered its military forces and beat down the movement the soviets disappeared.

Thus it was in 1905. In 1917 the war had weakened government through the defeats at the front and the hunger in the towns, and now the soldiers, mostly peasants, took part in the action. Besides the workers' councils in the town soldiers' councils were formed in the army; the officers were shot when they did not acquiesce in the soviets taking all power into their hands to prevent entire anarchy. After half a year of vain attempts on the part of politicians and military commanders to impose new governments, the soviets, supported by the socialist parties, were master of society.

Now the soviets stood before a new task. From organs of revolution they had to become organs of reconstruction. The masses were master and of course began to build up production according to their needs and life interests. What they wanted and did was not determined, as always in such cases, by inculcated doctrines, but by their own class character, by their conditions of life. What were these conditions? Russia was a primitive agrarian country with only the beginning of industrial development. The masses of the people were uncivilized and ignorant peasants, spiritually dominated by a gold glittering church, and even the industrial workers were strongly connected with their old villages. The village soviets arising everywhere were self-governing peasant committees. They seized the large estates of the former great landowners and divided them up. The development went in the direction of small freeholders with private property, and presented already the distinctions between larger and smaller properties, between influential wealthy and more humble poor farmers.

In the towns, on the other hand, there could be no development to private capitalist industry because there was no bourgeoisie of any significance. The workers wanted some form of socialist production, the only one possible under these conditions. But their minds and character, only superficially touched by the beginnings of capitalism, were hardly adequate to the task of themselves regulating production. So their foremost and leading elements, the socialists of the Bolshevist Party, organized and hardened by years of devoted fight, their leaders in the revolution became the leaders in the reconstruction. Moreover, were these working class tendencies not to be drowned by the flood of aspirations for private property coming from the land, a strong central government had to be formed, able to restrain the peasants' tendencies. In this heavy task of organizing industry, of organizing the defensive war against counter-revolutionary attacks, of subduing the resistance of capitalist tendencies among the peasants, and of educating them to modern scientific ideas instead of their old beliefs, all the capable elements among the workers and intellectuals, supplemented by such of the former officials and officers as were willing to co-operate, had to combine into the Bolshevist Party as the leading body. It formed the new government. The soviets gradually were eliminated as organs of self-rule, and reduced to subordinate organs of the government apparatus. The name of Soviet-Republic, however, was preserved as a camouflage, and the ruling party retained the name of Communist Party.

The system of production developed in Russia is State socialism. It is organized production with the State as universal employer, master of the entire production apparatus. The workers are master of the means of production no more than under Western capitalism. They receive their wages and are exploited by the State as the only mammoth capitalist. So the name State capitalism can be applied with precisely the same meaning. The entirety of the ruling and leading bureaucracy of officials is the actual owner of the factories, the possessing class. Not separately, everyone for a part, but together, collectively, they are possessors of the whole. Theirs the function and the task to do what the bourgeoisie did in Western Europe and America: develop industry and the productivity of labor. They had to change Russia from a primitive barbarous country of peasants into a modern, civilized country of great industry. And before long, in often cruelly waged class war between the peasants and the rulers, State-controlled big agrarian enterprises replaced the backward small farms.

The revolution, therefore, has not, as deceptive propaganda pretends, made Russia a land where the workers are master and communism reigns. Yet it meant progress of enormous significance. It may be compared with the great French revolution: it destroyed the power of monarch and feudal landowners, it began by giving the land to the peasants, and it made the masters of industry rulers of the State. Just as then in France the masses from despised "canaille" became free citizens, recognized even in poverty and economic dependence as personalities with the possibility to rise, so now in Russia the masses rose from unevolving barbarism into the stream of world progress, where they may act as personalities. Political dictatorship as form of government can no more prevent this development once it has started than the military dictatorship of Napoleon hampered it in France. Just as then in France from among the citizens and peasants came up the capitalists and the military commanders, in an upward struggle of mutual competition, by good and by bad means, by energy and talent, by jobbery and deceit—so now in Russia. All the good brains among the workers and peasants' children rushed into the technical and farming schools, became engineers, officers, technical and military leaders. The future was opened to them and aroused immense tensions of energy; by study and exertion, by cunning and intrigue they worked to assert their places in the new ruling class—ruling, here again, over a miserable exploited class of proletarians. And just as at that time in France a strong nationalism sprang up proclaiming the new freedom to be brought to all Europe, a brief dream of everlasting glory—so now Russia proudly proclaimed its mission, by world revolution to free all peoples from capitalism.

For the working class the significance of the Russian revolution must be looked for in quite different directions. Russia showed to the European and American workers, confined within reformist ideas and practice, first how an industrial working class by a gigantic mass action of wild strikes is able to undermine and destroy an obsolete State power; and second, how in such actions the strike committees develop into workers' councils, organs of fight and of self-management, acquiring political tasks and functions. In order to see the influence of the Russian example upon the ideas and actions of the working class after the first world war, we have to go a step backward.

The outbreak of the war in 1914 meant an unexpected breakdown of the labor movement all over capitalist Europe. The obedient compliance of the workers under the military powers, the eager affiliation, in all the countries, of the union and socialist party leaders to their governments, as accomplices in the suppression of the workers, the absence of any significant protest, had brought a deep disappointment to all who before put their hopes of liberation on proletarian socialism. But gradually among the foremost of the workers came the insight that what had broken down was chiefly the illusion of an easy liberation by parliamentary reform. They saw the bleeding and exploited masses growing rebellious under the sufferings of oppression and butchery, and, in alliance with the Russian revolutionaries, they expected the world-revolution to destroy capitalism as an outcome of the chaos of the war. They rejected the disgraced name of socialism and called themselves communists, the old title of working class revolutionaries.

Then as a bright star in the dark sky the Russian revolution flared up and shone over the earth. And everywhere the masses were filled with anticipation and became restive, listening to its call for the finishing of the war, for brotherhood of the workers of all countries, for world revolution against capitalism. Still clinging to their old socialist doctrines and organizations the masses, uncertain under the flood of calumnies in the press, stood waiting, hesitating, whether the tale might still come true. Smaller groups, especially among the young workers, everywhere assembled in a growing communist movement. They were the advance guard in the movements that after the end of the war broke out in all countries, most strongly in defeated and exhausted Central Europe. It was a new doctrine, a new system of ideas, a new tactic of fight, this communism that with the then new powerful means of government propaganda was propagated from Russia. It referred to Marx's theory of destroying capitalism by means of the workers' class fight. It was a call for fight against world capital, mainly concentrated in England and America, that exploited all peoples and all continents. It summoned not only the industrial workers of Europe and America, but also the subjected peoples of Asia and Africa to rise in common fight against capitalism. Like every war, this war could only be won by organization, by concentration of powers, and good discipline. In the communist parties, comprising the most gallant and able fighters, kernel and staff were present already; they have to take the lead, and at their call the masses must rise and attack the capitalist governments. In the political and economic crisis of the world we cannot wait until by patient teaching the masses have all become communists. Nor is this necessary; if they are convinced that only communism is salvation, if they put their trust in the Communist Party, follow its directions, bring it to power, then the Party as the new government will establish the new order. So it did in Russia, and this example must be followed everywhere. But then, in response to the heavy task and the devotion of the leaders, strict obedience and discipline of the masses are imperative, of the masses towards the Party, of the party members towards the leaders. What Marx had called the dictatorship of the proletariat can be realized only as the dictatorship of the Communist Party. In the Party the working class is embodied, the Party is its representative.

In this form of communist doctrine the Russian origin was clearly visible. In Russia, with its small industry and undeveloped working class, only a rotten Asiatic despotism had to be overthrown. In Europe and America a numerous and highly developed working class, trained by a powerful industry, stands over against a powerful capitalist class disposing of all the resources of the world. Hence the doctrine of party dictatorship and blind obedience found strong opposition here. If in Germany the revolutionary movements after the close of the war had led to a victory of the working class and it had joined Russia, then the influence of this class, product of the highest capitalist and industrial development, would soon have out-weighed the Russian character. It would have strongly influenced the English and the American workers; and it would have carried away Russia itself along new roads. But in Germany the revolution failed; the masses were kept aloof by their socialist and union lenders, by means of atrocity stories and promises of well-ordered socialist happiness, whilst their advance guards were exterminated and their best spokesmen murdered by the military forces under the protection of the socialist government. So the opposing groups of German communists could not carry weight; they were expelled from the party. In their place discontented socialist groups were induced to join the Moscow International, attracted by its new opportunist policy of parliamentarism, with which it hoped to win power in capitalist countries.

Thus world revolution from a war cry became a phrase. The Russian leaders imagined world revolution as a big scale extension and imitation of the Russian revolution. They knew capitalism only in its Russian form, as a foreign exploiting power impoverishing the inhabitants, carrying all the profits out of the country. They did not know capitalism as the great organizing power, by its richness producing the basis of a still richer new world. As became clear from their writings, they did not know the enormous power of the bourgeoisie, against which all the capabilities of devoted leaders and a disciplined party are insufficient. They did not know the sources of strength that lie hidden in the modern working class. Hence the primitive forms of noisy propaganda and party terrorism, not only spiritual, but also physical, against dissenting views. It was an anachronism that Russia, newly entering the industrial era out of its primitive barbarism, should take command over the working class of Europe and America, that stood before the task of transforming a highly developed industrial capitalism into a still higher form of organization.

Old Russia essentially, in its economic structure, had been an Asiatic country. All over Asia lived millions of peasants, in primitive small scale agriculture, restricted to their village, under despotic far distant rulers, whom they had no connection with but by the paying of taxes. In modern times these taxes became ever more a heavy tribute to Western capitalism. The Russian revolution, with its repudiation of Czarist debts, was the liberation of the Russian peasants from this form of exploitation by Western capital.

So it called upon all the suppressed and exploited Eastern peoples to follow its example, to join the fight and throw off the yoke of their despots, tools of the rapacious world capital. And far and wide, in China and Persia, in India and Africa the call was heard. Communist parties were formed, consisting of radical intellectuals, of peasants revolting against feudal landowners, of hard pressed urban coolies and artisans, bringing to the hundreds of millions the message of liberation. As in Russia it meant for all these peoples the opening of the road to modern industrial development, sometimes, as in China, in alliance with a modernizing national bourgeoisie. In this way the Moscow International even more than a European became an Asiatic institution. This accentuated its middle class character, and worked to revive in the European followers the old traditions of middle class revolutions, with the preponderance of great leaders, of sounding catchwords, of conspiracies, plots, and military revolts.

The consolidation of State capitalism in Russia itself was the determining oasis for the character of the Communist Party. Whilst in its foreign propaganda it continued to speak of communism and world revolution, decried capitalism, called upon the workers to join in the fight for freedom, the workers in Russia were a subjected and exploited class, living mostly in miserable working conditions, under a strong and oppressive dictatorial rule, without freedom of speech, of press, of association, more strongly enslaved than their brethren under Western capitalism. Thus an inherent falsehood must pervade politics and teachings of that party. Though a tool of the Russian government in its foreign politics, it succeeded by its revolutionary talk to take hold of all the rebellious impulses generated in enthusiastic young people in the crisis-ridden Western world. But only to spill them in abortive sham-actions or in opportunist politics—now against the socialist parties styled as traitors or social fascists, then seeking their alliance in a so-called red front or a people's front—causing its best adherents to leave in disgust. The doctrine it taught under the name of Marxism was not the theory of the overthrow of highly developed capitalism by a highly developed working class; but its caricature, product of a world of barbarous primitivity, where fight against religious superstitions means spiritual, and modernized industrialism—economic progress—with atheism as philosophy, party-rule the aim, obedience to dictatorship as highest commandment. The Communist Party did not intend to make the workers independent fighters capable by their force of insight themselves to build their new world, but to make them obedient followers ready to put the party into power.

So the light darkened that had illuminated the world; the masses that had hailed it were left in blacker night, either in discouragement turning away from the fight, or struggling along to find new and better ways. The Russian revolution first had given a mighty impulse to the fight of the working class, by its mass direct actions and by its new council forms of organization—this was expressed in the widespread rise of the communist movement all over the world. But when then the revolution settled into a new order, a new class rule, a new form of government, State capitalism under dictatorship of a new exploiting class, the Communist Party needs must assume an ambiguous character. Thus in the course of ensuing events it became most ruinous to the working class fight, that can only live and grow in the purity of clear thought, plain deeds and fair dealings. By its idle talk of world revolution it hampered the badly needed new orientation of means and aims. By fostering and teaching under the name of discipline the vice of submissiveness, the chief vice the workers must shake off, by suppressing each trace of independent critical thought, it prevented the growth of any real power of the working class. By usurping the name communism for its system of workers' exploitation and its policy of often cruel persecution of adversaries, it made this name, till then expression of lofty ideals, a byword, an object of aversion and hatred even among workers. In Germany, where the political and economic crises had brought the class antagonisms to the highest pitch, it reduced the hard class fight to a puerile skirmish of armed youths against similar nationalist bands. And when then the tide of nationalism ran high and proved strongest, large parts of them, only educated to beat down their leaders' adversaries, simply changed colors. Thus the Communist Party by its theory and practice largely contributed to prepare the victory of fascism.

6. THE WORKERS' REVOLUTION

The revolution by which the working class will win mastery and freedom, is not a single event of limited duration. It is a process of organization, of self-education, in which the workers gradually, now in progressing rise, then in steps and leaps, develop the force to vanquish the bourgeoisie, to destroy capitalism, and to build up their new system of collective production. This process will fill up an epoch in history of unknown length, on the verge of which we are now standing. Though the details of its course cannot be foreseen, some of its conditions and circumstances may be a subject of discussion now.

This fight cannot be compared with a regular war between similar antagonistic powers. The workers' forces are like an army that assembles during the battle! They must grow by the fight itself, they cannot be ascertained beforehand, and they can only put forward and attain partial aims. Looking back on history we discern a series of actions that as attempts to seize power seem to be so many failures: from Chartism, along 1848, along the Paris Commune, up to the revolutions in Russia and Germany in 1917–1918. But there is a line of progress; every next attempt shows a higher stage of consciousness and force. Looking back on the history of labor we see, moreover, that in the continuous struggle of the working class there are ups and downs, mostly connected with changes in industrial prosperity. In the first rise of industry every crisis brought misery and rebellious movements; the revolution of 1848 on the continent was the sequel of a heavy business depression combined with bad crops. The industrial depression about 1867 brought a revival of political action in England; the long crisis of the 1880's, with its heavy unemployment, excited mass actions, the rise of social-democracy on the continent and the "new unionism" in England. But in the years of industrial prosperity in between, as 1850–70, and 1895–1914, all this spirit of rebellion disappeared. When capitalism flourishes and in feverish activity expands its realm, when there is abundant employment, and trade union action is able to raise the wages, the workers do not think of any change in the social system. The capitalist class growing in wealth and power is full of self-confidence, prevails over the workers and succeeds in imbuing them with its spirit of nationalism. Formally the workers may then stick to the old revolutionary catchwords; but in their subconscious they are content with capitalism, their vision is narrowed; hence, though their numbers are growing, their power declines. Till a new crisis finds them unprepared and has to rouse them anew.

Thus the question poses itself, whether, if previously won fighting power again and again crumbles in the contentment of a new prosperity, society and the working class ever will be ripe for revolution. To answer this question the development of capitalism must be more closely examined.

The alternation of depression and prosperity in industry is not a simple swinging to and fro. Every next swing was accompanied by an expansion. After each breakdown in a crisis capitalism was able to come up again by expanding its realm, its markets, its mass of production and product. As long as capitalism is able to expand farther over the world and to increase its volume, it can give employment to the mass of the population. As long as thus it can meet the first demand of a system of production, to procure a living to its members, it will be able to maintain itself, because no dire necessity compels the workers to make an end of it. If it could go on prospering at its highest stage of extension, revolution would be impossible as well as unnecessary; then there were only the hope that a gradual increase of general culture could reform its deficiencies.

Capitalism, however, is not a normal, in any case not a stable system of production. European, and afterwards American capitalism could increase production so continuously and rapidly, because it was surrounded by a wide non-capitalist outer world of small-scale production, source of raw materials and markets for the products. An artificial state of things, this separation between an active capitalist core and a dependent passive surrounding. But the core ever expanding. The essence of capitalist economy is growth, activity, expansion; every standstill means collapse and crisis. The reason is that profits accumulate continuously into new capital that seeks for investment to bring new profit, thus the mass of capital and the mass of products increase ever more rapidly and markets are sought for feverishly. So capitalism is the great revolutionizing power, subverting old conditions everywhere and changing the aspect of the earth. Ever new millions of people from their secluded, self-sufficient home production that reproduced itself during long centuries without notable change, are drawn into the whirl of world commerce. Capitalism itself, industrial exploitation, is introduced there, and soon from customers they became competitors. In the 19th century from England it progressed over France, Germany, America, Japan, then in the 20th it pervades the large Asiatic territories. And first as competing individuals, then organized in national States the capitalists take up the fight for markets, colonies, world power. So they are driven on, revolutionizing ever wider domains.

But the earth is a globe, of limited extent. The discovery of its finite size accompanied the rise of capitalism four centuries ago, the realization of its finite size now marks the end of capitalism. The population to be subjected is limited. The hundreds of millions crowding the fertile plains of China and India once drawn within the confines of capitalism, its chief work is accomplished. Then no large human masses remain as objects for subjection. Surely there remain vast wild areas to be converted into realms of human culture; but their exploitation demands conscious collaboration of organized humanity; the rough rapine methods of capitalism—the fertility-destroying "rape of the earth"— are of no avail there. Then its further expansion is checked. Not as a sudden impediment, but gradually, as a growing difficulty of selling products and investing capital. Then the pace of development slackens, production slows up, unemployment waxes a sneaking disease. Then the mutual fight of the capitalists for world domination becomes fiercer, with new world wars impending.

So there can hardly be any doubt that an unlimited expansion of capitalism offering lasting life possibilities for the population, is excluded by its inner economic character. And that the time will come that the evil of depression, the calamities of unemployment, the terrors of war grow ever stronger. Then the working class, if not yet revolting, must rise and fight. Then the workers must choose between inertly succumbing and actively fighting to win freedom. Then they will have to take up their task of creating a better world out of the chaos of decaying capitalism.

Will they fight? Human history is an endless series of fights; and Clausewitz, the well-known German theorist on war, concluded from history that man is in his inner nature a warlike being. But others, skeptics as well as fiery revolutionists, seeing the timidity, the submissiveness, the indifference of the masses, often despair of the future. So we will have to look somewhat more thoroughly into psychological forces and effects.

The dominant and deepest impulse in man as in every living being is his instinct of self-preservation. It compels him to defend his life with all his powers. Fear and submissiveness also are the effect of this instinct, when against powerful masters they afford the best chances for preservation. Among the various dispositions in man those which are most adapted to secure life in the existing circumstances will prevail and develop. In the daily life of capitalism it is impractical, even dangerous for a worker to nurture his feelings of independence and pride; the more he suppresses them and tacitly obeys, the less difficulty he will encounter in finding and keeping his job. The morals taught by the ministers of the ruling class enhance this disposition. And only few and independent spirits defy these tendencies and are ready to encounter the incumbent difficulties.

When, however, in times of social crisis and danger all this submissivity, this virtuousness, is of no avail to secure life, when only fighting can help, then it gives way to its contrary, to rebelliousness and courage. Then the bold set the example and the timid discover with surprise of what deeds of heroism they are capable. Then self-reliance and high-spiritedness awake in them and grow, because on their growth depend their chances of life and happiness. And at once, by instinct and by experience, they know that only collaboration and union can give strength to their masses. When then they perceive what forces are present in themselves and in their comrades, when they feel the happiness of this awakening of proud self-respect and devoted brotherhood, when they anticipate a future of victory, when they see rising before them the image of the new society they help to build, then enthusiasm and ardor grow to irresistible power. Then the working class begins to be ripe for revolution. Then capitalism begins to be ripe for collapse.

Thus a new mankind is arising. Historians often wonder when they see the rapid changes in the character of people in revolutionary times. It seems a miracle; but it simply shows how many traits lay hidden in them, suppressed because they were of no use. Now they break forth, perhaps only temporarily; but if their utility is lasting, they develop into dominant qualities, transforming man, fitting him for the new circumstances and demands.

The first and paramount change is the growth of community-feeling. Its first traces came up with capitalism itself, out of the common work and the common fight. It is strengthened by the consciousness and the experience that, single, the worker is powerless against capital, and that only firm solidarity can secure tolerable life conditions. When the fight grows larger and fiercer, and widens into a fight for dominance over labor and society, on which life and future depend, solidarity must grow into indissoluble all-pervading unity. The new community-feeling, extending over the entire working class, suppresses the old selfishness of the capitalist world.

It is not entirely new. In primeval times, in the tribe with its simple mostly communistic forms of labor the community-feeling was dominant. Man was completely bound up with the tribe; separate from it he was nothing; in all his actions the individual felt as nothing compared with the welfare and the honor of the community. Inextricably one as he was with the tribe primitive man had not yet developed into a personality. When afterwards men separated and became independent small-scale producers, community feeling waned and gave way to individualism, that makes the own person the centre of all interests and all feelings. In the many centuries of middle class rising, of commodity production and capitalism, the individual personality-feeling awoke and ever more strongly grew into a new character. It is an acquisition that can no more be lost. To be sure, also in this time man was a social being; society dominated, and in critical moments, of revolution and war, the community-feeling temporarily imposed itself as an unwanted moral duty. But in ordinary life it lay suppressed under the proud fancy of personal independence.

What is now developing in the working class is not a reverse change, as little as life conditions are a return to bygone forms. It is the coalescence of individualism and community-feeling into a higher unity. It is the conscious subordination of all personal forces in the service of the community. In their management of the mighty productive forces the workers as their mightier masters will develop their personality to a yet higher stage. The consciousness of its intimate connection with society unites personality-feeling with the all-powerful social feeling into a new life-apprehension based on the realization of society as the source of man's entire being.

Community-feeling from the first is the main force in the progress of revolution. This progress is the growth of the solidarity, of the mutual connection, of the unity of the workers. Their organization, their new growing power, is a new character acquired through fight, is a change in their inner being, is a new morality. What military authors say about ordinary war, namely, that moral forces therein play a dominant role, is even more true in the war of the classes. Higher issues are at stake here. Wars always were contests of similar competing powers, and the deepest structure of society remained the same, whether one won or the other. Contests of classes are fights for new principles, and the victory of the rising class transfers the society to a higher stage of development. Hence, compared with real war, the moral forces are of a superior kind: voluntary devoted collaboration instead of blind obedience, faith to ideals instead of fidelity to commanders, love for the class companions, for humanity, instead of patriotism. Their essential practice is not armed violence, not killing, but standing steadfast, enduring, persevering, persuading, organizing; their aim is not to smash the skulls but to open the brains. Surely, armed action will also play a role in the fight of the classes; the armed violence of the masters cannot be overcome in Tolstoian fashion by patient suffering. It must be beaten down by force; but, by force animated by a deep moral conviction.

There have been wars that showed something of this character. Such wars as were a kind of revolution or formed part of revolutions, in the fight for freedom of the middle class. Where rising burgherdom fought for dominance against the home and the foreign feudal powers of monarchy and landownership—as in Greece in antiquity, in Italy and Flanders in the Middle Ages, in Holland, England, France in later centuries—idealism and enthusiasm, arising out of deep feelings of the class-necessities, called forth great deeds of heroism and self-sacrifice. These episodes, such as in modern times we meet with in the French revolution, or in Italy's liberation by Garibaldi's followers, count among the most beautiful pages in human history. Historians have glorified and poets have sung them as epochs of greatness, gone for ever. Because the sequel of the liberation, the practice of the new society, the rule of capital, the contrast of impudent luxury and miserable poverty, the avarice and greed of the business men, the job-hunting of officials, all this pageant of low selfishness fell as a chilling disappointment upon the next generation. In middle-class revolutions egotism and ambition in strong personalities play an important role; as a rule the idealists are sacrificed and the base characters come to wealth and power. In the bourgeoisie everybody must try to raise himself by treading down the others. The virtues of community-feeling were a temporary necessity only, to gain dominance for their class; once this aim attained, they give way to the pitiless competitive strife of all against all.

Here we have the fundamental difference between the former middle-class revolutions and the now approaching workers' revolution. For the workers the strong community-feeling arising out of their fight for power and freedom is at the same time the basis of their new society. The virtues of solidarity and devotion, the impulse to common action in firm unity, generated in the social struggle, are the foundations of the new economic system of common labor, and will be perpetuated and intensified by its practice. The fight shapes the new mankind needed for the new labor system. The strong individualism in man now finds a better way of asserting itself than in the craving for personal power over others. In applying its full force to the liberation of the class it will unfold itself more fully and more nobly than in pursuing personal aims.

Community-feeling and organization do not suffice to defeat capitalism. In keeping the working class in submission, the spiritual dominance of the bourgeoisie has the same importance as has its physical power. Ignorance is an impediment to freedom. Old thoughts and traditions press heavily upon the brains, even when touched already by new ideas. Then the aims are seen at their narrowest, well-sounding catchwords are accepted without criticism, illusions about easy successes, half-hearted measures and false promises lead astray. Thus the importance of intellectual power for the workers is shown. Knowledge and insight are an essential factor in the rise of the working class.

The workers' revolution is not the outcome of rough physical power; it is a victory of the mind. It will be the product of the mass power of the workers, certainly; but this power is spiritual power in the first place. The workers will not win because they have strong fists; fists are easily directed by cunning brains, even against their own cause. Neither will they win because they are the majority; ignorant and unorganized majorities regularly were kept down, powerless, by well-instructed organized minorities. Majority now will win only because strong moral and intellectual forces cause it to rise above the power of their masters. Revolutions in history could succeed because new spiritual forces had been awakened in the masses.

Brute stupid physical force can do nothing but destroy. Revolutions, however, are the constructive epochs in the evolution of mankind. And more than any former the revolution that is to render the workers master of the world demands the highest moral and intellectual qualities.

Can the workers respond to these demands? How can they acquire the knowledge needed? Not from the schools, where the children are imbibed with all the false ideas about society which the ruling class wishes them to have. Not from the papers, owned and edited by the capitalists, or by groups striving for leadership. Not from the pulpit that always preaches servility and where John Balls are extremely rare.

Not from the radio, where, unlike the public discussions in former times, for the citizens a powerful means of training their minds on public affairs—

one-sided allocations tend to stultify the passive listeners, and by their never-easing obtrusive noise allow of no reposed thinking. Not from the film that—unlike the theatre, in early days for the rising burgher class a means of instruction and sometimes even of fight—appeals only to visual impression, never to thinking or intelligence. They all are powerful instruments of the ruling class to keep the working class in spiritual bondage. With instinctive cunning and conscious deliberation they are all used for the purpose. And the working masses unsuspectingly submit to their influence. They let themselves be fooled by artful words and outside appearances. Even those who know of class and fight leave the affairs to leaders and statesmen, and applaud them when they speak dear old words of tradition. The masses spend their free time in pursuing puerile pleasures unaware of the great social problems on which their and their children's existence depends. It seems an insolvable problem, how a workers' revolution is ever to come and to succeed, when by the sagaciousness of the rulers and the indifference of the ruled its spiritual conditions remain lacking.

But the forces of capitalism are working in the depths of society, stirring old conditions and pushing people forward even when unwilling. Their inciting effects are suppressed as long as possible, to save the old possibilities of going on living; stored in the subconscious they only intensify the inner strains. Till at last, in crisis, at the highest pitch of necessity they snap and give way in action, in revolt. The action is not the result of deliberate intention; it comes as a spontaneous deed, irresistibly. In such spontaneous action man reveals to himself of what he is capable, a surprise to himself. And because the action is always collective action, it reveals to each that the forces dimly felt in himself, are present in all. Confidence and courage are raised by the discovery of the strong class forces of common will, and they stir and carry away ever wider masses.

Actions break out spontaneously, enforced by capitalism upon the unwilling workers. They are not so much the result as the starting point of their spiritual development. Once the fight is taken up the workers must go on in attack and defense; they must exert all their forces to the utmost. Now falls away the indifference that was only a form of resistance to demands they felt themselves unequal to respond to. Now a time of intense mental exertion sets in. Standing over against the mighty forces of capitalism they see that only by the utmost efforts, by developing all their powers can they hope to win. What in every fight appears in its first traces now broadly unfolds; all the forces hidden in the masses are roused and set in motion. This is the creative work of revolution. Now the necessity of firm unity is hammered into their consciousness, now the necessity of knowledge is felt at every moment. Every kind of ignorance, every illusion about the character and force of the foe, every weakness in resisting his tricks, every incapacity of refuting his arguments and calumnies, is revenged in failure and defeat. Active desire, by strong impulses from within, now incites the workers to use their brains. The new hopes, the new visions of the future inspire the mind, making it a living active power, that shuns no pains to seek for truth, to acquire knowledge.

Where will the workers find the knowledge they need? The sources are abundant; an extensive scientific literature of books and pamphlets, explaining the basic facts and theories of society and labor already exists and more will follow. But they exhibit the greatest diversity of opinion as to what is to be done; and the workers themselves have to choose and to distinguish what is true and right. They have to use their own brains in hard thinking and intent discussion. For they face new problems, ever again, to which the old books can give no solution. These can supply only general knowledge about society and capital, they present principles and theories, comprehending former experience. The application in ever new situations is our own task.

The insight needed can not be obtained as instruction of an ignorant mass by learned teachers, possessors of science, as the pouring of knowledge into passive pupils. It can only be acquired by self-education, by the strenuous self-activity that strains the brain in fell desire to understand the world. It would be very easy for the working class if it had only to accept established truth from those who know it. But the truth they need does not exist anywhere in the world outside them; they must build it up within themselves. Also what is given here does not pretend to be established final truth to be learned by heart. It is a system of ideas won by attentive experience of society and the workers' movement, formulated to induce others to think over and to discuss the problems of work and its organization. There are hundreds of thinkers to open new viewpoints, there are thousands of intelligent workers who, once they give their attention to them, are able, from their intimate knowledge, to conceive better and in more detail the organization of their fight and the organization of their work. What is said here may be the spark that kindles the fire in their minds.

There are groups and parties pretending to be in the exclusive possession of truth, who try to win the workers by their propaganda under the exclusion of all other opinions. By moral and, where they have the power, also by physical constraint, they try to impose their views upon the masses. It must be clear that one-sided teaching of one system of doctrines can only serve, and indeed should serve, to breed obedient followers, hence to uphold old or prepare new domination. Self-liberation of the working masses implies self-thinking, self-knowing, recognizing truth and error by their own mental exertion. Exerting the brains is much more difficult and fatiguing than exerting the muscles; but it must be done, because the brains govern the muscles; if not their own, then foreign brains.

So unlimited freedom of discussion, of expressing opinions is the breathing air of the workers' fight. It is more than a century ago that against a despotic government, Shelley, England's greatest poet of the 19th century, "the friend of the friendless poor," vindicated for everybody the right of free expression of his opinion. "A man has the right to unrestricted liberty of discussion." "A man has not only the right to express his thoughts, but it is his duty to do so" . . . "nor can any acts of legislature destroy that right." Shelley proceeded from philosophy proclaiming the natural rights of man. For us it is owing to its necessity for the liberation of the working class that freedom of speech and press is proclaimed. To restrict the freedom of discussion is to prevent the workers from acquiring the knowledge they need. Every old despotism, every modern dictatorship began by persecuting or forbidding freedom of press; every restriction of this freedom is the first step to bring the workers under the domination of same kind of rulers. Must not, then, the masses be protected against the falsehoods, the misrepresentations, the beguiling propaganda of their enemies? As little as in education careful withholding of evil influences can develop the faculty to resist and vanquish them, as little can the working class be educated to freedom by spiritual guardianship. Where the enemies present themselves in the guise of friends, and in the diversity of opinions every party is inclined to consider the others as a danger for the class, who shall decide? The workers, certainly; they must fight their way in this realm also. But the workers of to-day might in honest conviction condemn as obnoxious opinions that afterwards prove to be the basis of new progress. Only by standing open to all ideas that the rise of a new world generates in the minds of man, by testing and selecting, by judging and applying them with its own mental capacities, can the working class gain the spiritual superiority needed to suppress the power of capitalism and erect the new society.

Every revolution in history was an epoch of the most fervent spiritual activity. By hundreds and thousands the political pamphlets and papers appeared as the agents of intense self-education of the masses. In the coming proletarian revolution it will not be otherwise. It is an illusion that, once awakened from submissiveness the masses will be directed by one common clear insight and go their way without hesitation in unanimity of opinion. History shows that in such awakening an abundance of new thoughts in greatest diversity sprouts in man, expressions all of the new world, as a roaming search of mankind in the newly opened land of possibilities, as a blooming richness of spiritual life. Only in the mutual struggle of all these ideas will crystallize the guiding principles that are essential for the new tasks. The first great successes, result of spontaneous united action, by destroying previous shackles, do no more than fling open the prison gates; the workers, by their own exertion, must then find the new orientation towards further progress.

This means that those great times will be full of the noise of party strife. Those who have the same ideas form groups to discuss them for their own and to propagate them for their comrades' enlightenment. Such groups of common opinion may be called parties, though their character will be entirely different from the political parties of the previous world. Under parliamentarism these parties were the organs of different and opposite class interests. In the working class movement they were organizations taking the lead of the class, acting as its spokesmen and representatives and aspiring at guidance and dominance. Now their function will be spiritual fight only. The working class for its practical action has no use for them; it has created its new organs for action, the councils. In the shop organization, the council organization, it is the entirety of the workers itself that acts, that has to decide what must be done. In the shop assemblies and in the councils the different and opposite opinions are exposed and defended, and out of the contest the decision and the unanimous action has to proceed. Unity of purpose can only be reached by spiritual contest between the dissenting views. The important function of the parties, then, is to organize opinion, by their mutual discussion to bring the new growing ideas into concise forms, to clarify them, to exhibit the arguments in a comprehensible form, and by their propaganda to bring them to the notice of all. Only in this way the workers in their assemblies and councils can judge their truth, their merits, their practicability in each situation, and take the decision in clear understanding. Thus the spiritual forces of new ideas, sprouting wildly in all the heads, are organized and shaped so as to be usable instruments of the class. This is the great task of party strife in the workers' fight for freedom, far nobler than the endeavor of the old parties to win dominance for themselves.

The transition of supremacy from one class to another, which as in all former revolutions is the essence of the workers' revolution, does not depend on the haphazard chances of accidental events. Though its details, its ups and downs depend on the chance of various conditions and happenings that we cannot foresee, viewed at large there is a definite progressive course, which may be an object of consideration in advance. It is the increase of social power of the rising class, the loss of social power of the declining class. The rapid visible changes in power form the essential character of social revolutions. So we have to consider somewhat more closely the elements, the factors constituting the power of each of the contending classes.

The power of the capitalist class in the first place consists in the possession of capital. It is master of all the factories, the machines, the mines, master of the entire productive apparatus of society; so mankind depends on that class to work and to live. With its money-power it can buy not only servants for personal attendance; when threatened it can buy in unlimited number sturdy young men to defend its domination, it can organize them into well-armed fighting groups and give them a social standing. It can buy, by assuring them;

honorable places and good salaries, artists, writers and intellectuals, not only to amuse and to serve the masters, but also to praise them and glorify their rule, and by cunning and learning to defend their domination against criticism.

Yet the spiritual power of the capitalist class has deeper roots than the intellect it can buy. The middle class, out of which the capitalists rose as its upper layer, always was an enlightened class, self-reliant through its broad world conception, basing itself, its work, its production system, upon culture and knowledge. Its principles of personal ownership and responsibility, of self-help and individual energy pervade the entire society. These ideas the workers have brought with them, from their origin out of impoverished middle-class layers; and all the spiritual and physical means available are set to work to preserve and intensify the middle-class ideas in the masses. Thus the domination of the capitalist class is firmly rooted in the thinking and feeling of the dominated majority itself.

The strongest power factor of the capitalist class, however, is its political organization, State-power. Only by firm organization can a minority rule over a majority. The unity and continuity of plan and will in the central government, the discipline of the bureaucracy of officials pervading society as the nervous system pervades the body, and animated and directed by one common spirit, the disposal, moreover, when necessary, over an armed force, assure its unquestioned dominance over the population. Just as the strength of the fortress consolidates the physical forces of the garrison into an indomitable power over the country, so State power consolidates the physical and spiritual forces of the ruling class into unassailable strength. The respect paid to the authorities by the citizens, by the feeling of necessity, by custom and education, regularly assure the smooth running of the apparatus. And should discontent make people rebellious, what can they do, unarmed and unorganized, against the firmly organized and disciplined armed forces of the Government? With the development of capitalism, when the power from a numerous middle class ever more concentrated in a smaller number of big capitalists, the State also concentrated its power and through its increasing functions took ever more hold of society.

What has the working class to oppose to these formidable factors of power?

Ever more the working class constitutes the majority, in the most advanced countries the large majority of the population, concentrated here in large and giant industrial enterprises. Not legally but actually it has the machines, the productive apparatus of society in its hands. The capitalists are owners and masters, surely; but they can do no more than command. If the working class disregards their commands they cannot run the machines. The workers can. The workers are the direct actual masters of the machines; however determined, by obedience or by self-will, they can run them and stop them. Theirs is the most important economic function; their labor bears society.

This economical power is a sleeping power as long as the workers are captivated in middle-class thinking. It grows into actual power by class consciousness. By the practice of life and labor they discover that they are a special class, exploited by capital, that they have to fight to free themselves from exploitation. Their fight compels them to understand the structure of the economic system, to acquire knowledge of society. Notwithstanding all propaganda to the contrary this new knowledge dispels the inherited middle-class ideas in their heads, because it is based on the truth of daily experienced reality, whereas the old ideas express the past realities of a bygone world.

Economic and spiritual power are made an active power through organization. It binds all the different wills to unity of purpose and combines the single forces into a mighty unity of action. Its outer forms may differ and change as to circumstances, its essence is its new moral character, the solidarity, the strong community-feeling, the devotion and spirit of sacrifice, the self-imposed discipline. Organization is the life principle of the working class, the condition of liberation. A minority ruling by its strong organization can be vanquished only, and certainly will be vanquished, by organization of the majority.

Thus the elements constituting the power of the contending classes stand over against one another. Those of the bourgeoisie stand great and mighty, as existing and dominating forces, whereas those of the working class must develop, from small beginnings, as new life growing up. Number and economic importance grow automatically by capitalism; but the other factors, insight and organization, depend on the efforts of the workers themselves. Because they are the conditions of efficient fight they are the results of fight; every setback strains nerves and brains to repair it, every success swells the hearts into new zealous confidence. The awakening of class-consciousness, the growing knowledge of society and its development, means the liberation from spiritual bondage, the awakening from dulness to spiritual force, the ascension of the masses to true humanity. Their uniting for a common fight, fundamentally, means already social liberation; the workers, bound into the servitude of capital resume their liberty of action. It is the awakening from submissiveness to independence, collectively, in organized union challenging the masters. Progress of the working class means progress in these factors of power. What can be won in improvement of working and living conditions depends on the power the workers have acquired; when, either by insufficiency of their actions, by lack of insight or effort, or by inevitable social changes their power, compared with the capitalist power, declines, it will be felt in their working conditions. Here is the criterion for every form of action, for tactics and methods of fight, for forms of organization: Do they enhance the power of the workers? For the present, but, still more essential, for the future, for the supreme goal of annihilating capitalism? In the past trade unionism has given shape to the feelings of solidarity and unity, and strengthened their fighting power by efficient organization. When, however, in later times it had to suppress the fighting spirit, and it put up the demand of discipline towards leaders against the impulse of class solidarity the growth of power was impeded. Socialist party work in the past highly contributed to raise the insight and the political interest of the masses; when, however, it tried to restrict their activity within the confines of parliamentarism and the illusions of political democracy it became a source of weakness.

Out of these temporary weaknesses the working class has to lift its power in the actions of the coming times. Though we must expect an epoch of crisis and fight this may be alternated with more quiet times of relapse or consolidation. The traditions and illusions may act temporarily as weakening influences. But then also making them times of preparation, the new ideas of self-rule and council organization by steady propaganda may take a broader hold on the workers. Then, just as now, there is a task for every worker once he is seized by the vision of freedom for his class, to propagate these thoughts among his comrades, to rouse them from indifference, to open their eyes. Such propaganda is essential for the future. Practical realization of an idea is not possible as long as it has not penetrated the minds of the masses at large.

Fight, however, is always the fresh source of power in a rising class. We cannot foresee now what forms this fight of the workers for their freedom will assume. At times and places it may take the harsh form of civil war, so common in former revolutions when it had to give the decisions. There heavy odds may seem to be against the workers, since Government and the capitalists, by money and authority, can raise armed forces in unlimited numbers. Indeed the strength of the working class is not situated here, in the bloody contest of massacring and killing. Their real strength rests in the domain of labor, in their productive work, and in their superiority in mind and character. Nevertheless, even in armed contest capitalist superiority is not unquestioned. The production of arms is in the hands of the workers; the armed bands depend on their labor. If restricted in number, such bands, when the entire working class, united and unafraid, stands against them, will be powerless, overwhelmed by sheer numbers. And if numerous, these bands consist of recruited workers too, accessible to the call of class solidarity.

The working class has to find out and to develop the forms of fight adapted to its needs. Fight means that it goes its own way according to its free choice, directed by its class interests, independent of, hence opposed to the former masters. In fight its creative faculties assert themselves in finding ways and means. Just as in the past it devised and practiced spontaneously its forms of action: the strike, the ballot, the street demonstration, the mass meeting, the leaflet propaganda, the political strike, so it will do in future. Whatever the forms may be, character, purpose and effect will be the same for all: to raise the own elements of power, to weaken and dissolve the power of the foe. So far as experience goes mass political strikes have the strongest effects; and in future they may be still more powerful. In these strikes, born out of acute crises and strong strains, the impulses are too fierce, the issues go too deep to be directed by unions or parties, committees or boards of officials. They bear the character of direct actions of the masses. The workers do not go into strike individually, but shopwise, as personnel collectively deciding their action. Immediately strike committees are installed, where delegates of all the enterprises meet, assuming already the character of workers' councils. They have to bring unity in action, unity also, as much as possible, in ideas and methods, by continual interaction between the fighting impulses of the shop-assemblies and the discussions in the council meetings. Thus the workers create their own organs opposing the organs of the ruling class.

Such a political strike is a kind of rebellion, though in legal form, against the Government, by paralyzing production and traffic trying to exert such a pressure upon the government that it yields to the demands of the workers. Government, from its side, by means of political measures, by prohibiting meetings, by suspending the freedom of press, by calling up armed forces, hence by transforming its legal authority into arbitrary though actual power, tries to break the determination of the strikers. It is assisted by the ruling class itself, that by its press monopoly dictates public opinion and carries on a strong propaganda of calumny to isolate and discourage the strikers. It supplies volunteers not only for somehow maintaining traffic and services, but also for armed bands to terrorize the workers and to try to convert the strike into a form of civil war, more congenial to the bourgeoisie. Because a strike cannot last indefinitely, one of the parties, with the lesser inner solidity, must give way.

Mass actions and universal strikes are the struggle of two classes, of two organizations, each by its own solidity trying to curb and finally to break the other. This cannot be decided in one action; it demands a series of struggles that constitute an epoch of social revolution. For each of the contending classes disposes of deeper sources of power that allow it to restore itself after defeat. Though the workers at a time may be defeated and discouraged, their organizations destroyed, their rights abolished, yet the stirring forces of capitalism, their own inner forces, and the indestructible will to live, once more puts them on their feet. Neither can capitalism be destroyed at one stroke; when its fortress, State Power, is shattered, demolished, the class itself still disposes of a great deal of its physical and spiritual power. History has instances how governments entirely disabled and prostrate by war and revolution, were regenerated by the economic power, the money, the intellectual capacity, the patient skill, the class-consciousness—in the form of ardent national feeling—of the bourgeoisie. But finally the class that forms the majority of the people, that supports society by its labor, that has the direct disposal over the productive apparatus, must win. In such a way that the firm organization of the majority class dissolves and crumbles State power, the strongest organization of the capitalist class.

Where the action of the workers is so powerful that the very organs of Government are paralyzed the councils have to fulfill political functions. Now the workers have to provide for public order and security, they have to take care that social life can proceed, and in this the councils are their organs. What is decided in the councils the workers perform. So the councils grow into organs of social revolution; and with the progress of revolution their tasks become ever more all-embracing. At the same time that the classes are struggling for supremacy, each by the solidity of its organization trying to break that of the other class, society must go on to live. Though in the tension of critical moments it can live on the stores of provisions, production cannot stop for a long time. This is why the workers, if their inner forces of organization fall short, are compelled by hunger to return under the old yoke. This is why, if strong enough, if they have defied, repelled, shattered State Power, if they have repulsed its violence, if they are master in the shops, they immediately must take care of the production. Mastery in the shops means at the same time organization of production. The organization for fight, the councils, is at the same time organization for reconstruction.

Of the Jews in olden times building the walls of Jerusalem it is said that they fought sword in one, trowel in the other hand. Here, differently, sword and trowel are one. Establishing the organization of production is the strongest, nay, the only lasting weapon to destroy capitalism. Wherever the workers have fought their way into the shops and taken possession of the machines, they immediately start organizing the work. Where capitalist command has disappeared from the shop, disregarded and powerless, the workers build up production on the new basis. In their practical action they establish new right and new Law. They cannot wait till everywhere the fight is over; the new order has to grow from below, from the shops, work and fight at the same time.

Then at the same time the organs of capitalism and Government decline into the role of unessential foreign and superfluous things. They may still be powerful to harm, but they have lost the authority of useful and necessary institutions. Now the roles, more and more manifestly to everybody, are reverted. Now the working class, with its organs, the councils, is the power of order; life and prosperity of the entire people rests on its labor, its organization. The measures and regulations decided in the councils, executed and followed by the working masses, are acknowledged and respected as legitimate authority. On the other hand the old governmental bodies dwindle to outside forces that merely try to prevent the stabilization of the new order. The armed bands of the bourgeoisie, even when still powerful, get ever more the character of unlawful disturbers, of obnoxious destroyers in the rising world of labor. As agents of disorder they will be subdued and dissolved.

This is, in so far as we now can foresee, the way by which State Power will disappear, together with the disappearance of capitalism itself. In past times different ideas about future social revolution prevailed.

First the working class had to conquer the political power, by the ballot winning a majority in Parliament, helped eventually by armed contests or political strikes. Then the new Government consisting of the spokesmen, leaders, and politicians, by its acts, by new Law, had to expropriate the capitalist class and to organize production. So the workers themselves had only to do half the work, the less essential part; the real work, the reconstruction of society, the organizing of labor, had to be done by the socialist politicians and officials. This conception reflects the weakness of the working class at that time; poor and miserable, without economic power, it had to be led into the promised land of abundance by others, by able leaders, by a benignant Government. And then, of course, to remain subjects; for freedom cannot be given, it can only be conquered. This easy illusion has been dispelled by the growth of capitalist power. The workers now have to realize that only by raising their own power to the highest height can they hope to win liberty; that political dominance, mastery over society must be based upon economic power, mastery over labor.

The conquest of political power by the workers, the abolition of capitalism, the establishment of new Law, the appropriation of the enterprises, the reconstruction of society, the building of a new system of production are not different consecutive occurrences. They are contemporary, concurrent in a process of social events and transformations. Or, more precisely, they are identical. They are the different sides, indicated with different names, of one great social revolution: the organization of labor by working humanity.

III. The Foe

1. THE ENGLISH BOURGEOISIE

Knowledge of the foe, knowledge of his resources, of his forces and his weaknesses, is the first demand in every fight. The first requisite to protect us, when seeing his superior powers, against discouragement; after partial success, against illusions. Hence it is necessary to consider how, with the evolution of society, the present ruling class has developed.

This development was different in different countries. The workers of each country are exploited and dominated by their own bourgeoisie [the property owning and capitalist class]; it is the foe they have to deal with. So it might seem sufficient to study its character only. But at present we see that the capitalist classes of all countries and all continents grow together into one world class, albeit in the form of two fiercely fighting coalitions. So the workers cannot restrict their attention to their direct masters. Already in the past, when taking up their fight, they themselves immediately felt an international brotherhood. Now the capitalist classes of the entire world are their opponents, and so they must know and understand them all.

Old capitalism is best seen in England. There for the first time it came to power; from there it spread over the world. There it developed most of the institutions and the principles imitated and followed afterwards in other countries. Yet it shows a special character different from the others.

The English revolution, of the time of Pym and Cromwell, was not a conquest of power by the capitalist class, won from a previously ruling feudal class of landowners. Just as earlier in Holland, it was the repulse of a kind to establish absolute monarchical power. In other countries, by means of their standing armies and of the officials and judges appointed by them and obeying them, the kings subdued the independent nobility as well as the privileged town governments. Making use of the money power of rising capitalism, they could establish strong central governments and turn the tumultuous nobles into obedient courtiers and military officers, securing them their feudal rights and properties, and at the same time protecting commerce and industry, the source of the taxes from the business people. Their power was based on a kind of equilibrium between the rising power of capital and the declining power of land ownership. In England, however, in consequence of the local self-rule of the counties, of the traditional coalition of landowners and town-citizens in the House of Commons, and of the lack of a standing army, the Stuart kings failed in their striving for absolute monarchy. Though it broke out in defense of the medieval rights and privileges, the revolutionary fight, convulsing the depth of society, to a great extent modernized institutions. It made Parliament, especially the House of Commons, the ruling power of the land.

The middle class, thus becoming the ruling class in England, consisted chiefly of the numerous class of squires, independent landowners, the gentry, forming the lower nobility; they were associated with the influential merchants of London, and with the wealthy citizens ruling in the smaller towns. By means of local self-government, embodied in their office of Justices of the Peace, they dominated the countryside. The House of Commons was their organ, by means of which they determined the home and foreign policy of the country. Government itself they left mostly to the nobility and the kings, who were now their instruments and steadily controlled by Parliament. Because England as an island was protected by her fleet, there was hardly any army; the ruling class having learned to hate and fear it as an instrument of governmental despotism, jealously kept it insignificant. Neither was there a police to restrain personal liberty.

Thus the government had no means to keep down by force new rising powers. In other countries this keeping down of course could only be temporary, till at last a violent revolution broke out and swept away the entire old system of domination. In England, on the contrary, when after long resistance the ruling class in public opinion and social action felt the irresistible force of a rising class, it had no choice but to yield. Thus by necessity originated the policy grown into an English tradition, of resisting rising forces as long as it is possible, in the end to yield before the breaking point is reached. The governing class then retained its power by sharing it with the new class, accepting its leading figures into its midst, often by knighting them. The old forms remained, even though the contents changed. No revolution, as a cleansing thunderstorm, did away with the old traditions and the old wigs, with the meaningless ceremonials and the antiquated forms of thinking. Respectfully the English people look up to the aristocratic families ruling with such sensible policy. Conservatism permeates all forms of social life. Not the contents; by the unlimited personal liberty labor and life develop freely according to practical needs.

The industrial revolution broke into the careless life of old England of the 18th century, an irresistible new development and a destructive catastrophe. Factories were built, provided with the newly invented spinning machines, driven by water, and then by steam power, soon to be followed by weaving, and then by machine factories. The new class of factory owners arose and grew rich by the exploitation of the new class of miserable workers, formed out of the impoverished artisans beaten down by the superiority of the new machines. Under the indifference of the old authorities that were entirely inactive and incapable of coping with the new situation, industrial capitalism grew up in a chaos of free competition, of the most horrible working conditions, of utter neglect of the simplest exigencies of health and careless waste of the nation's vigor.

A fierce struggle ensued, in a complicated triangular way. Repeatedly the workers broke out into revolts against the miserable working conditions combined with cruel oppression from the old political institutions, against the employers, as well as against the governing land owner class. And at the same time the new industrial bourgeoisie growing in wealth and social influence, vindicating its share in government, organized itself ever more strongly. Under this double pressure the landowners were forced to yield; in the Reform Act of 1832 modernizing the constituencies, the capitalist class of factory owners got their representation in Parliament. And in 1846, by a special repeal of the corn laws that raised the price of wheat by import duties, they succeeded in throwing off the heavy tribute to the landowners. Thus the way was free for producing and accumulating capital in unlimited quantity. The working class, however, stormed in vain against the ramparts of the State stronghold, now fortified by an additional garrison of defenders. The rulers had, it is true, no forces to suppress the working class movement by violence. Capitalist society resisted by its inner toughness, by its deep-seated solidity, instinctively felt by the entire middle class to be a rising form of production destined to conquer the world. It yielded by steps, by granting such reforms as were unavoidable; so in ever new fights the workers obtained the right of association, the ten hour day, and finally, gradually, the franchise.

The English bourgeoisie was undisputed master; its Parliament was the sovereign power of the realm. The first and strongest industrial and capitalist class of the world, it dominated world commerce and world markets. During the entire 19th century it was master on the seven seas and powerful in all continents. Riches flowing from all sides, from industry, from commerce, from the colonies, accumulated in its hands. The other classes shared in its enormous profits. In the first place the landowner class, the ruling nobility, from olden times was strongly affiliated to business and commercial life. It was not feudal at all, not of mediaeval descent—the feudal class had exterminated itself in civil wars—but of middle class origin, owing its elevation to wealth, services, to mere favor, the more jealous therefore of the outer appearances and ceremonies of prerogative. Now in the new system of unlimited profit-production it coalesced with the industrial capitalists into one powerful ruling and exploiting class.

Where an aristocracy finds its place in capitalist society, its special pursuit, besides government offices, is the profession of arms. So the standing of the landowner class is shown by the power of militarism. In Prussian Germany the supremacy of the landed nobility was expressed in the ascendancy of military above civil forms. There, even under modern capitalism, civilians were despised as second rate, and the highest ambition for a wealthy business man or a deserving scientist was to don the uniform of reserve officer, "the king's coat." In England, with its small and chiefly colonial army, the same process took place in the navy. For continental wars there was an army recruited from the lowest classes, called "scum of the earth" by their honored chief, the Duke of Wellington; fighting in the stiff linear tactics of hirelings at a time when in France and Germany enthusiastic popular armies practiced the free skirmishing method of fighting; only as late as 1873 flogging of the soldiers was abolished. Military office was not esteemed, and the spirit of militarism was entirely absent. Civilian life was supreme above military forms; when the professional daily duties were absolved, the English officer put on civilian dress, to be simply a gentleman—the word expressing a civilian code of honor not known in other countries. Thus the absence of continental militarism is an indication of how completely the landowning aristocracy in England is absorbed into the entirety of the capitalist class.

The working class also got its part. Not all of course; only its most influential groups, "skilled labor," that by its trade unions was able to display fighting power. From its profits secured by world monopoly the capitalist class could grant them a share sufficient to turn them into contented adherents of the existing order. They separated from the miserable unskilled masses that filled the slums. Every thought that another system of production might be possible or necessary, disappeared. So capitalism was entirely secure; the solidity of a system of exploitation depends on the lack of capacity of the exploited class to discern its exploitation. Among the workers the middle class doctrine prevailed that everybody is master of his own fate. They took over all middle class ideas and traditions, even the reverence paid to the upper classes and their ceremonies.

During the long years of exploitation and gradual development capital in private hands could increase along with the need for larger installations, brought about by the progress of technics. There was no need for organization of capital; banking operations found sufficient scope in interchanging and lending money for facilitating intercourse. There was also little organization of the industrial enterprises into large combines; the employers, themselves disposing of sufficient capital, remained independent owners of their shops. Hence a wilful individualism was the salient character of the English bourgeoisie. Hence also little concentration in the realm of production; numerous independent small shops kept up alongside of the large factories. Thus in the coal industry the demands of security and health put up by the workers and by the Sankey

Commission, ever again were frustrated by the small mine owners not having the means to modernize their backward installations.

Entire freedom in social life allows every new idea to be tried out and to be put into practice, every impulse of will; whereas the lack of this liberty causes the impeded wishes and inapplicable ideas to develop into consistent theoretical systems. So, contrasted to the broadly worked-out theoretical character of science and activity on the continent, the English became men of practical deeds. For every problem or difficulty an immediate practical solution was sought without regard to further consequences, in technics as well as in politics. Science played a small part in the progress of technics. This is also a cause of much backwardness in English business life.

In this way England in the 19th century became the model country of old capitalism with its free competition, careless and improvident, full of hard egoism against the weak, persons as well as peoples, full of obsolete institutions and senseless old forms, full of downtrodden misery viewed with indifference alongside the display of luxury. Already such books as William Booth's "Darkest England" and Robert Blatchford's "Dismal England" indicate a state of dirty neglect not tolerated in other civilized countries, entirely left to the individual initiative of single philanthrophists. In the later years only, and in the new century, social reforms began to play a noticeable role; and, especially after the first world war, a stronger concentration of capital set in.

In this way at the same time, however, the English bourgeoisie developed that master character that was the envy of all capitalists of other countries, who in vain tried to imitate it. For many centuries it has been living in a state of complete freedom and unchallenged power. Through its monopoly of industry and commerce in the 19th century it felt itself master of the world, the only cosmopolitans, at home in every continent and on every ocean. It never learned to fear; never was it faced by a superior foe attacking from outside or a revolution threatening from within, suggesting the idea of mortality. With unlimited self-assurance it confronts every new difficulty, sure to overcome it, by force if it can, by concessions if it must. In foreign politics, in the founding and defense of its world power, the English ruling class showed the capacity of ever again adapting itself to new situations, of defying its most solemn proclamations of yesterday by the opposite practice of tomorrow, of "shaking hands with murderers" where it was necessary, and, in seeming generosity, of making allies of vanquished opponents of whom it feels that they cannot be permanently kept down. All this not by a wide knowledge and foresight; on the contrary, it is a class rather ignorant, narrow-minded and conservative—hence much blundering before finally the new arrangement is found—but it has the self-sure instinct of power. The same instinctive sagacity to solve its problems by practical conduct was used in home politics to keep the working class in spiritual and actual dependence; here with equal success.

Modern development, certainly, caused the English bourgeoisie to lose a good deal of its exceptional position in the world; but ever again it knew how to resign and to adapt itself to the rise of other equal powers. Already in the latter part of the 19th century German industry made its appearance as a serious competitor in the world market, whilst afterwards Japan came to oust the products of British industry. Britain's financial supremacy was lost to America in the first world war. But its main character, acquired in an unchallenged rule of so many centuries was unshaken. In home politics also it knew how to adapt its rule to the demands of the working class, by introducing a system of social reforms and provisions. The English bourgeoisie had the good luck that the formation of the Labor Party, transferring all workers' votes from Liberal politicians to Labor leaders entirely filled with middle class ideas, rendered the working class an active agent in consolidating capitalist rule—though it had to pay for it the price of a modernizing reform of some of the worst abominations of capitalism. In leaders of the Labor Party it found able Cabinet Ministers, entirely devoted to the maintenance of the capitalist system, therein representing, when these temporarily had to prevail, the pacifist tendencies.

This character of the English bourgeoisie is essential in determining the forms of the prospective rise of the working class. What must be overcome, the power of the bourgeoisie, weakness of the workers, is not physical force but spiritual dependence. Doubtless physical force may play its role, too, at critical moments; English capitalism, in defense of its existence, will be able to bring up, when necessary, strong powers of violence and restraint. But the weakness of the English working class consists chiefly in its being entirely dominated by middle class ideas. Self-centered individualism, the conviction that everybody has to forge his own fate, respect for traditional social relations, conservatism of thought, are firmly rooted in it by the unchallenged power of capitalism, at home and all over the world. Strong shocks will be needed to stir the petrified brains; and capitalist development is at work already. When political catastrophes or the irresistible rise of mighty competitors undermine the world power of the English bourgeoisie, when the privileged position of the English workers has gone, when their very existence is endangered, then also for them the only way will be the fight for power over production.

The fundamental ideas of council organization are not entirely foreign to the English workers. At the end of the first world war the shop steward movement arose, establishing a direct contact of shop representatives in preparing fighting actions, independent of the unions. Already earlier "guild socialism" presented many cognate conceptions; and "industrial unionism" put up the demand of control of production, by the workers, linked, though, with the ideas of the unions as the ruling bodies. The character of the English bourgeoisie and the freedom of all social relations make it probable that practical momentary solutions of the conflicts will be sought for, rather than fundamental decisions. So as an instance, we might conceive that as a temporary compromise, freedom of speech and discussion in the shop is established, and the capitalist's old right of hiring and firing is restricted by the workers' right to decide on the seniority issues of the personnel; this would keep the road open to further progress. In such a course of development, when at last the partial concessions should amount to an important loss of power, attempts of the capitalist class to regain supremacy by serious decisive class war cannot be avoided. Yet it seems possible that, if anywhere, in England the mastery of the workers over production may be won by successive steps along intermediary forms of divided rule; each step unsatisfactory, and urging further steps until complete freedom is reached.

2. THE FRENCH BOURGEOISIE

The development in France took place along quite different lines. In a great political revolution the bourgeoisie, combined with the farmers, overthrew the absolute monarchy with all its mediaeval forms, and deprived the nobility and the church of its landed property. In explicit acts and laws the Revolution abolished all feudal privileges, proclaimed the "rights of man," with private property as their main foundation, and asserted legal equality of all citizens. Constrained to a pitched revolutionary fight the bourgeoisie made a sharp division between itself, garbed as the third estate, as the entire people, and the defeated feudal classes, now completely excluded from political power. It had to do the governing work entirely by itself. There was a clear consciousness of the middle class character of its institutions, formulated in precise paragraphs; the rights of Parliament, differently from English custom, were exactly circumscribed. These formulations of Parliamentary constitution then served as a model for other countries. Political freedom, in England a practical fact, in France was conscious theory. The need of explaining and formulating it created a wealth of political literature, in books and speeches, full of lucid expression of principles. But what was lacking was the immediate feeling of complete mastership. Practice at the same time was imperfect; the French bourgeoisie had first to suffer military despotism, and then, in gradual steps, in a series of smaller political revolutions, in 1830, 1848, 1870, had to win complete power over the State.

In these revolutions, fought chiefly by the popular classes, the petty burghers, the artisans, the workers, these learned to distinguish their own class interests, as contrasted to capitalist interests. The workers aspired to a further revolution that should break the new class power of capitalism, but in the armed conflicts, in 1848 and 1871, they were defeated and butchered; partly by their own class fellows, hired by the bourgeoisie, partly by the aid of the petty burgherdom, shopkeepers, farmers, who all came to the rescue as defenders of private property. Thus it was shown that the bourgeoisie had a firm grip on society, that the working class was not yet ripe for mastery, and that a further development of capitalism was needed.

Though in these fierce class fights the bourgeoisie had been victorious, it did not come out without injury. It had lost its self-confidence. It knew that ever it would have to defend itself against the growing power from beneath, that ever its rule would be threatened by the working class. So it sought for protection by a strong State Power. The centralization of all political power in the Government at Paris, introduced already by the Convention and by Napoleon, was intensified in the 19th century. Together with the absence of a ruling aristocracy it gave a political aspect to France quite different from England.

Moreover, economic development took a different course. After a strong growth about the middle of the century industrial development slackened. The countryside gave no strong surplus of population flowing to the towns to provide labor power for a growing industry. The savings of small business men, collected in the banks, were not used as industrial capital in founding new enterprises, but mostly invested in governmental loans. Certainly in regions with rich coal and ore deposits a strong iron and steel industry developed, with powerful capitalists at the head, often in family relation with the landed aristocracy. Besides, in the big towns, especially in Paris, as the centre of fashion for the entire European bourgeoisie, the old small-scale industry of luxuries, founded on personal skill and taste of a numerous class of wage-earning artisans, strongly developed. But the chief character of French capitalism, especially after 1870, ever more became the prevalence of financial capital as supreme power.

The banks, under the lead of the central "Banque de France," collected the money of small capitalists, shareholders and farmers into a huge mass of bank capital. Wherever governments in Europe or other continents wanted loans they were procured by the French banks; the bonds and shares were recommended and urged upon the clients as a good investment. Thus the small-property-class in France consists mainly of rentiers, stock-holders, living upon the exploitation of foreign peoples, receiving their income from the taxes squeezed by foreign governments out of their subjects. The loans of these governments usually had to serve for buying war materials or building railways. So bank capital worked in close collaboration with the lords of the steel industry, usually imposing the condition that the money was to be spent in the affiliated French steel works. Thus the savings of the French rentiers went to the coffers of the steel capitalists, and the interest for the rentiers was provided by foreign taxpayers.

This predominant character of French capital determined French politics, foreign, as well as home. Foreign politics served to protect the interests of bank capital and the rentiers, by alliances fortifying its international power and its influence over smaller backward countries. By military power when necessary, it secured the payments from unwilling debtor-governments; or it converted some barbarian chieftain into a dependent prince, providing him with European arms to subjugate and exploit the formerly free tribes; which was called bringing order and civilization.

The problem of home politics in big capitalism is always how to make parliaments chosen by universal suffrage, hence dependent on the votes of small business men, of farmers and of workers, instruments of the interests of big capital. In countries with a rapid industrial development this is not difficult. The entire bourgeoisie is carried away, its business prospers through the fervent economic action, and the workers, too, fully occupied as they are, and able to win good wages, are conciliated. Big capital, with assured self-confidence proclaims its interests to be the common interests of society at large. It is quite different, however, with bank capital. Its exploitation of foreign peoples and capturing of the savings of their own people, through violence and deceit, bears the character of usury and robbery. Its interests must be served behind the scenes, by secret arrangements with influential politicians. For its purposes cabinet ministers must be installed or deposed, party leaders must be won over, members of parliament must be manipulated, papers must be bribed–all dirty intrigues that cannot bear the light of day. The politicians, mostly lawyers or other intellectuals, forced by the party-machines upon the farmers and citizens as their representatives, consider politics as business, aiming at high and remunerative offices as their share in the spoils. Parliamentarianism everywhere in modern times is degenerating because it has to put up the semblance of the common good while serving capitalist interests. But where financial capital rules, it must deteriorate into sheer corruption. For financial capital, as represented by the French banks, has no direct connection with labor. Its politics, not founded on the actual fight of a class in command of production, must live on false slogans, on deceitful promises and sounding rhetoric.

Because in Paris during most of the 19th century small scale enterprises were dominant, the working class, not sharply separated from the mass of the small independent artisans and employers, could not develop a clear-cut class consciousness, though it was filled with an ardent republican and democratic fighting spirit. Seeing the capitalists rise by the protection of government, by using the political power for shameless personal enrichment, whereas they themselves were forcibly kept down, the workers considered State Power as the chief cause of their exploitation and their misery. So their feelings of free individuality, inheritance of the Great Revolution developed into some kind of anarchism, the doctrine that only by complete abolition of the State and its constraining power mankind can be free as an agglomeration of independent collaborating individuals.

When, in later years, with the gradual development and concentration of industry, trade unions arose, these, just as in England, took the central place in the social ideas of the working class. Not so much as practical means of participating in prosperity, but rather, French capitalism lacking industrial and commercial world power, as the theoretical basis of a better society. So towards the end of the century syndicalism became the theory of social reconstruction occupying the minds of the workers not only in France, but spreading over Spain, Italy and other countries also. Syndicats is simply the French name for trade unions. In the doctrine of syndicalism, "labor the basis of the new world," means that the syndicat, the union will be its organization unit. The union, it says, is the free creation of the workers, their field of self-government, whereas in the State the officials and politicians, and in the political parties the intellectuals dominate. A political revolution that should make the State master of production would mean a more oppressive slavery for the workers. Liberation of the workers by revolution is only possible as a destruction of State and Government. It must be brought about by a universal strike, a common action of all its workers. In its place shall come the free association of all the unions; the unions will be the bodies to organize and direct production.

These principles clearly expound their dependence on the forms of French capitalism. Since the contents of politics stood at a wide distance from the productive work of society with its struggle of real class interest, the working class held itself at a wide distance from politics. Since politics was a dirty business of personal intrigue, the workers disdained to get mixed up with politics. Their practice, proclaimed as class war, theoretically for abolishing exploitation, practically for better working conditions, was comprised entirely within the field of production, where it acted by means of the syndicates. Syndicalism did not intend to yield or to submit to bank capital; in the syndicalist slogans of anti-patriotism, antimilitarism, and universal strike, it expressed its refusal to be carried away in the militaristic policy of bank capital. But this was only a negative form of opposition, not a positive form of fight; it underrated the powerful hold of capital through the power of nationalistic ideas. In the principle: that every member of the syndicat may individually take part in politics by voting "according to his philosophic or political ideas" is expressed the primitive helplessness of a class that contents itself with trying to exclude from its immediate struggle differences of opinion on society at large. The insight was lacking that against big capital in industry solid big organizations needs must arise, involving a bureaucracy of leading officials. And that production directed by the syndicats means production under the direction of union leaders and not by self-management of the workers.

Practically syndicalism went down when at the outbreak of the first world war its leaders joined their Government and submitted to their capitalist class. This prepared the transition to overt reformist policy after the war, when in international collaboration the differences in theory between the English, German and French unions receded behind their common practice. In these later years also the differences in character of capitalism in different countries, strongly emphasized before, became less marked in the growth of industry everywhere, in the merging of financial and industrial capital, in their common imperialist policy of subduing foreign peoples and of preparing for future wars for world supremacy.

The power of the French bourgeoisie consists, as everywhere, in its economic and financial power, its spiritual power and its State power. Different from the English bourgeoisie, its economic power is not in the first place mastery over industry and world commerce, but money power; with this money it buys propaganda and armed force, and dominates politics. The spiritual power of French capitalism is based on the tradition of the Great Revolution and the social institutions created by it. The proud feeling of having thrown off despotism and, an example for others, established legal freedom and equality, lives as a strong tradition in the entire people. Only by nursing these feelings, by acknowledging the democratic forms, by respecting the freedom in public opinion, can capital rule over the masses who take the outer appearances for reality. And should they become rebellious, they find a strong centralized State Power over them. The basic weakness of the French working class, notwithstanding its gallant fights in the past, rests on the slowness of modern economic development, the masses of the farmers, the citizens, the workers being dispersed over numerous petty enterprises. French capitalism lagged behind the old power of English and the rising power of German and American capitalism; no fresh stream of impulses pushed the classes into strong action and energetic fight.

3. THE GERMAN BOURGEOISIE

At the end of the Middle Ages a proud, free and martial burgherdom, rich through its commerce from Italy and the East to Northern and Western Europe, filled the flourishing German towns. Then by the discovery of America and India world trade shifted to the shores of the Atlantic. The economic decline found its sequel in internecine wars and invasions by foreign powers, ransacking and murdering, entirely destroying the old wealth. The Thirty-Years' War left Germany a devastated and impoverished country, without commerce and industry, cut off from the economic development of the West, divided into a hundred small independent States under petty princes, powerless outside their domain, arbitrary despots at home. The largest among them, the rising Prussian monarchy, was dominated completely by the landed aristocracy, the "Junkers," who kept the miserable farmers in servitude, masters of the army as an instrument of conquest. The French revolution and the rise of the English industry gave a first impulse to the German poets and philosophers, exponents of the nascent aspirations of burgherdom. Through the Napeolonic domination the rise of nationalism had a reactionary character finding its theoretical expression in the solemn confession of servility; the French revolution proclaimed the rights of man, we proclaim the duties of man.

Towards the middle of the 19th century industry began to develop, and with it a first spirit of freedom, of criticism against the narrow-minded suppression by absolutism and police arbitrariness. The rising bourgeoisie prepared to extort political rights from the Prussian monarchy, which meant a revolution by the help of the working masses. But then, in 1848, it saw the working class proclaim its radical demands, and even fight the propertied classes in a fierce class struggle, at the Paris barricades. So it shrank back; the way of revolution, of winning freedom and power for itself by winning political freedom for the masses, was barred. When in the following years industry developed ever more, the German bourgeoisie alongside of itself saw the working class organizing into an independent power. So it was pinched between an old ruling power above, monarchy, aristocracy and army, and a rising new power beneath, workers already talking communism. Because it wanted police protection in every strike, because it felt the working class to be its genuine economic antagonist, it could not venture a serious fight against State Power. And should it eventually talk of revolution, then the aristocratic rulers would not hesitate to rouse the workers against their employers by promising social laws restricting the arbitrariness in the factory, and by even hinting at a "social monarchy," protecting the working class against capitalism.

So the German bourgeoisie learned fear. Fear for the power above, fear for the power beneath determined its social character. Never it knew that proud feeling that only self-won freedom can waken in a social class.

Other causes aided to develop this character. Unlike France and England that many centuries ago already had acquired their rational unity, Germany was still divided in several dozens of insignificant Statelets. It was an annoying and cumbersome impediment to the development of industry and commerce; so many different governments and laws and rules, different systems of taxes and coinage, custom duties at the several frontiers, every petty government plaguing business through stupid officials, and powerless to protect it on foreign markets. The German bourgeoisie deeply resented the lack of a powerful united State. A free and united Germany had been its hope at the outset of 1848; but the courage had failed to join in the fight of the people. And now it perceived that there was another way to acquire, not freedom, but unity: by means of Prussian militarism. The Prussian aristocracy had made its army an excellent instrument of conquest. In a series of wars, a revolution from above, the surrounding Powers were defeated or overawed, and the small German States were subjected and combined into a powerful German Empire. And now the bourgeoisie changed its policy, left its parliamentary spokesmen alone to make speeches against militarism, and enthusiastically hailed the "iron chancellor" and the Prussian king as its heroes.

"Despotism under Bismarck," wrote the English historian Trevelyan "had become an active principle in the van of progress; it was no longer timidly hostile to the mercantile class, to the press, education and science, but harnessed them all to the coach of government." Formerly, in other countries, progress—i.e., the development of capitalism—was always linked with increasing freedom—i.e., mastery of the bourgeoisie over government. Now, here, on the contrary, despotic government became the instrument for the development of capitalism. The constitution of the newly created Empire was animated by a modern daring spirit, and its policy by brutal energy, adequate to a strongly developing capitalism. Social reform laws and universal suffrage for the Diet secured participation of the masses in its world politics, and the adaptation to changing conditions. At the same time the separate States remained, with their obsolete constitutions, with their narrow-minded officialdom, covering the field of administration, of home affairs, of police and education, keeping the masses subjected and continually supervised.

Thus a strong State power was put into the service of rising capitalism without giving political supremacy to the capitalists themselves. The Prussian landowning aristocracy remained master of modern Germany; but only by serving the demands of capitalism. It took its share of the increasing mass of surplus value, not only occupying the lucrative ruling posts in government, but also using its political power to increase—by corn laws—the money produce of its landed property. The bourgeoisie remained a class of obedient subjects, socially influential by its money, but regarded as second class citizens, content to conduct their business and respectfully glorifying monarchy and nobility. In contrast to England and France, parliament had no power over government; it could not by its vote enforce the dismissal of a cabinet. If a parliamentary majority had tried such a thing by using its right of control of the budget, the bourgeoisie would have forsaken and discarded it; rather than be dependent on a parliament elected by the masses it preferred to be ruled from above.

Now the way was open for capitalist development without political freedom. Whereas the working class, continually struggling for breathing and fighting space, was kept down by a strong hand, Germany as a mighty new Power played its role in European politics. Industry and commerce developed with a marvellous rapidity, overtaking all other European countries, equalled only by the United States of America.

This was not only the fresh energy of a people, kept back through years of adverse political conditions. In Germany industry came up half a century later than in England, at a time of more highly developed technics. It had to begin at the outset by introducing big machines and expensive installations requiring science and capital. Science it had; long before already its scientists had taken an honorable part in international research. Just because technical application had been restricted better theoretical foundations could be laid, that now were the basis, at a rapidly growing number of universities and technical schools, of a thorough scientific training for the needs of industry. Personal wealth, however, great capital, such as the factory owners in England, had accumulated out of the profits of half a century, was lacking in Germany. There the capital needed for big enterprises had to be provided by carefully collecting all small bits of savings from the separate small capitalists. This was the function of the banks.

Thus German industry acquired a special character. To increase the profits for a rapid accumulation of capital the productivity was raised by conscious amelioration of its scientific basis. So from a number of markets German competition was able to oust the English, confident in their tried and proved methods. At the same time the close connection of banks and industry created new form of organization. The bank, interested in the success of enterprises because it provided them with capital, supervised and advised their policy and brought them into connection. This led to mutual assistance and favorite treatment between such enterprises, to an intertwining of interests, often to the formation of cartels, in every case to organization. The interpenetration of the directions of the banks and big industries created a conscious common policy of continuously extending their power over new branches. By investing capital here, by enlarging existing business there, by the well-planned founding of new enterprises, the banks, a few groups of fiercely competing financial powers, organized industry in a systematical way, increasing profits and still more their own share in it. Thus what first appeared as a weakness, the lack of private capital, turned into strength. Against the self-willing independence of English business men, confident in their traditional wealth and clientele, German industry rapidly rose to power through its purposeful organization. With restless energy and fresh ambition the German bourgeoisie forced its way up in production and world commerce, began to export capital to colonies and foreign continents, and prepared to conquer its share in world power.

In England militarism never got a footing in society. In Germany the forms and spirit of militarism pervaded and dominated society; its code of honor, coarse and touchy, was aped by the middle class youth at the universities; and to the caste of officers the business man was the despised civilian. The middle class German looked up with deep veneration at the army, its refuge and its instrument of power, and equally worshiped the masters of the army, the monarch and his officers. In German constitution, Parliament, the Diet, had no power over the army, it had solely to provide the money. This militarism embodied the submissiveness of the German bourgeoisie, its lack of personal pride, its feeling of inferiority, often camouflaged as rough brutality. The German bourgeoisie never knew freedom. Entirely foreign to them is the proud feeling of independence, as personal freedom pervading all classes in the Western countries.

This, however, made the German bourgeoisie better adapted to the exigencies of big capitalism. Organization of capitalism, based as it is on subordination under a stronger power, came easier to the German than to a capitalist class accustomed to personal independence. The same disposition enabled the German bourgeoisie twice to engage in the fight for world power with an unequalled, well nigh irresistible war machine, the efficiency of which was based on carefully prepared military and capitalist organization, technically as well as spiritually. So that its opponent, the world-commanding English bourgeoisie, careless and unprepared, staggering under the fierce assault, had to put up its defense by summoning all the deepest forces of its inner nature.

The American entomologist Howard, in his "Man and Insect," makes a comparison of nature's two most successful adaptations to the "struggle for life" in animal structure: the insects covering all their weak parts by an unassailable hard and flexible skin, the mammals supporting them by a skeleton within; and their contest over the domination of the world, the author says, is not yet decided. This image fits for a comparison of the two contending capitalist classes; the German bourgeoisie covering its inner softness by an outer steel armor and assailing with the sharpest arms the apparently unprotected foe; but the English bourgeoisie has bones in its body.

This character of the German bourgeoisie at an early date brought the German workers to political independence. Left alone in their struggle against the oppressive police State, they were not attached to the middle class by the tradition of a common fight for political freedom. Whereas in other countries the hard industrial boss commanded respect by seizing power over the State and modernizing it, in Germany the gruff master in the shop proved the submissive coward in politics, giving examples in servility only. The German workers stood directly over against the allied classes of land owners and capitalists; they had to fight on the political at the same time as on the economic field. Concentrated by the rapid development of industry in large numbers in the factories and the towns, they had to build their organizations and find their own way, independent of middle class influences and traditions.

The rapid rise of social democracy demonstrated this political independence. Its name expresses the basic idea that socialist production must be won by means of democracy, by the masses conquering power over the State. Its propaganda of class struggle aroused the increasing numbers of workers to devoted fight, its papers and pamphlets educated them to knowledge of society and its development. It was the energy and rapidity of capitalist development that aroused the energy of the German working class and soon made them the foremost and directing power in the international workers' movement. It was the submissive politics of the German capitalist class, in placing them directly over against the entire ruling class, that rendered them class-conscious, that forced them by theory to deepen their insight in social forces, and that made them the teachers of the workers of all countries. Just as in France the sharp opposition between middle class and nobility had given origin to an extensive literature on political theory, so in Germany the sharp opposition between working class and bourgeoisie gave origin to an extensive literature on social theory, mostly based on the scientific work of Marx. This intellectual superiority, together with the gallant fight against oppression and despotism, alone against the mighty rulers, attracted all progressive and idealistic elements among the other classes, and collected around them all who longed for liberty and hated the degrading Prussian militarism. In Germany a deep gap, social as well as spiritual, separated two worlds, one of insolent power and wealth, where servility glorified oppression and violence, the other of idealism and rebelliousness, embodied in the workers' class struggle for liberation of humanity.

The infiltration with idealistic middle class and intellectual elements tended to call up ideas of peaceful petty capitalist reform and democracy, though they were entirely at variance with the actual big capitalist conditions. Other influences went in the same direction. The increased power of the workers—politically, by finally, in 1912, mustering one-third of all the vote, economically by the rapid growth of the trade unions to giant organizations—awakened the desire for direct progress in social reform. Though traditional program and theory spoke of revolution as the goal of all activity, the real outcome was to ascertain to the workers their place in capitalism, acknowledged not officially, but actually, and only at the cost of continual fight. So reformist tendencies got an increasing hold on the workers. At the deepest root of reformist mood lay, of course, the economic prosperity that in the twenty years before the first world war enormously swelled German capitalism. All this meant a strong influence of capitalist and middle class ideas upon the workers.

The spiritual power of the German bourgeoisie over the working masses was not due to its political, but to its economic achievements. Leaving politics and government to others, concentrating all its attention on industry and commerce, the capitalist class here unfolded such capacities and energy as to push German economy in an unrivaled tempo to the forefront of world development. This vigour commanded respect in the workers and carried them along in the feeling of participating in a mighty world process. They felt the enormous and enormously increasing power and brunt of capital, against which their organizations appeared insufficient and against which even their own ideals seemed to fade. So, in their sub-consciousness, they were to a certain extent dragged on in the middle class stream of nationalism, in the desire for national greatness and world power that burst out in the first world war.

In the Western countries the early political ascendency of the bourgeoisie kept the workers in political dependence; the economic forces and crises had to awaken them to class consciousness and class fight. In Germany the late, therefore more thorough economic ascendency of the bourgeoisie bound the workers into spiritual dependence; here the political forces drove them into fight and awakened their class consciousness. Opposed to a bourgeoisie entirely addicted to despotism and violence the German workers will have to win their freedom along the difficult way of political crises and catastrophes.

4. NATIONALISM

Nationalism is the essential creed of the bourgeoisie. What for this class stands above the individuality of separate man is the community indicated, with small differences of meaning, by the different names of nation, people, fatherland or State.

Nation and national feeling came up and developed along with the bourgeoisie. Original peasant life knew only the community of the village and of the larger tribe or county or canton; for the rising burgher class the town was their community. Their common interests did not stretch beyond these small realms. The spoken languages varied over larger regions; their similarity over limited regions facilitated their connection under the domination of one prince. But usually such domination, by conquest and inheritance, extended over countries with entirely different speech. For the farmers it hardly mattered what prince reigned far away and over what other people.

This changed with the rise of commercial, and still more with that of industrial capital. The merchant trading over wide countries and seas needs a strong Power that protects him, fights his competitors and subdues backward tribes; if this is lacking he himself founds a town federation. The industrialist needs security on the roads, unity of law, protection by a power mightier than a town. Where by insular isolation, as in England, or by conquests of princes, as with France, larger realms had been joined, they need only be consolidated and strengthened from within. In other cases, as with Italy and Germany, strong States had to be built in modern times, through wars and revolutions, through the force of the nationalist feeling of the bourgeoisie.

This does not mean that State and nation are identical or coincide. The State is a power structure, provided with physical means of coercion and suppression; the nation is a community bound by inner forces. So the State has the greatest inner solidity when it coincides with the nation. But States to increase their power try to include regions and peoples as much as possible, though they may belong to other nations, mixed up one with another by chance migrations in olden times. So Denmark formerly included Germans, Germany later included Danes and Poles, Hungary included Roumanians, Slavs and

Germans, Roumania afterwards included Hungarians and Germans. The Austrian Monarchy comprised seven different nationalities, never grown together. In such cases the growth of national feeling, accompanying the rise of a modern bourgeoisie, acts as a destructive force. In cases of a seaport town with a hinterland of different race and language (as Fiume or Dantzig) the economic interests demanding political unity are impaired by national enmity.

A common language, as the instrument of understanding, is the strongest force to connect people into one State and one nation. This does not mean, however, that nations are simply communities of speech. The Swiss, in their majority, speak German; yet they are a separate nation, different from the Germans. The English and the American nations speak the same language. The Swiss people during five centuries already has gone its own way, different from the way of other German-speaking people. They lived under their special institutions, ruling themselves as free peasants in a primitive democracy, whilst the Germans were oppressed under the yoke of some hundred small tyrants. The Swiss all experienced the same historical happenings, that molded their mind in the same way; in continual actual and spiritual intercourse they grew together into a similarity of character and ideas, different from those on the other side of the frontier. It is not only the passive qualities acquired in this way, but much more the active will, the mutual feeling of belonging together in a community of life, that connects and separates mankind into nations. It is the same with the English and the Americans: their separate history in different continents each following its own fate, often in sharp hostility of capitalist interests, made them different nations. And within each nation the community of fate, the subjection to the same historical influences impressed a common stamp upon all; the common fight for common interest, for common freedom, welded them into a firm unity. It produced a community of ideas embodied in and strengthened by literature, by art, by the daily papers, constituting national culture, itself an important factor in developing the sense of nationality. Even the bitter struggle of the classes takes place on this common ground of common experience in the ups and downs of mutual fight as direct face-to-face opponents.

So a nation is not a community of State, not a community of language, but a community of lot [of destiny arising out of their common social-economic practice]. Of course, these different types of community are mutually strongly dependent. Language is a strong nation-building agent. Nationality is the strongest State-building power. On the reverse political State power strongly reacts in making and unmaking nations, by uniting and separating the peoples, by establishing or destroying lot-community [a feeling of common destiny]. In the Middle Ages Northern and Southern France, differing in language as much as France and Spain, were united by conquest; during the rise of the bourgeoisie they formed one country, and as a unity they experienced later revolutions. Simultaneously with the Swiss mountaineers the Low Countries bordering the ocean separated politically from the large German body. A dozen of rich merchant towns, protecting themselves on the land side by a chain of allied provinces, they formed an independent State, raising the Holland dialect into a separate language with its own literature and culture; and by their special history becoming a separate nation. The Flemish, though speaking the same language as the Dutch, by their entirely separate and different history cannot be considered to belong to the same nation, whereas their political unity with the Wallons is thwarted by difference of language. Political measures, dictated by economic interests gradually melted the Scots with the English into one nation, whereas by such measures the Irish were driven into the consciousness of being a separate and hostile nation.

Thus nation is a product of history. All the happenings in the past, experienced in common, determining character, feelings, culture, have settled in the form of nationality. Nationality is congealed history, perpetuated outcome of the past as a living force.

National character and still more national feeling, thus spontaneously growing out of society, constitute the inner strength of national States. They are needed by the bourgeoisie, praised as patriotism, and furthered by special measures. The differences within the boundaries are effaced as much as possible, the differences with the outside world are emphasized and enhanced. One common language, necessary for intercourse, is taught all over the realm, suppressing the old dialects and even minority languages—as Gaelic in Wales, Provensal in Southern France—that only remain as curiosities and in remote villages. And a vast literature in this common language is at work, from first childhood onward, to impress identical ideas and identical feelings upon the entire population. An intentional propaganda works to intensify the mutual feelings of connection, and to render the antagonism to everything foreign more conscious. The doctrine of class struggle that draws a cleavage through national community is denounced as a danger and even persecuted as a crime against national unity. What as a spontaneous living product of society develops and changes with society itself, nationalism proclaims to be an eternal fact of nature and a duty of man.

Nationality is congealed history—but history goes on, adding continuously to the former deposit. New economic developments, growth of capital, wars and conquests produce new interests, change frontiers, awaken new directions of will and feeling, combine or separate peoples, break old communities and engender new ones. So nationality, together with its deeper generating forces, is fluctuating, in extent and content, and shows a variety of aspects.

Just as petty trade remains within big capitalism, provincialisms, remnants of old customs and ideas, persist, and they sometimes extend across the State frontiers. In the time of ascending capitalism with its free trade reaching all over the world, feelings of cosmopolitism of international brotherhood of all mankind gained ground in the bourgeoisie. Afterwards, when competition became fierce and the ensuing fight for world power deepened nationalism, this was ridiculed and suppressed as a childish illusion. In such parts of the world where capitalism is just beginning to take a footing, where it begins to undermine primitive economy and to overthrow worn-out despotisms, we see nations in the making. Besides profit-hungry business men, gambling adventurers, agents of foreign capital and rapacious politicians, forming the beginning of a bourgeoisie, it is chiefly the intellectuals, educated by European sciences and ideas, who come forward as the spokesmen of nationalism. On the Balkans the chance results of war often decided what adjacent valleys with cognate dialects would be included into the Serbian or into the Bulgarian nation. In China the class of merchants and landowners, spiritually united already by an old culture, assisted by a Western educated class of intellectuals, gradually develops into a modern bourgeoisie, animated by a growing spirit of nationalism. In India such growth, though rooted in native capitalist industry, is severely hampered by an obsolete diversity of religions. In all colonies with no bourgeoisie as yet, nationalism propagated by small groups of intellectuals, is the first theoretical form of rebellion against foreign exploitation. Where, on the other hand, in groups of a single million speaking a separate dialect nationalism arises, as wish or only whim of intellectuals, it may work as a disruptive force in the coherence of great units.

In the countries of modern capitalism nationalism has gone through different forms, corresponding to the development of the bourgeoisie. When burgherdom in its first rise becomes master in its town or realm it is freedom for which it fights. It not only breaks the power of nobility, of land ownership in its domain it has also to beat foreign powers that suppress or threaten its freedom. The rise of the bourgeoisie as a ruling class is connected with war against foreign feudal or absolutistic or previously dominant capitalistic powers. Such wars are wars of liberation, and are a kind of revolution; all enthusiasm, all devotion nascent from the establishment of a higher system of production manifests itself as national passion and exalts nationalism to lofty idealism. Thus it was with Holland in the 16th century freeing itself from the Spanish King, with the English at the same time fighting against Spanish world power, with America 1776 against England, with the French in the Great Revolution against Europe led by England, with the Italians in the 19th century against Austria; and even the German war against France 1870 had some traits of it. Such wars of liberation and consolidation, establishing its independence and power, in all later years are exalted by the bourgeoisie as the sublime summits of national history.

But then, gradually, the image changes. Capitalism is exploitation, is domination of an exploited class by a ruling class. The bourgeoisie, liberating itself from domination by land ownership, establishes new suppression. Throwing off the yoke of foreign oppression it soon begins to lay its yoke upon weaker peoples, adjacent or in far away colonies. Specially with the development of big capitalism. And always under the same slogans of nationalism. But now nationalism has another color. Not the freedom but the greatness of the nation is its slogan. It appeals to the feelings of pride, to the instincts of power, in all the other classes who have to serve the bourgeoisie as its helpers and underlings, as spokesmen, as military and civil officers, and who take part in its power. Now the own people is proclaimed the chosen people, superior in force and virtue, the "grande nation," the "Herrenvolk," the "finest race among mankind," destined to lead or to dominate other nations. As the contest for world power, the fight for supremacy in the world between the capitalist classes becomes fiercer, nationalism grows into a feverish passion, often carrying away the entire population in a common struggle for existence.

Nationalism is not simply an artificial doctrine imposed by the rulers upon the masses. Like every system of thoughts and feelings it arises out of the depth of society and proceeds from the economic realities and necessities. For the bourgeoisie the nation is the community to which its weal and woe is tied; so all the old instincts of community feeling are put in its service and develop to mighty forces of idealism. More than the adults the youth, not yet permeated by the spirit of selfish profit-seeking, is susceptible to enthusiastic response to the call of the community. For the working masses, as long as they have no possibility and no thought to fight for themselves against the bourgeoisie. Spiritually dependent on the master-class, they have to accept, more or less willingly, its ideas and its aims. All these influences work as spiritual forces in the realm of instinctive spontaneity.

But then, added to it, come the deliberate efforts of the bourgeosie to intensify the spontaneous feelings by artificial means. The entire education in the schools and the propaganda in literature and papers are directed to foster and strengthen the spirit of nationalism. Not of course by showing its connection with the profit for capital; a clear consciousness of this connection, as in all ideologies of an exploiting class, is lacking, and must be carefully withheld from the exploited masses. So other foundations must be sought for, other usually deceptive arguments must be found, drawn mostly from existing traditions based on former social conditions. The love for the birthplace where our cradle stood, the remembrance of the world of our youth, of villages or town quarter, small communities of peasant or artisan life, must serve to fix the adherence to the nationalist State Power, where it fights foreign Powers, for the profit of capital. History is colored and doctored to convert the strict objective truth about the past into a brilliant one-sided image of the nation's life, apt to awaken strong feelings of intercommunity, of enthusiasm, of pride and admiration in young people, to elate their hearts, to strain their minds, to instigate emulation, hence to solidify the inner strength of the national community.

To give a still greater solidity to the national ideology, it sometimes is founded upon a material, physical base, on consanguinity and race. The races of mankind have been formed in the many thousands of years of prehistoric times. We meet with them at the dawn of history, and afterwards in surrounding barbaric countries and continents, as groups with similar qualities. They have been shaped by migrations, conquests, exterminations and blendings of primitive groups, when in more quiet times or in isolated regions the mixture settled to specific types. The fight for living space and for possession of the sources of life continued in later civilized history. But now, by the development of new forms of production, as a fight of States and nations. Though both are communities of lot [of common destiny] and are designated by the same name of "people," there is a fundamental difference between the original races and the later nations. The races are groups connected by the ties of blood, by consanguinity; the nations, formed in the ages of production of commodities, are groups connected by the spiritual ties of common consciousness, ideas, experience and culture.

Written history of the great migrations in later times attests how almost all modern peoples, the nations, have been shaped by a thorough mixture of different races. And this process of mixing is going on though in more quiet forms, under modern industrial conditions. Large numbers of people migrate from the poor agrarian regions into foreign industrial towns or districts; such as the Irish into English towns, the Czechs into Vienna, the Poles into Rhineland, the Europeans into America. Mostly they assume language and habits from their new surroundings as well as the ideas, and so are dissolved and assimilated into its national community. Only when the migration comprises greater connected masses, especially when touched already by the consciousness of fervid national strife, the assimilation ceases.

When a modern nation is claimed to be the pure descendants of one original race, how can it be decided? The evidence of history, usually uncertain, points to strong blending. Neither is the community of language decisive. It is true that peasant communities tenaciously stick to their language as long as their life and work is not influenced by other dominant languages. But it is known quite well how often in the mixing up of peoples the language of the victors is assumed by the vanquished or the language of more civilized intruders. Community of language later on is a strong force in the making of nations; but it cannot make certain a community of descent. There are, further, bodily differences in color, hair, bodily structure and form of the skull, manifest and large between the main groups, Europeans, Mongolians, Negroes. But they are small in subordinate groups. And in all modern peoples these bodily characteristics show the most embarrassing diversity. Ethnologists, especially in

Germany, speak of a "Nordic" race, dolichocephalic [with oblong skull], blonde, and blue-eyed, of which the Teuton peoples were descendants and representatives, contrasted to the darker "alpine" race, brachycephalic [with round skull], living in Central Europe. But modern Europe shows dolichocephaly dominant only in Norway, North-western Germany, Holland, England, whereas the chief part of Germany is brachycephalic, increasingly so in the later centuries. The American ethnologist Dixon pointed out that the inhabitants of the then existing Austrian monarchy as to bodily characteristics and shape of the skull formed a nearly homogeneous race, whereas they were divided into some seven fiercely quarreling nations, speaking as many different languages, and brought together by different ancient wanderings and adventures. On the other hand the French, bodily showing a mixture of most different racial characteristics, feel and act as one homogeneous consolidated nation.

Race community as the foundation of nationality is only a fantastic theory, devised and propagated for political purposes. The strength of German nationalism is not rooted in the blood of the ancient Teutons but in the needs of modern capitalism. The strong real roots of nationalism are situated in economy, in the mode of production. So it must be different for different classes.

On the working class nationalism never got much hold. In the petty-burgher and farmer classes from which it proceeded national feeling played no great role; and its own exploitation by capital gave another direction to the ideas, not towards community, but towards fight with the bourgeoisie. They perceived nationalism to be the ideology of their exploiters, often a form of hypocrisy when the most greedy capitalists used patriotic talk to fill their own pockets. When by unemployment they were driven to wander they found in other countries other workers, comrades, exploited like themselves. Practically, by their fight, and then theoretically, in their consciousness, they drew a dividing line across the nation. Another community of lot, the class-community determined their feelings and thoughts, extending over all countries. The dividing line of the classes crosses that of the nations. To the nationalist propaganda of the bourgeoisie they opposed the reality of their life by the statement that the workers have no fatherland. Socialist propaganda fundamentally opposing capitalism proclaimed internationalism to be the principle of the working class.

But beneath the conscious thoughts and avowed doctrines there was in the workers, in their sub-consciousness, still a certain national feeling, revealing itself at the outbreak of the world war. Practically they had to acquiesce in the rule of the bourgeoisie and were its subordinates; practically their fight could do no more than ascertain their place in capitalism; so in their ideas they could not attain complete independence. When the workers politically and socially follow the bourgeoisie they remain middle-class-minded. In England they participated in the profits that world commerce, industrial monopoly and colonial exploitation bestowed upon the bourgeoisie. In Germany the energy of the bourgeoisie to win industrial world power carried them away in the vague feeling that industrial power and prosperity is a workers' interest, too. So nationalism in the working class was the companion of reformism, in England as a quiet hardly conscious conservative tradition, in Germany as an impetuous instinct driven by a turbulent economic expansion. It must be remarked that working class nationalism always was pacifistic, rooted in the tradition of petty-burgher illusions, in contrast to the aggressive violent nationalism of the bourgeoisie.

When the working class takes up its revolutionary fight, nationalism is dropped entirely. In the new workers' organization of production there is no antagonism of interests with other peoples; it extends over the countries disregarding all former frontiers. In the reconstruction of society fight is only needed against the capitalist class; in this fight the workers all over the world have to rely on one another as brothers in arms; together belonging to one army. They speak different languages, certainly; but these differences relate only to the outer forms of their thoughts. The essential contents, their ideas, their feelings, their culture, determined as they are by the same class struggle, the common fight as the chief life experience, the common lot, are identical. From having been subjected to different national influences in previous history there may remain differences in passive character and culture; but in active character, in the direction of will, they form one unity. This new state of thought of the working class cannot well be indicated by calling it international; it is more and higher than a peaceful collaboration of free and equal nations. It is the entire absence of nationality; for the workers the nations do not exist, they see before them the unity of mankind all over the world, a community of production, of life, of culture. Over all diversity of bodily qualities and natural surroundings, of local speech and traditional habits stretches the interconnection of all mankind as one great community of lot. Thus nationalism disappears from the earth together with the class that was its author.

This is of the future. For the time being nationalism exists as a strong power obstructing the way. For the workers it is necessary not only to destroy all nationalist tradition in themselves, but also, in order to avoid illusions, to understand its strength in the hostile class. Nationalism does not belong to the ideologies that as traditions of the past times are gradually extinguished under modern conditions. It is a living ideology, drawing its forces ever anew from a fertile economic soil, standing in the centre of fight, the flag of the foe. German history of the last quarter of a century offers an example of how after the downbreak of her State power the bourgeoisie was able to resuscitate itself by means of spiritual power, through nationalism, and thus to build up a new more powerful state.

The outbreak of the first world war 1914 was the catastrophe of social democracy and labor movement. The party and union leaders placed all the power of their organization, its press, its moral authority at the service of the Government in Germany, considered as the foremost example for the working class, and in all other countries. It was the collapse of all the proud program slogans of class struggle and of internationalism. The workers having put all their confidence, their faith into their party, their organization , now were powerless against the nationalist propaganda, against the combined pressure of the military and the party apparatus.

Then came 1918–the downbreak of the German military power. The rebellion of the sailors, the strikes and demonstrations in the chief towns, the formation of workers' and soldiers' councils carried the socialist leaders into power. They were the only men to keep the working class in check and to prevent a real workers' revolution, which they hated and feared no less than did the generals and the capitalists. The working masses found the political power fallen into their hands; but they did not know what to do with it. Again they put their faith into the party, in their leaders, and passively suffered the small advance groups of revolutionary fighters and spokesmen to be massacred by military forces at the command of the socialist rulers. They had always been taught that the party would bring them socialism. Now the party, now their leaders were in office; now socialism was to come.

What they got was capitalism. The socialist leaders did not touch capitalist property, not even aristocratic land ownership. By convoking a National Assembly they immediately restored parliamentarism, which had always been their life element. So the bourgeoisie gained an official centre of organized power. It was quite content that socialist and democratic politicians, beguiling the masses with the illusion of power, occupied the upper places; afterwards they could be turned out gradually and replaced by liberals and reactionaries. Capitalism acted as it always acts: it exploited the masses, expropriated the middle classes, aggravated the economic chaos by gambling with the means of production, bribed the officials, and threw society into ever new crises of unemployment. And all discontent and exasperation turned against the new republic and its parliamentary leaders.

Now the bourgeoisie began to build up its fighting power but of all the elements that were depressed and embittered by the new conditions: the middle class youth, flung down from its high hopes for victory and future greatness; the dismissed military officers, exasperated by defeat, entirely living in the old conceptions; the young intellectuals, in despair at seeing the governmental offices once considered as their monopoly now occupied by despised socialists and Jews. All impoverished by the devaluation of the money, all filled with bitterness over the humiliation of their country, all driven by a fierce will to take up again the fight for world power. Their binding force was an ardent nationalism, blasted into white heat by the enforced humiliating peace conditions, animated by hatred against the slack nationality of the meek rulers no less than against the foreign victorious enemies. They stood up as the bearers of sublime national ideas, whereas the workers over against them could show no more than either contentment over the mock democracy of a worthless republic, or the sham revolutionist talk of bolshevist party dictatorship. Thus the most active elements among the up-growing youth were assembled and drilled into fighting bands, inspired by fiery nationalist teachings. Big capital provided the means for a continuous propaganda among the population. Until the world crisis of 1930 raised them to political importance. The impotent socialist leaders did not even venture to call upon the armed workers for resistance. The "world-liberating" social democracy ignominiously went to ruin as a worm-eaten wreck. Nationalism now raised to the highest pitch, easily annihilated the parliamentary republic, and began to organize all the forces of the nation for a new war for world power.

5. AMERICAN CAPITALISM

The white population of the U.S.A. descends from European immigrants who, most energetic and independent elements of their peoples, crossed the ocean to escape oppression, persecution and poverty. From the first settlements on the Eastern coast, with its commercial towns, they gradually expanded over the entire continent exterminating in continuous fight the Indian natives, clearing the forests, subduing the wilderness, and converting it into cultivated land. In all these pioneers, as a necessary character developed a strong individualism, a daring adventurous spirit, self-reliant, hard, alert, watchful and relentless in the surrounding dangers, and a love of liberty taking and making its own right. Not only in the forerunners, the trappers and farmers, but also in the dealers, the artisans, the business men, who followed them, populating the new towns and creating a new existence for themselves. Whereas in old Europe everybody found himself in fixed conditions, here everything had to be shaped anew. In the hard and pitiless struggle for life, that left no time for spiritual concentration, in the creation of great enterprises and fortunes, respect for success in life and business became the outstanding character of American society.

Thus conditions for both capital and labor were different from Europe. To keep the workers from trying their luck as pioneers in the wide spaces, high wages must be paid, thus furthering the introduction of labor-saving machines. This privileged position, fixed by craft unions, could be upheld until modern times. Then in the last decades of the 19th century, destitute masses of immigrants from Southern and Eastern Europe began to pour in and fill the factories and slums of the Eastern towns with cheap labor power.

And in the present century free soil came to an end.

Capital was the leading power in the 19th century expansion. It had not to fight a feudal power or class; with the throwing off, in the war of independence, of the domination of English 18th century commercial capital, it had won complete mastery. The absence of any feudal tradition, of all respect for privilege of birth made respect for property, for the reality of dollar power paramount. American capital soon played the chief role in opening up the Western wilds by digging canals and building railways. Through its friends in Congress it was rewarded for this service to the nation with big allotments for exploitation, paying not more than the bribes, the form by which the politicians got their share of the profits. The timber of the endless woods, the fertile soil along the railways, the rich ore deposits in the earth, all became property of the capitalists. And in their wake colonists from the Eastern States or from Europe populated the West, farmers and business men finding their villages and towns ready made, lumber workers and miners ordering their life by the law of the wild, soon to be substituted by the organs of Government and public law.

The seizure of the natural riches of an immense virgin continent laid the foundation for the rapid growth of big fortunes. In Europe this seizure and exploitation had been the task of a large citizen class during many centuries; thus the profit—economically a form of rent—was spread out in the form of moderate wealth for the many, only exceptionally—as with the Fugger family in Augsburg—creating big fortunes. In America this process in the second half of the 19th century concentrated within a short time, raising rapidly a small class of supercapitalists, of multimillionaires.

The big American fortunes have not been formed by regular accumulation of industrial profit, but in the first instance by the accession, partly through traffic monopolies, partly through political corruption, of valuable primary materials. In stubborn mutual fight, destroying or subduing larger and smaller competitors, big monopolies were erected that laid a heavy tribute upon the entire population and snatched part of the industrial surplus value from the hands of the industrial capitalists. More rapidly and more ruthlessly than elsewhere the supremacy of big capital over the entire bourgeoisie, the power of big finance over industry, and the concentration of capitalist power in a small number of big concerns was established. Monopoly of course does not mean a full hundred per cent control over a branch: if it reaches only, say, 80 per cent, outsiders are harmless and usually follow the lead of the monopolists. So there remains a border region for individual efforts of smaller capitalists to wrestle themselves up to secondary importance. Neither are all of the profits pocketed by the monopolists themselves; part of the shares is left to the capitalist public to gamble with and to enjoy the dividends without thereby having any share in the leading of the business. In this way at the same time all the smaller capitalists' property comes at the disposal of the monopolist, to use it in their strategy of mutual capital warfare, just as in olden times the kings made use of the combined fighting power of the dependent barons.

Yet, what remains as income for the monopolists is so enormous that it cannot be consumed or spent by themselves. With such boundless richness the motive of securing wealth for luxurious satisfaction of all needs is absent; many of the monopolist leaders, indeed, live rather frugally. What drives them is the striving for power, for expansion of their domination over ever wider domains of economic life–an automatic impulse of business instinct swollen to irrationality. The example was set long ago already by John D. Rockefeller, whose yearly income was then estimated at nearly a hundred millions of dollars. No luxury, however crazy, was able to absorb the stream of gold flowing into his hands; he did not concern himself with the spending, and left it to an office of secretaries. No young spendthrifts could, as in olden times, destroy the fortunes collected by their fathers; this property has now become an unassailable family possession. As a new feudal class "America's sixty families" hold sway over the sources of life of society, living in their castles and large estates, sometimes possessors of almost a whole State, as the Dupont family in Delaware. They are mightier than the kings of old, who only could try to squeeze their share out of the profits of the capitalist class; they are the masters of the very capital power of society, of all the rapidly growing productive forces of a rapidly developing continent.

Power over production means power over politics, because politics is one of the basic means to secure power over production. Politics in America was always different from politics in Europe, because here there was no feudal class to beat down. In its fight against the domination of the feudal class the European bourgeoisie acquired its sense for the supremacy of class interests above personal interests, thus in their pursuit developing idealism and self-sacrifice. So in Europe politics was a domain where disinterested politicians could work for sublime principles, for the "public interest." In America there was no need and no room for such class-politics; interests from the beginning were personal or group interests. Thus politics was business, a field for pursuit of personal interests like any other field of activity. Only in later years, when the working class awoke and began to talk of socialism, as its counterpart came up some talk of public interests of society, and the first traces of reform politics.

The result, accepted as inevitable, was that politics often is graft. In their first rise the monopolists had no other means than direct bribing. Often the word is quoted as spoken by John D., that everybody can be bought if you only know his price. A continuous fight on the part of the smaller capitalists, of competitors, and of spokesmen of public honesty, before the courts in the legislative bodies tried in vain either to punish or to redress fraud, or to so much as disclose truth. It was on such an occasion that a senator friend of the accused millionaire exclaimed: "We ought to pass a law that no man worth a hundred of million dollars should be tried for a crime." Indeed, the masters of capital stand above law; why, then, maintain the troublesome appearance that they are equal citizens, subject to law?

When the power of big business becomes more firmly rooted and unassailable, these coarse methods gradually became superfluous. Now it had a large attendance of friends, of clients and agents, of dependent proxies, all men of standing, put into well-paid honorable offices, influential in politics as in all public life. They are or they influence the party leaders, they form the caucuses, they manage everything behind the scenes at the party congresses and select congress members, senators and candidates for the presidency. The hundred thousands of dollars necessary for the noisy election campaigns are paid by big business; each of the big interests has one of the two great contending parties as its agent, and some of the largest even pay both. To fight this "corruption," or at least to expose it by publicity their adversaries succeeded in enacting that each party had to give public account of its finances, thus to show the sources of its funds. It was a blow in the air; it created no sensation and not even surprise: it appeared that public opinion was entirely prepared to accept the domination of politics by big business as a self-evident fact of common knowledge.

The press of course is entirely in the hands of big capital. The big papers are bought, or an unlimited amount of dollars is spent to have new papers founded by its retainers. Most important here are the popular local paper providing the spiritual nurture for the millions of voters. At the same time the leading papers offer to the educated classes, in order to direct their opinions, able articles on science, art, literature, foreign politics, carefully written by good experts. No independent press of wide circulation is possible. Sometimes a cross-headed rich idealist founded a paper open to exposure and criticism of the secret dealings of the capitalists. Attempts were then made to capture or to undermine it; if they failed, its revelations, its opinions, its existence even were never alluded to in the other papers, in a conspiracy of silence, so that its influence remained entirely negligible.

This press dominates the spiritual life of the American people. The most important thing is not even the hiding of all truth about the reign of big finance. Its aim still more is the education to thoughtlessness. All attention is directed to coarse sensations, everything is avoided that could arouse thinking. Papers are not meant to be read–the small type is already a hindrance–but in a rapid survey of the fat headlines to inform the public on unimport news items, on family triflngs of the rich, on sexual scandals, on crimes of the underworld, or boxing matches. The aim of the capitalist press all over the world, the diverting of the attention of the masses from the reality of social development, from their own deepest interests, nowhere succeeds with such thoroughness as in America.

Still more than by the papers the masses are influenced by broadcasting and film. These products of most perfect science, destined at one time to be the finest educational instruments of mankind, now in the hands of capitalism have been turned into the strongest means to uphold its rule by stupefying the minds. Because after nerve-straining fatigue the movie offers relaxation and distraction by means of simple visual impressions that make no demand on the intellect, the masses get used to accept thoughtlessly and willingly all its cunning and shrewd propaganda. It reflects the ugliest sides of middle-class society. It turns all attention either to sexual life, in this society—by the absence of community feelings and fight for freedom—the only source of strong passions, or to brutal violence; masses educated to rough violence instead of to social knowledge are not dangerous to capitalism. Broadcasting by its very nature is an organ of rulership for dominating the masses, through incessant one-sided allocations forcing its ideas, its viewpoints, its truths and its lies upon the listeners, without possibility of discussion or protest. As the genuine instruments of spiritual domination of the millions of separate individuals by an organized dictatorship it is used by big capital to assert its power.

Not only to the coarse work of mass propaganda through the papers, but also to the more subtle influencing of deeper spiritual life the masters of capital extend their care. Reviews are bought or founded, richly illustrated Weeklies or Monthlies are edited and composed by able men of letters and expert collaborators. They are full of instructive and attractive stuff carefully selected in such a way that the cultured and intellectual part of the citizens learn to feel and to think just as monopolist capital wishes them to, namely, that their country is a great country, and a free country, and a young country, destined to a far greater future, and—though there are some defects to be corrected by deserving citizens—the best possible of worlds. Here the young intellectuals find their opportunities; if they should be inclined to thwarting the mighty, to independent criticism, to sharp opposition they are ejected, ignored, and silenced, hampered everywhere, perhaps morally ruined; if docile and ready to serve the masters the way is open to well remunerated positions and public honors.

Science, too, is subject to the millionaire class. The English tradition of private endowment not only of churches, hospitals and orphanages, but also of universities, professorships and libraries, has been followed in America from the beginning. Enormous sums of money have been spent by American millionaires of course not all of them, and not even the richest—on institutes of arts and sciences, on museums, galleries, universities, laboratories, hospitals, observatories, libraries. Sometimes from idealistic motives, sometimes in commemoration of a relative, sometimes for mere pride, always with an instinct of justice in it: where they had seized for their own the riches that elsewhere went to society at large, theirs was the duty to provide for such special, large, cultural expenses not immediately felt as needed but yet necessary as the basis of society in the long run. Spending in this way only a small part of their wealth they acquired fame as protectors of science, as benefactors of mankind. Their names are inscribed in big golden letters on the fronts of the proud buildings: Field Museum, McCormick University, Widener Library, Carnegie Institute, Lick Observatory, Rockefeller Foundation. And this means more than simply the satisfaction of personal pride. It means that the entire world of science becomes their adherents and considers their exploitation of the American people more desirable condition for the advancement of science than when in other countries money for science must be extorted in meagre amounts from uninterested governments. Founding and endowing universities means controlling them; thus the millionaires, by means of their agents who act as presidents and overseers, can see to it that no dangerous elements as teachers may influence the ideas of the students.

The spiritual power that big capital wields in this way hardly requires any sacrifices on their side. If it left all these expenses to Government to provide it would have to pay for them in the form of taxes. Now such foundations are exempt from taxes and often are used as a means to escape taxation. The donations consist of shares of large enterprises; what these institutions receive is the dividend, and money produce for which the capitalists have no other use. The voting power attached to the shares, however, needed in the manipulation and financial strategy of the masters, the only thing that concerns them, by carefully devised statutes is securely kept in the hands of their agents.

Thus in a firm grip the monopoly capitalists dominate industry, traffic, production, public life, politics, the church of course, the press, the reviews, the universities, science and art. It is the most highly developed form of class domination, of an all powerful small minority over the entire bourgeoisie, and thus over the entire American people, "United States incorporated." It is the most perfect form of capitalist rule, because it is based on democracy. By the democratic forms of life it is firmly rooted in society; it leaves all the other classes—the smaller bourgeoisie, the intellectuals, the farmers, the mass of the workers—convinced that they are free men in a free country, struggling of course against mighty social forces, but still master of their lot, choosing their own way. It has been built up, gradually and instinctively, in a shrewdly composed organization of all economic and spiritual forces. The main part of business, as well as of spiritual life is interwoven into a system of dependencies, accepted as existing conditions, camouflaged in an appearance of independent action and free individuality. Whoever tries opposition is thrown out and destroyed; whoever collaborates willingly, though obliged to continual struggle with competitors, finds his place in the system.

Against this domination of the big monopolists the capitalist world has no means of resistance or redress. Hundreds of times, in the most varied ways, attempts have been made to break their power, by action before the courts, by legislation against trusts and combinations, by election campaigns, by new political parties with new slogans. But it was all in vain. Of course; for it would have meant return to unorganized small business, contrary to the essential nature of social development. Attempts to prepare the way for further development towards collective production, by means of fundamental criticism, were made in the propaganda of "technocracy" by a group of intellectuals and engineers, as well as in the action of the Social-Democratic Party. But their forces were too weak. The bulk of the intellectual class feels well off and content with the system. And as long as skilled labor succeeds in maintaining its position by means of its unions, a powerful revolutionary class-action of the workers cannot be expected.

The American workers have always felt the hard hand of capital and had to fight ever again against its pressure. Though simply a fight over wages and working conditions, it was fought with all the fierceness that under the wild conditions of unbridled business egotism accompanied all fight for mere personal interests. What appeared in such conflicts between labor and capital was first the solidarity of the entire class of business men with big capital. It was an instinctive class-consciousness, fanned to white-heat by the press that, entirely in the hands of capital's servants, denounced the strikers for forged outrages and called them anarchists and criminals. And secondly the spirit of lawlessness and violence in the same class, inheritance of the pioneer conditions, especially vivid in the far West. The old methods of wild warfare against the Indians and of taking law into their own hands were now used against the new foe, the rebelling class, the strikers. Armed bands of citizens promoted to civic guards and thus qualified to any lawless deed of violence, imprisoned and ill-treated the strikers and applied every form of terrorism. The workers, their old independent pioneer spirit not yet broken, resisted with all means, so that strikes often took the character of small civil wars in which case of course the workers usually had the worst of it. In the industrial towns of the East a well organized police force, strong fellows convinced that strikers are criminals, stand in the service of mayors and town councils who themselves are installed as its agents by big capital. When in big plants or in mining districts strikes broke out, troops of rowdies from the underworld, procured by the Pinkerton office, sworn in by the authorities as special constables, were let loose upon the workers. Thus in America only in extreme cases the workers on strike might hope for the amount of right and order as is the rule, e.g., in England.

All this was no hindrance for the workers to fight. The American labor movement has shown brilliant examples of fighting spirit, courage and devotion, though they always acted in separate groups only. From now on, however, new methods of fight, greater unity, new forms of organization will gradually be enforced upon them. Conditions are changing; there is no more open land to be settled by pioneers—though, more broadly considered, with better methods the continent might feed many more millions of inhabitants. Now it will be more difficult to uphold the old wage standards. Since the stream of immigration has been stopped the process of Americanization of the old immigrants is equalizing the working and fighting conditions, and prepares the basis for an all encompassing unity of class. The further conditions will have to be created by the further expansion of capitalism.

American capital is now entering upon world politics. Up till now all its time and force was occupied by organizing and raising itself by taking possession of its continent. Then the first world war made it the paramount financial power. The American supply of war materials to Europe had to be paid, first with European property of American shares, and then with gold and obligations. London lost to New York its place as money-center of the world. All the European gold assembled in America, property of the American capitalist class. Its congestion already brought a world crisis, because there was no market for an industrial production built upon this abundance of gold.

Such a market, however, can be created. Thronged in the fertile plains and valleys of Eastern and Southern Asia, many hundreds of millions of people, nearly half the population of the earth, are living as yet in home production or small scale craft and tillage. To convert these intelligent and industrious masses first into buyers of industrial products and then into industrial and agrarian workers in the service of capital is the big opportunity that now faces American capitalism. The supplying of this enormous market will secure an age of rise and prosperity for American industry. The investment of capital, the building of railways and factories, the founding of new industries in those thickly populated countries, promises immense profits from capitalist exploitation and immense increase of power. It is true that, by creating of a capitalist China a mighty competitor will be raised for the future, with the prospect of future world war farther ahead; but that is of no concern now. For the moment the concern is to secure this market by ousting other world powers, especially the strongly developed Japanese capitalism that was at work to found an East-Asiatic Empire under its lead. World politics means wars; that will introduce militarism in America, with all its constraint, with its barrack drill, with its restriction of old liberties, with more violence and heavier pressure. Camouflaged of course in democratic forms, but still creating new conditions of life, new feelings and ideas, a new spiritual outlook, somehow resembling those of old Europe. Then the American workers, partly participating in the power and prosperity of the rise, partly pressed down more heavily by more powerful masters, will needs develop more powerful forms of class fight.

American capitalism built up a power over society and the working class unequalled over the world. Social and political democracy afford a far more solid foundation than any dictatorship could give. Its power rests on its concentrated ownership of all means of production, on its money, on its unrestricted power over State and Government, on its spiritual domination over the entire society. Against a rebellious working class it will be able to bring all the organs of the State into sharper action, to organize still larger bodies of armed defenders, through its press monopoly to incite public opinion into a spiritual terrorism; and when necessary, democracy may even be replaced by open dictatorship. So the working class also will have to rise to a far greater height of power than ever before. Against a more powerful foe higher demands of unity, of insight, of devotion must be satisfied anywhere else in the world were needed. Their development doubtless requires a long period of fight and growth. The chief weakness of the American working class is its middle class mentality, its entire spiritual subjection under middle class ideas, the spell of democracy. They will be able to throw it off only by raising their minds to a deeper class consciousness, by binding themselves together into a stronger class unity, by widening their insight to a higher class-culture than anywhere else in the world.

The working class in America will have to wage against world capitalism the most difficult, at the same time the decisive fight for their and the world's freedom.

6. DEMOCRACY

Democracy was the natural form of organization of the primitive communities of man. Self-rule and equality of all the tribe members determined in their assemblies all the common activities. The same was the case in the first rise of burgherdom, in the towns of Greece in antiquity, of Italy and Flanders in the Middle Ages. Democracy here was not the expression of a theoretical conception of equal rights of all mankind, but a practical need of the economic system; so the journeymen in the guilds took as little part in it as the slaves in antiquity; and larger property usually carried larger influence in the assemblies. Democracy was the form of collaboration and self-rule of free and equal producers, each master of his own means of production, his soil or his shop and his tools. In ancient Athens it was the regular citizens' assemblies that decided on the public affair, whereas the administrative functions, held for small periods only, circulated by lot. In the mediaeval towns the artisans were organized in guilds, and the town government, when not in the hands of patrician families, consisted of the leaders of the guilds. When at the end of the middle ages the mercenaries of the princes got ascendancy over the armed citizens the freedom and democracy of the towns were suppressed.

With the rise of capitalism the era of middle class democracy begins, fundamentally though not at once actually. Under capitalism all men are independent owners of commodities, all having the same right and freedom to sell them at their will–the unpropertied proletarians own and sell their labor power. The revolutions that abolished feudal privileges, proclaimed freedom, equality and property. Because in this fight the combined force of all citizens was need-ed, the promulgated constitutions bore a strongly democratic character. But the actual constitutions were different; the industrial capitalists, as yet not very numerous and powerful, were in fear lest the lower classes whom they trod down by competition and exploitation, should control legislation. So to these classes, excluded from the ballot, during the entire 19th century political democracy is program and goal of their political activities. They are animated by the idea that through the establishment of democracy, through universal suf-frage, they will win power over government and in that way be able to restrain or even to abolish capitalism.

And, to all appearance, this campaign succeeds. Gradually the suffrage is extended, and finally in nearly all countries the equal vote for all men and women for the election of members of parliament is established. So this time often is spoken of as the age of democracy. Now it becomes apparent that democracy is not a danger for capitalism, not weakness but strength. Capitalism stands on a solid basis; a numerous middle class of wealthy indus-trial employers and business men dominates society and the wage earning workers have found their acknowledged place. It is now understood that a social order gains in solidity when all the grievances, all the misery and dis-content, otherwise a source of rebellion, find a regular and normalized outlet in the form of criticism and charge, of parliamentary protest and party strife. In capitalist society there is a perpetual contest of interests between the classes and groups; in its development, in the continuous changes of structure and shifting of industries new groups with new interests arise and demand recogni-tion. With suffrage universal, not artificially limited, they all find their spokes-men; any new interest, according to its significance and power, can carry its weight in legislation. Thus parliamentary democracy is the adequate political form for rising and developing capitalism.

Yet the fear for the rule of the masses could not do without warrants against "misuse" of democracy. The exploited masses must have the conviction that by their ballot they are master of their fate, so that if they are not content it is their own fault. But the structure of the political fabric is devised in such a way that government through the people is not government by the people. Parliamentary democracy is only partial, not complete democracy.

Only one day in four or five years the people have power ever the dele-gates; and on election day noisy propaganda and advertising, old slogans and new promises are so overwhelming that there is hardly any possibility of criti-cal judgment. The voters have not to designate trusted spokesmen of their own: candidates are presented and recommended by the big political parties, selected by the party caucuses; and they know that every vote on an outsider is practically thrown away. The workers adapted themselves to the system by forming their own party—in Germany the Social Democratic Party, in England the Labor Party–playing an influential role in parliament, sometimes even providing cabinet ministers. Then, however, its parliamentarians had to play the game. Besides their special concern, social laws for the workers, most questions subjected to their decisions relate to capitalist interests, to problems and difficulties of capitalist society. They get used to be caretakers of these interests and to deal with these problems in the scope of existing society. They become skilled politicians, who just like the politicians of other parties constitute an almost independent power, above the people. .

Moreover, these parliaments chosen by the people have not full power over the State. Next to them, as a guarantee against too much influence of the masses stand other bodies, privileged or aristocratic–Senate, House of Lords, First Chamber–whose consent is necessary for the laws. Then the ultimate decision is mostly in the hands of princes or presidents, living entirely in circles of aristocratic and big capitalist interests. They appoint the State secretaries or cabinet ministers directing the bureaucracy of officials, that do the real work of governing. By the separation of the legislative and the executive part of government the chosen parliamentarians do not themselves govern; besides law-making they can only indirectly influence the actual governors, by way of criticism or of refusing money. What is always given as the characteristic of real democracy: that the people chooses its rulers, is not realized in parliamentary democracy. Of course not; for its purpose is to secure the rule of capitalism through the illusion of the masses that they have to decide their own fate.

So it is idle talk to speak of England, of France, of Holland as democratic countries–only for Switzerland this may fit in a way. Politics is the reflection of the state of feelings and ideas in the people. In custom and feeling there is the spirit of inequality, the respect for the "upper" classes, old or new; the worker as a rule stands cap in hand before the master. It is a remnant of feudalism, not eradicated by the formal declaration of social and political equality, adapted to the new conditions of a new class rule. The rising bourgeoisie did not know how to express its new power otherwise than by donning the garb of the feudal lords and demanding from the exploited masses the corresponding professions of respect. Exploitation was made still more irritating by the arrogance of the capitalist asking servility also in manners. So in the workers' struggle the indignation of humiliated self-respect gives a deeper coloring to the fight against misery.

In America it is just the reverse. In the crossing of the ocean all remembrances of feudalism are left behind. In the hard struggle for life on a wild continent every man was valued for his personal worth. As an inheritance of the independent pioneer spirit a complete democratic middle class feeling pervades all classes of American society. This inborn feeling of equality neither knows nor tolerates the arrogance of birth and rank; the actual power of the man and his dollar is the only thing that counts. It suffers and tolerates exploitation the more unsuspectingly and willingly, as this exploitation presents itself in more democratic social forms. So American democracy was the firmest base and is still the strongest force of capitalism. The millionaire masters are fully conscious of this value of democracy for their rule, and all spiritual powers of the country collaborate to strengthen these feelings. Even colonial policy is dominated by them. Public opinion in America abhors the idea that it should subjugate and dominate foreign peoples and races. It makes them its allies, under their own free government; then the automatic power of financial supremacy makes them more dependent than any formal dependence could do. It must be understood, moreover, that the strong democratic character of social feelings and customs does not implicate corresponding political institutions. In American government, just as in Europe, the constitution is composed in such a way as to secure the rule of a governing minority. The President of the U.S. may shake hands with the poorest fellow; but president and Senate have more power than King and upper houses have in most European governments.

The inner untruthfulness of political democracy is not an artful trick invented by deceitful politicians. It is the reflection, hence an instinctive consequence, of the inner contradictions of the capitalist system. Capitalism is based upon the equality of citizens, private owners, free to sell their commodities—the capitalists sell the products, the workers sell their labor power. By thus acting as free and equal bargainers they find exploitation and class antagonism as the result: the capitalist master and exploiter, the worker actually the slave. Not by violating the principle of juridical equality, but by acting according to it the result is a situation that actually is its violation. This is the inner contradiction of capitalist production, indicating that it can be only a transition system. So it can give no surprise that the same contradiction appears in its political form.

The workers cannot overcome this capitalist contradiction, their exploitation and slavery proceeding from their legal liberty, as long as they do not recognize the political contradiction of middle-class democracy. Democracy is the ideology they brought along with them from the former middle-class revolutionary fights; it is dear to their hearts as an inheritance of youthful illusions. As long as they stick to these illusions, believe in political democracy and proclaim it their program they remain captives in its webs, struggling in vain to free themselves. In the class struggle of today this ideology is the most serious obstacle to liberation.

When in 1918 in Germany military Government broke down and political power fell to the workers unrestrained by a State Power above, they were free to build up their social organization. Everywhere workers' and soldiers' councils sprang up, partly from intuition of necessities, partly from the Russian example. But the spontaneous action did not correspond to the theory in their heads, the democracy theory, impressed by long years of social-democratic teaching. And this theory now was urged upon them with vehemence by their political and union leaders. To these leaders political democracy is the element where they feel at home, in managing affairs as spokesmen of the working class, in discussion and fight with opponents in parliament and conference room. What they aspired at was not the workers master of production instead of the capitalists, but they themselves at the head of State and society, instead of the aristocratic and capitalist officials. This for them was meaning and contents of the German revolution. So they gave out, in unison with the entire bourgeoisie, the slogan of a "National Assembly" to establish a new democratic constitution. Against the revolutionary groups advocating council organization and speaking of dictatorship of the proletariat they proclaimed legal equality of all citizens as a simple demand of justice. Moreover, the councils, they said, if the workers were set on them, could be included into the new constitution and thereby even get an acknowledged legal status. Thus the mass of the workers, wavering between the opposite slogans, their heads full of the ideas of middle-class democracy, offered no resistance. With the election and meeting of the National Assembly at Weimar the German bourgeoisie acquired a new foothold, a centre of power, an established Government. In this way started the course of events that finally led to the victory of National Socialism.

Something analogous, on a minor scale, was what happened in the civil war in Spain, 1935–1936. In the industrial town of Barcelona the workers having at the revolt of the generals stormed the barracks and drawn the soldiers to their side, were master of the town. Their armed groups dominated the street, maintained order, took care of the food provision, and, whilst the chief factories were kept at work under the direction of their syndicalist unions, waged war upon the fascist troops in adjoining provinces. Then their leaders entered into the democratic government of the Catalan republic, consisting of middle-class republicans allied with socialist and communist politicians. This meant that the workers instead of fighting for their class had to join and to adjust themselves to the common cause. Weakened by democratic illusions and inner dissensions their resistance was crushed by armed troops of the Catalan government. And soon, as a symbol of restored middle-class order, you could see as in olden times workers' women, waiting before the bakers shops, brutalized by mounted police. The working class once more was down, the first step in the downfall of the republic, that finally led to the dictatorship of the military leaders.

In social crisis and political revolution, when a government breaks down, power falls into the hands of the working masses; and for the propertied class, for capitalism arises the problem how to wrest it out of their hands. So it was in the past, so it may happen in the future. Democracy is the means, the appropriate instrument of persuasion. The arguments of formal and legal quality have to induce the workers to give up their power and to let their organization be inserted as a subordinate part into the State structure.

Against this the workers have to carry in them a strong conviction that council organization is a higher and more perfect form of equality. It realizes social equality; it is the form of equality adapted to a society consciously dominating production and life. It might be asked whether the term democracy fits here, because the ending–'-cracy'–indicates domination by force, which here is lacking. Though the individuals have to conform to the whole there is no government above the people; people itself is government. Council organization is the very means by which working mankind, without need of a ruling government, organizes its vital activities. Adhering, then, to the emotional value attached of old to the word democracy we may say that council organization represents the higher form of democracy, the true democracy of labor. Political democracy, middle-class democracy, at its best can be no more than a formal democracy; it gives the same legal rights to everybody, but does not care whether this implies security of life; because economic life, because production is not concerned. The worker has his equal right to sell his labor power; but he is not certain that he will be able to sell it. Council democracy, on the contrary, is actual democracy since it secures life to all collaborating producers, free and equal masters of the sources of their life. The equal right in deciding needs not to be secured by any formal regulating paragraph; it is realized in that the work, in every part, is regulated by those who do the work. That parasites taking no part in production automatically exclude themselves from taking part in the decisions, cannot be considered as a lack in democracy; not their person but their function excludes them.

It is often said that in the modern world the point of dispute is between democracy and dictatorship; and that the working class has to throw in its full weight for democracy. The real meaning of this statement of contrast is that capitalist opinion is divided whether capitalism better maintains its sway with soft deceitful democracy, or with hard dictatorial constraint. It is the old problem of whether rebellious slaves are kept down better by kindness or by terror. The slaves, if asked, of course prefer kind treatment to terror; but if they let themselves be fooled so as to mistake soft slavery for freedom, it is pernicious to the cause of their freedom. For the working class in the present time the real issue is between council organization, the true democracy of labor, and the apparent, deceitful middle-class democracy of formal rights. In proclaiming council democracy the workers transfer the fight from political form to economic contents. Or rather–since politics is only form and means for economy– for the sounding political slogan they substitute the revolutionizing political deed, the seizure of the means of production. The slogan of political democracy serves to detract the attention of the workers from their true goal. It must be the concern of the workers, by putting up the principle of council organization, of actual democracy of labor, to give true expression to the great issue now moving society.

7. FASCISM

Fascism was the response of the capitalist world to the challenge of social-ism. Socialism proclaimed world revolution that was to free the workers from exploitation and suppression. Capitalism responds with a national revolution curbing them, powerless, under heavier exploitation. The socialist working class was confident that it could vanquish the middle-class order by making use of the very middle-class right and law. The bourgeoisie responds by snapping its fingers at right and law. The socialist workers spoke of planned and organized production to make an end of capitalism. The capitalists respond with an organization of capitalism that makes it stronger than ever before. All previous years capitalism was on the defense, only able apparently to slacken the advance of socialism. In fascism it consciously turns to attack.

The new political ideas and systems, for which from Italy the name Fascism came into use, are the product of modern economic development. The growth of big business, the increase in size of the enterprises, the subjection of small business, the combination into concerns and trusts, the concentration of bank capital and its domination over industry brought an increasing power into the hands of a decreasing number of financial magnates and kings of industry. World economy and society at large were dominated ever more by small groups of mutually fighting big capitalists, sometimes successful stock jobbers, sometimes pertinacious shrewd business tacticians, seldom restricted by moral scruples, always active sinewy men of energy.

At the end of the 19th century these economic changes brought about a corresponding change in the ideas. The doctrine of equality of man, inherited from rising capitalism with its multitude of equal business men, gives way to the doctrine of inequality. The worship of success and the admiration for the strong personality—leading and treading down the ordinary people—distorted in Nietzsche's "superman"—reflect the realities of new capitalism. The lords of capital, risen to power through success in gambling and swindling, through the ruin of numberless small existences, are now styled the "grand old men" of their country. At the same time the "masses" ever more are spoken of with contempt. In such utterances it is the down trodden petty bourgeoisie, dependent, without social power and without aspirations, bent entirely on silly amusements—including the congenial working masses without class consciousness—that serves as the prototype for the will-less, spiritless, characterless mass destined to be led and commanded by strong leaders.

In politics the same line of thought appears in a departure from democracy. Power over capital implies power over Government; direct power over Government is vindicated as the natural right of the economic masters. Parliaments evermore serve to mask, by a flood of oratory, the rule of big capital behind the semblance of self-determination of the people. So the cant of the politicians, the lack of inspiring principles, the petty bargaining behind the scenes, intensifies the conviction in critical observers not acquainted with the deepest causes that parliamentarism is a pool of corruption and democracy a chimera. And that also in politics the strong personality must prevail, as independent ruler of the State.

Another effect of modern capitalism was the increasing spirit of violence. Whereas in the rise of capitalism free trade, world peace and collaboration of the peoples had occupied the minds, reality soon had brought war between new and old capitalist Powers. The need of expansion in foreign continents involves big capital into a fierce fight for world power and colonies. Now forcible subjection, cruel extermination and barbarous exploitation of colored races are defended by the doctrine of the superiority of the white race, destined to dominate and to civilize them and justified in exploiting natural richness wherever it may be. New ideals of splendor, power, world domination of the own nation replace the old ideals of freedom, equality and world peace. Humanitarianism is ridiculed as an obsolete effeminacy; force and violence bring greatness.

Thus the spiritual elements of a new social and political system had silently grown up, visible everywhere in moods and opinions of the ruling class and its spokesmen. To bring them to overt action and supremacy the strong concussions of the world war with ensuing distress and chaos were necessary. It is often said that fascism is the genuine political doctrine of big capitalism. This is not true; America can show that its undisturbed sway is better secured by political democracy. If, however, in its upward struggle it falls short against a stronger foe, or is threatened by a rebellious working class, more forcible and violent modes of domination are needed. Fascism is the political system of big capitalism in emergency. It is not created by conscious premeditation; it sprang up, after much uncertain groping, as a practical deed, followed afterwards by theory.

In Italy the post-war crisis and depression had brought discontent among the bourgeoisie, disappointed in its national hopes; and had brought an impulse to action among the workers, excited by the Russian and the German revolutions. Strikes gave no relief, owing to soaring prices; the demand for workers' control, inspired by syndicalist and bolshevist ideas, led to shop occupation, not hindered by the weak and wavering government. It looked like a revolution, but it was only a gesture. The workers, without clear insight or purpose, did not know what to do with it. They tried, in vain, to produce for the market as a kind of productive co-operation. After an arrangement of the trade unions with the employers they peacefully cleared out.

But this was not the end. The bourgeoisie, terror-stricken for a moment, attained in its deepest feelings, fuming revenge now that disdain succeeded fear, organized its direct action. Bands of active pugnacious middle-class youths, fed with strong nationalist teachings, full of instinctive hatred against the workers, their unions, their co-operatives, their socialism, encouraged by bourgeoisie and land-owners providing money for arms and uniforms, began a campaign of terrorism. They destroyed workers' meeting rooms, ill-treated labor leaders, sacked and burnt co-operatives and newspaper offices, attacked meetings, first in the smaller places, gradually in the bigger towns. The workers had no means of efficient response; wont to peaceful organizing work under the protection of law, addicted to parliamentarism and trade union fight, they were powerless against the new forms of violence.

Soon the fascist groups combined into stronger organization, the fascist party, its ranks ever more joined by energetic youths from the bourgeoisie and the intellectuals. Here, indeed, these classes saw a rescue from the impending threat of socialism. Now the riots grew into a systematic destruction and annihilation of everything the workers had built up, the ill-treatment grew into unpunished murder of prominent socialists. When at last the liberal ministers made some hesitating attempts to suppress the outrages they were turned out, on the menace of civil war, and the leaders of fascism, appointed in their place, became masters of the State. An active organized minority had imposed its will upon the passive majority. It was not a revolution; the same ruling class persisted; but this class had got new managers of its interests, proclaiming new political principles.

Now fascist theory, too, was formulated. Authority and obedience are the fundamental ideas. Not the good of the citizens but the good of the State is the highest aim. The State, embodying the community, stands above the entirety of the citizens. It is a supreme being, not deriving its authority from the will of the citizens, but from its own right. Government, hence, is no democracy, but dictatorship. Above the subjects stand the bearers of authority, the strong men, and uppermost the—formally at least—all-powerful dictator, the Leader.

Only in outer forms does this dictatorship resemble the ancient Asiatic despotisms over agrarian peoples or the absolutism in Europe some centuries ago. These primitive monarchial governments, with a minimum of organization, soon stood powerless over against the rising social power of capitalism. The new despotism, product of highly developed capitalism, disposes of all the power of the bourgeoisie, all the refined methods of modern technics and organization. It is progress, not regress; it is not return to the old rough barbarism but advance to a higher more refined barbarism. It looks like regression because capitalism, that during its ascent evoked the illusion of the dawn of humanity, now strikes out like a cornered wolf.

A special characteristic of the new political system is the Party as support and fighting force of dictatorship. Like its predecessor and example, the Communist Party in Russia, it forms the bodyguard of the new Government. It came up, independent from and even against Government, out of the inner forces of society, conquered the State, and fused with it into one organ of domination. It consists chiefly of petty-bourgeois elements, with more roughness and less culture and restraint than the bourgeoisie itself, with fell desire to climb to higher positions, full of nationalism and of class hatred against the workers. Out of the equable mass of citizens they come to the front as an organized group of combative fanatical volunteers, ready for any violence, in military discipline obeying the leaders. When the leaders are made masters over the State they are made a special organ of Government, endowed with special rights and privileges. They do what lies outside the duties of the officials, they do the dirty work of persecution and vengeance, they are secret police, spies and organ of propaganda at the same time. As a devoted semi-official power with undefined competencies they permeate the population; only by their terrorism dictatorship is possible.

At the same time, as counterpart, the citizens are entirely powerless; they do not influence government. Parliaments may be convoked, but only to listen and applaud to speeches and declarations of the leaders, not to discuss and decide. All decisions are taken in the set assemblies of party chiefs. Surely this was usually the case under parliamentarism also; but then secretly, and publicly denied and always there was control by party strife and public criticism. These have disappeared now. Other parties than the One are forbidden, their former leaders have fled. All newspapers are in the hands of the Party; all publicity is under its control; free speech is abolished. The former source of power of Parliament, its financial control of Government by voting or refusing money, has gone, too. Government disposes at its will over all State revenues without rendering account; it can spend unknown and unlimited sums of money for party purposes, for propaganda or anything else.

State power now takes up the care for economic life, making it at the same time subservient to its own purposes. In a country where capitalism is still in its development, this means collaboration with big capital, not as in former times in secret, but as a normal duty. Big enterprise is furthered by subsidies and orders; public services are actuated for business life, the old laziness disappears, and foreign tourists in praise of the new order relate that the trains conform to schedule. Small enterprise is organized in "corporations" where employers and directors collaborate with controlling State officials. "Corporatism" is put up as the character of the new order against parliamentarism; instead of deceitful talk of incompetent politicians comes the expert discussion and advice of the practical business man. Thus labor is acknowledged as the basis of society: capitalist labor, of course.

The fascist State through its regulations strengthens the economic power of big capital over small business. The economic means of big capital to impose its will are never entirely adequate; in a free State ever again small competitors come up, take a stand against the big ones, refuse to conform to agreements, and disturb the quiet exploitation of customers. Under fascism, however, they have to submit to the regulations established in the corporations according to the most influential interests and given legal validity by decree of government. Thus the entire economic life is subjected more thoroughly to big capital.

At the same time the working class is made powerless. Classwar, of course, is "abolished." In the shop all are collaborating now as comrades in the service of the community; the former director, too, has been turned into a worker and a comrade; but as he is the leader, clad with authority, his commands must be obeyed by the other workers. Trade unions, being organs of fight, of course are forbidden. The workers are not allowed to fight for their interests; State power takes care of them, and to the State authorities they have to bring forward their complaints – usually neutralized by the greater personal influence of the employers. So a lowering of working conditions and standard of life was unavoidable. As a compensation the workers, now assembled in fascist organizations with Party members as designated dictatorial leaders, were regaled with brilliant speeches on the eminence of labor, now for the first time acknowledged in its worth. For capital times were good now, times of strong development and high profits, notwithstanding the often troublesome control of ignorant fascist officials demanding their share. Capitalists of other countries visited with troubles and strikes, looked with envy at the industrial peace in Italy.

More consciously than elsewhere nationalism uprises as the all dominating ideology, because it affords a basis to theory and practice of State omnipotence. The State is the embodiment, the organ of the nation; its aim the greatness of the nation. For the raising of the power needed in the world fight of capitalism fascism in many points is superior to other political systems. With all the forces of State-paid propaganda national feelings and pride are aroused; the ancient Romans are exalted as the great ancestors, the Emperor Augustus is celebrated as the great Italian, the Mediterranean is called "our sea," the glory of ancient Rome has to be restored. At the same time military power is built up; war industry is promoted and subsidized; for armaments Government through lack of any public control can secretly spend as much money as it wants. The Italian Government and bourgeoisie grew boastful and aggressive. They wanted their country not to be admired as a museum of ancient art any more, but respected as a modern country of factories and guns.

For many years Italy was the only European country, besides Russia, that had a dictatorial government. So it might seem a result of special chance conditions there. Then, however, other countries followed. In Portugal, after many bickerings between parties in Parliament and military officers, the generals seized power, but felt incapable of solving the many economic difficulties. So they appointed a well known fascist-minded professor of economy to act as dictator under the name of prime minister. He introduced corporatism to take the place of parliamentarism, and was much praised for the undisturbed firmness of his reign. The petty-capitalist stage of development in this country is shown in that his most praised reform was economizing in finance by cutting the government expenses.

It seems a contradiction that fascism, a product of big capitalism should happen to rule in backward countries, whereas the countries of biggest capitalism reject it. The latter fact is easily explained, because democratic parliamentarism is the best camouflage for its sway. A system of government is not connected automatically with a system of economy. The economic system determines the ideas, the wishes, the aims; and then people with these aims in mind adjust their political system according to their needs and possibilities. The ideas of dictatorship, of the sway of some few strong individuals, countered by other strong social forces in countries where big capital reigns, in distant regions also strike the mind where big capitalism is no more than aspiration of future development.

In backward countries, when capitalism begins to come up and to stir the minds, the political forms of advanced countries are initiated. Thus in the second part of the 19th century parliamentarism held its triumphal course through the world, in the Balkans, in Turkey, in the East, in South America, though sometimes is parody forms. Behind such parliaments stood no strong bourgeoisie to use them as its organ; the population consisted in large landowners and small farmers, artisans, petty dealers, with chiefly local interest. Parliaments were dominated by jobbers enriching themselves through monopolies, by lawyers and generals ruling as ministers and bestowing well-paid offices on their friends, by intellectuals making business out of their membership, by agents of foreign capital preying upon the richness of timber and ore.

A dirty scene of corruption showing that parliamentarism did not sprout from sound and natural roots here.

Such new countries cannot repeat the gradual line of development of the old capitalist countries in first ascent. They can and must introduce highly developed technics at once: on their precapitalist conditions they must implant big industry directly; acting capital is big capital. So it is not strange that the political forms generated by petty capitalism in Europe do not fit here. There parliamentarism was firmly rooted in the consciousness of the citizens and had time gradually to adapt itself to the new conditions. Here, at the outskirts, the fascist ideas of dictatorship could find adherence, since the practice of politics was already conforming to it. Landowners and tribe chieftains easily convert their old power into modern dictatorial forms; new capitalist interests can work better with some few mighty men than with a host of greedy parliamentarians. So the spiritual influences of big world capital find a fertile field in the political ideas of rulers and intellectuals all over the world.

8. NATIONAL SOCIALISM

Far more important are the forms of fascism presented by the most strongly developed country of capitalist Europe. After having lost the first world war and after being pressed down to entire powerlessness, Germany through fascism was enabled to prepare for a second, more formidable attempt at world power.

In the post-war years of misery and humiliation the gradually assembling nationalist youth felt by instinct that its future depended on organization of power. Among the many competing organizations the National Socialist Party crystallized as the group with the greatest growing faculty, and afterwards absorbed the others. It prevailed by having an economic program, sharply anti-capitalist—hence denoted socialist—fit to attract the petty bourgeoisie, the farmers and part of the workers. Directed of course against capital such as these classes know it as their suppressor, the usury capital, the real estate banks, the big warehouses, especially against Jewish capital therefore. Its anti-semitism expressed the feelings of these classes as well as of the academic circles who felt threatened by Jewish competition now that the republic had given equal civil rights. Its acute nationalism gave expression to the feelings of the entire bourgeoisie, by sharply protesting against Germany's humiliation, by denouncing Versailles, and by the call to fight for new power, for new national greatness. When then the great crisis of 1930 reduced the middle class masses to a panic fright, when these, through their millions of votes, made national socialism a powerful party, German big capital saw its chance. It gave money for an overwhelming propaganda that soon beat the wavering liberal and socialist politicians out of the field, made national socialism the strongest party and its leader chief of the government.

Unlike other parties in government its first provisions were to make sure that it never should loose its government power. By excluding the Communist Party as criminals from the Reichstag and affiliating the lesser nationalist groups it secured a majority to start with. All important government and police offices were filled by party members; the communist fighting groups were suppressed, the nationalist ones were privileged. Protected by the authorities the latter, by deeds of violence, with impunity could spread so much terror that every idea of resistance was quelled in the people. The daily press first was muzzled, then gradually captured and "equalized" into organs of national socialism. Socialist and democratic spokesmen had to flee to other countries; the widely spread socialist and the not less hated pacifist literature was collected in violent searches and solemnly burned. From the first days began the persecutions of the Jews, that gradually became more cruel, and last proclaimed as their aim the extermination of the entire Jewish race. As a heavy steel armor the dictatorship of a resolute, well-organized minority closed around German society, to enable German capital as a well-armored giant to take up again the fight for world power.

All political practice and all social ideas of national socialism have their basis in the character of its economic system. Its foundation is organization of capitalism. Such among the first adherents who insisted upon the old anti-capitalist program were of course soon dismissed and destroyed. The new measures of state control over capital were now explained as the formerly promised subjection and destruction of capitalist power. Government decrees restricted capital in its freedom of action. Central government offices controlled the sale of products as well as the procuring of raw materials. Government gave prescripts for the spending of profits, for the amount of dividends allowed, for the reserves to be made for new investments, and for the share it required for its own purposes. That all these measures were not directed against capitalism itself, but only against the arbitrary freedom of capital dispersed over numerous small holders, is shown by the fact that herein Government was continually guided by the advice of big capitalists and bankers outside the party, as a more resolute sequel of what had been started already in collaboration with former less daring governments. It was an organization imposed by the condition of German capitalism, the only means to restore it to power.

Under capitalism capital is master; capital is money claiming the surplus value produced by labor. Labor is the basis of society, but money, gold, is its master. Political economy deals with capital and money as the directing powers of society. So it had been in Germany, as anywhere. But German capital was defeated, exhausted, ruined. It was not lost; it had maintained itself as master of the mines, the factories, of society, of labor. But the money had gone. The war reparations pressed as a heavy debt, and prevented rapid accumulation of new capital. German labor was tributary to the victors, and through them to America. Since America had secluded itself from the imports of goods it had to be laid in gold; gold disappeared from Europe and choked America, pushing both into a world crisis.

The German "revolution" of 1933—proudly called so by national socialism—was the revolt of German against American capital, against the rule of gold, against the gold form of capital. It was the recognition that labor is the basis of capital, that capital is mastery over labor, and that, hence, gold is not necessary. The real conditions for capitalism, a numerous intelligent and skilled working class and a high stage of technics and science, were present. So it repudiated the tribute, rejected the claims of foreign gold, and organized capitalist production on the basis of goods and labor. Thus, for the use of internal propaganda, always again it could speak of fight against capital and capitalism; for capital was money, was gold that reigned in America, in England, in France, as it had reigned formerly in Germany. The separating cleft, in this line of thought, gaped between the gambling and exploiting usurers and money capitalists on the one side, and the hard toiling workers and employers on the other side.

Under free capitalism the surplus value growing everywhere out of production piles up in the banks, looks out for new profits, and is invested by its owner or by the bank in new or in existing enterprises. Since in Germany money was scarce State government had to provide the means for founding new necessary enterprises. That could be done only by seizing the profits of all enterprises for this purpose, after allowance of a certain dividend for the shareholders. So it established itself as the central leader of economy. In the emergency of German capitalism the spending of capital could not be left to the will and whim of private capitalists, for luxury, for gambling or foreign investment. With strict economy all means must be used for reconstruction of the economic system. Every enterprise now depends on the credit assigned by the State and stands under continuous control of the State. The State for this purpose has its economic offices of experts, in which the leaders of the big enterprises and concerns by their advice are dominating. This means a complete domination of monopolist capital over the smaller capitalists in a system of planned economy. Conscious organization has replaced the automatism of gold.

Germany, though striving after autarchy, could not exist without importing raw materials from outside, paying for them, because it had no money, by exports of its own products. Hence commerce could not be left to the arbitrariness of private dealers, to the wish of the public for superfluous or foreign fancies. When all sales shall serve the necessary reconstruction Government has to supervise foreign commerce by rigid prescripts, or take it in its own hand. It controls and limits every transfer of money across the frontiers, even tourist travels; all drafts on foreign debtors must be delivered. The State itself takes up large-scale commerce, purchase as well as sale. The great difficulty of the old economic system, the transition of commodities into gold, the selling of the goods, the primary cause of so much faltering and crisis, is thereby automatically solved at the same time. The State, as universal dealer, is able in every purchase contract to stipulate that the same value of its product shall be bought, so that no money is needed. Or expressed in another way: in selling its goods it asks to be paid not in money but in kind, in other goods: German machines against Hungarian wheat or Roumanian oil. Gold is eliminated from business by direct barter of goods.

But now barter on a gigantic scale, of the produce and needs of entire countries at once. Private dealers in the other countries seldom have such monopolies as are needed here; moreover such big transactions, especially of materials serviceable to war have political consequences. Hence the foreign governments have to step in. If they were not yet adapted to such economic functions they now adapt themselves; they take in hand the disposal over the products, and in their turn go to regulating commerce and industry. Thus State control in a big country leads to state control in other countries. A new system of economy, the system of direct barter of goods, is introduced into international commerce. It is especially attractive to the rising countries that are purveyors of raw materials. They now get their machines and canons, without in Paris and London contracting heavy loans that would bring there into financial dependence. Thus German economic expansion is custing English and French capital from those countries; and it is accompanied by political expansion. With the new economic system the ruling classes there adopt the new political ideas, the fascist system of government, that increases their power at home and better fits their needs than an imitation of parliamentarism. Politically they were drawn nearer to Germany. Thus what at first, according to old economic ideas, looked a paralyzing weakness, the lack of gold, was now turned into a source of new force.

German capitalism saw a new road opened towards resurrection and power. This could not but have an enormous influence upon the ideas and feelings of the bourgeoisie, especially upon the capitalist and intellectual youth. It had experienced the poverty and dejection in the post-war years, the desperation and impotence under the Weimar republic; now again it saw a future full of hope. When a class, from pressure and dependence, sees looming up a future of greatness with as yet unlimited possibilities, enthusiasm and energy are awakened; it clothes the coming world with the garb of exalted ideologies inspiriting the minds. Thus national socialism speaks of its conquest of power as a grand social, political and spiritual revolution, far surpassing all previous ones, a revolution that ends capitalism, establishes socialism and community, one destined to renovate society for thousands of years.

What really happened was only a structural change of capitalism, the transition from free to planned capitalism. Yet this change is important enough to be felt as the beginning of a new grand epoch. Human progress always consisted in the replacing of instinctive action, of chance and custom by deliberate planning. In technics science had already replaced tradition. Economy, however, the social entirety of production, was left to the chance of personal guessing of unknown market conditions. Hence wasted labor, destructive competition, bankruptcy, crisis and unemployment. Planned economy tries to bring order, to regulate production according to the needs of consumption. The transition of free capitalism to capitalism directed by State-dictatorship means, fundamentally, the end of the pitiless fight of all against all, in which the weak were succumbing. It means that everybody will have his place assigned, an assured existence, and that unemployment, the scourge of the working class, disappears as a stupid spilling of valuable labor power.

This new condition finds its spiritual expression in the slogan of community. In the old system everybody had to fight for himself, only guided by egotism. Now that production is organized into a centrally directed unity, everybody knows that his work is part of the whole, that he is working for the national community. Where loss of old liberty might evoke resentment as intense propaganda accentuates the service of the community as the high moral principle of the new world. It is adequate to carry away especially young people into devoted adherence. Moreover the anti-capitalist fiction of the exclusion of the gold, by persistent propaganda is hammered into the minds as the new reign of labor. Community and labor find their common expression in the name socialism.

This socialism is national socialism. Nationalism, the mightiest ideology of the bourgeoisie, stands over all other ideas as the master they have to serve. The community is the nation, it comprises only the fellow people, labor is service of the own people. This is the new, the better socialism, entirely opposed to the international socialism of Jewish Marxism that by its doctrine of class war tore the national unity asunder. It had made the German people powerless; national socialism makes the national community a mighty unbreakable unity.

For national socialist doctrine the nations are the entities constituting mankind. The nations have to fight for their place on earth, their "living space"; history shows an almost uninterrupted series of wars in which strong peoples exterminated, drove out or subjected the weaker ones. Thus it was and thus it will be. War is the natural condition of mankind, peace is nothing but preparation of future war. So the first duty of every people is to make itself powerful against others; it has to choose between victory or downfall. Internationalism and pacifism are bloodless abstractions, yet dangerous because they are sapping the strength of the people.

The first aim of national socialism was to make a powerful unity of all German-speaking people. Through adversity of historical development it had been divided into a number of separate states, only incompletely united in Bismarck's former Reich—the Austrian part remaining an independent state— moreover mutilated by the victors of 1918. The call for national unity met with a wide response in the feelings, even of such isolated groups as the German settlers in Transylvania or in America. In consequence of the interlacing of living sites of different races, as well as by economic connections, the principle of political unity of course encounters many difficulties. The German-speaking town of Danzig, was the natural harbor for the surrounding Polish hinterland. The Czecho-Slovak State as a Slavonic protrusion separated the Northern and the Austrian Germans, and included on the inner slopes of the frontier ridges [Sudetes] an industrious German population. Under capitalism such abnormal cases are not solved by any fair principle of equable dealing, but by power against power. So they were the direct motives that gave rise to the present world war.

From the first day preparation for war was the leading thought of national socialism, the goal of all its measures. For this purpose industry was supervised and regulated by the State, for this purpose private profits and dividends were cut down, for this purpose the investment of capital and the founding of new enterprises was reserved to Government economic offices. All surplus value beyond a certain profit rate for the shareholders is taken by the State for its needs; these needs are the supreme common interest of the entire bourgeoisie. In old capitalism the State had to procure money for its needs by taxation, sometimes by the cunning method of unfair indirect taxes; or, if by direct taxes, conceded grudgingly and under suspicious control by the propertier citizens, and considered as an unrighteous incursion upon their personal expenditure. Now this is all changed. The State by its own right takes what it wants directly at the source, the chief part of the surplus value, and to the capitalist owners it leaves some remnant fixed at its own discretion. No more the State has to beg from the masters of the means of production; it is itself master now and they are the recipients. An enormous increase of financial power compared with other States; but indispensable for success in the world fight. And again national socialism in in this way shows off before the people's masses as the power that curbs capital, by enforcing it to deliver the main part of its profit to the common weal, to the community.

Moreover the State is direct master of production. In the old capitalism, when the State had with difficulty extorted money for expenses from Parliament, or borrowed it under fat provisions from the bankers, it had to spend it on the monopolistic private arms industry. These concerns, internationally connected, though they paraded as national firms, Krupp in Essen, Schneider in Le Creusot, Armstrong in England, not only took their big profits, but without conscientious scruples impartially supplied enemies and allies with the most perfect and newest inventions. It looked as if war were a puerile play of politicians to fatten some few armament capitalists. To national socialism, however, war is the most serious affair, for which an unlimited part of the entire industrial apparatus can be used. Government decides what big portion of the total steel and chemical industry shall serve for armaments. It simply orders the factories to be built, it organizes science and technics to invent and try new and better weapons, it combines the functions of military officer, engineer, and inventor, and makes war science [Wehrwissenschaft] the object of special training. Armored cars, dive bombers, big submarines with ever more perfect installations, rapid torpedo boats, rockets, all of new construction, can be built in secret. No information reaches the enemy, no sensational daily press can publish any notice, no parliament members can ask information, no criticism has to be encountered. Thus the arms are heaped up during years of feverish war preparation till the moment of attack has arrived.

In old capitalism war was a possibility, avoided as long as possible, or at least disclaimed, a war of defense mostly on the part of the old satisfied Powers. The new upgrowing powers, aggressive because they have to conquer their share in the world, have a positive aim that strains the energy much more intensely than does the negative aim of mere passive defense of existing conditions. They are "dynamic"; in military tactics this character is represented in the irresistible impulse of the well prepared mass offensive.

Thus German capitalism, by installing a national socialist government completely dominating the entire economic life, provided itself with an incomparable war machine. The question may by posed, however, whether it did not shoot past the aim. In striving for power over the world, did it not lose its mastery at home? Could the German bourgeoisie still be called the ruling class?

German state control is no state socialism. The State is not, as it is in Russia, owner of the means of production. In Russia the bureaucracy of State officials collectively owns the industrial apparatus; it is the ruling and exploiting class, appropriating the surplus value. In Germany there is a numerous bourgeoisie, directors of enterprises, free employers, officials, shareholders; they are the owners of the means of production living on surplus value. But now the two functions of the shareholder are separated; the right of disposal is detached from ownership. Under big capitalism the right of disposal is the most important function of capitalist ownership; we see it in America in the holding companies. Then the owner in his character of exploiter only retains the function of receiving part of the profits. In Germany Government took for itself the right of disposal, the right to manipulate with capital, to direct production, to increase the productivity and to distribute the profits. For the mass of the bourgeoisie there remained the detailed work of directing their enterprises and gambling with the shares. Since production and import both are determined by the State, private dividends could not be spent in another way other than by buying industrial shares, i.e., by returning the profits as new capital into State-controlled industry.

Thus big capital retained power. Surely its expectation when it put national socialism at the head of the State, of finding obedient servants, was disappointed; the old masters of industry and banks had to share their power with the new masters of the State, who not only partook in the directing but also in the pocketing. Big capital in Germany had not yet taken the American form of an unassailable property of some families; capable men of daring from anywhere could rise to the leadership of big concerns. Now they had to share their leading power with other men of daring risen to power by way of politics and party fight. In the economic offices the leaders of big business meet with the political leaders in the common task of regulating production. The dividing line between private capitalists and State officials disappears in the coalescing of functions. Together they are master of the State and of the means of production.

With the deep changes in economic and political conditions a new state of mind pervaded the German people. The mutual connection and dependence became stronger, gradations of value and rank were felt, the authority of leaders, the obedience of the masses imposed themselves; consciousness of subordination in large entities accompanies planned economy. And above all, in the entire middle class there is a strained nationalism, a passionate will to fight for world power. Though growing spontaneously out of the new conditions this new spirit was not left to develop freely; for in that case opposite ideas and forces would arise at the same time. It was the object of an intense one-sided propaganda. To make these feelings a spiritual force binding the entire nation into a fighting unity, they were fostered and developed by special means. Propaganda and education were made the task of a separate State department, endowed with unlimited financial means. All usable forces of publicity, of science, literature and art were set to work systematically to cram the national socialist ideas into all the heads, with exclusion all deviating spiritual influences.

This implied a complete spiritual despotism. Whereas under former systems of despotism the daily press was only muzzled or harassed by a stupid censorship, often outwitted by the wits of editors, now the entire press was annexed by the Party and provided with party members as editors. The national socialist State was not only master of the material life of man, it was also master of the spiritual life, by means of the Party. No books or writings expressing deviating opinions could be published; foreign publications were carefully controlled before being admitted. Secret printing of independent or opposite opinions was not only punished severely as capital crime, but also rendered difficult by State control of all materials. It is intellectual cowardice that shuns dispute on equal terms and dares to attack and insult the adversary only after he has been fettered and muzzled. But it was efficient; the party press was able, without compensation, day by day to force upon the readers not only its doctrine but also its biased representation or misrepresentation of facts and happenings, or to omit them entirely. Notwithstanding all preconceived distrust of one-sided information, the ever repeated, never contradicted views, so well confirmed by the facts presented, must in the long run take hold of the minds. The more so as they were presented as part and result of an attractive doctrine, the ideology of community and labor: the end of selfishness and exploitation, the new reign of devotion to the people's weal, regulated work and prosperity for all, the common exertion for the greatness and the future of the nation, with severe punishment of course for all its enemies.

At the same time all verbal intercourse was strictly controlled. The party everywhere had its members and adherents, in the offices, in the shops, all inspired with the moral duty to denounce for punishment, as enemies of the community, all who expressed other opinions, ventured criticism, or spread rumors. Thus no opposition could form, except in the extreme secrecy of insignificant groups; everywhere a feeling of utter powerlessness prevailed.

Thus, compared with the ancient forms of despotic rule, modern capitalism showed an enormous progress of efficiency in the technics of suppression. Whether we take the English Tory Government in the beginning of the 19th century, that had no police force, or the Prussian absolutism of Russian Czarism in later times, with their primitive barbarous cruelty, they all present the spectacle of stupid helplessness, normal for a government living far from the people. In the English courts editors and authors made a tough fight for reform and freedom of press, applauded by the people when they went to gaol. The Czarist gaolers often could not conceal their respect for the revolutionaries as representatives of superior culture. Repeatedly Prussian police, trapped by the better organization of the socialist workers, had to suffer exhibition as simpletons before the courts.

Now that was all over. The new despotism was equipped with all the engines of the modern State. All force and energy that capitalism evokes is combined with the most thorough-going tyranny that big capital needs in order to uphold its supremacy. No tribunal to do justice to the subject against the State. The judges are Party members, agents of the State, dismissed if they are soft, bound to no statute book, administering justice after decrees from above. Law suits are public only when needed for propaganda, to intimidate others; and then the papers bring only what the judge deems adequate. The police consist of strictly organized and disciplined ruffians provided with all weapons and methods to beat down the "Volksgenossen." Secret police again were all powerful, were more capable that it was in olden times. No law secured anybody from being put in gaol, for unlimited time, without trial. The concentration camp, formerly invented as a war measure against guerrillas, now was installed as a form of mass-prison with hard labor, often accompanied by systematic cruelties. No personal dignity was respected; it did not exist any more. Where petty bourgeois coarseness, turned into perverse abuse of unlimited power, was provided with all the inventiveness of modern capitalism, cruelty against the victims did not reach a pitch rivaling the worst barbarousness of former centuries. Cruelty as a rule is a consequence of fear, experienced in the past or felt for the future, thus betraying what is hidden in subconsciousness. But for the moment all adversaries were made powerless, silenced and intimidated.

Spiritual tyranny was supplemented by incessant propaganda, especially adapted to the younger generation. The rulers know quite well that they can win over only very few of the older generation of workers who, grown up in the nobler ideas of Social Democracy, preserved these as a precious remembrance, though bereft of practical use. Only for the younger adults who experienced Social Democracy in its decline, as ruling party, the propaganda could be effective. But it was the growing youth which it did itself educate and shape, that national socialism placed its hope as material for its new world.

It cannot surprise that it met with great success. As no party or group before it concerned itself with youth. National socialism appointed able leaders well versed in modern psychology, disposing of ample financial means, who, with entire devotion assembled and educated the youth in an all-embracing organization. All the innate feelings of comradeship, of mutual aid, of attachment, of activity, of ambition could develop in young people. They were filled with the self-confidence of being an important part of the national community with an important task of their own. Not to win a good position for oneself, the highest ideal of the youngsters in capitalist society, but to serve and forward the national community. The boys had to feel future fighters, preparing for great deeds, not by learned studies but by vigour, pluck, fighting capacity and discipline. The girls had to prepare for the future of being heroic German mothers; increase of population, as rapid as possible, was a condition for strength in the world fight.

With ardor the children imbibed the new teachings that far outweighed the spiritual influence of their parents and teachers. Against these they acted as fervent champions and spokesmen of the new creed, especially educated for that task. Not simply to extend the propaganda into home and school, but still more to report to their new leaders home disputes and controversies. Hence to act as spies and denuciators of their own parents, who under the threat of severe punishment had to abstain from any attempt to educate their children in their own spirit. The children belonged to the State, not to the parents. Thus for the future war an army of missions was prepared unrivaled for enthusiasm and devotion. Such an education implies careful protection against any opposite influence that could evoke doubts, uncertainties and inner conflicts. Doubts and inner conflicts, to be sure, produce strong characters, independent thinkers; but for such national socialism had no use. What it needed, and what it tried to rear by one-sided teaching of the one sole truth, was blind faith and, based thereon, fanatical devotion, expedient for irresistible assault.

The strength of national socialism lay in its organization of the material production, of physical forces. Its weakness lay in its attempt to uniformize the mentalities, the intellectual forces, in both cases by brutal constraint. Most of its adherents and spokesmen came from the lower middle class, rough, ignorant, narrow-minded, desirous to win a higher position, full of prejudices, easily addicted to brutality. They came to power not through intellectual but through physical and organizational superiority, by daring and combativeness. They imposed their spirit of violence upon the dominated intellectuals and workers. Thus respect for brute strength, contempt for science and knowledge was bred in the upgrowing generation; for the ambitious, instead of painful patient study, an easier way to high positions led through party service that demanded no knowledge but only sturdy drilling, physical training, rough force and discipline.

German big capitalism, however, cannot develop without science is the basis of technical progress, and without an intellectual class with important functions, economic and social. Furthering and encouragement of science is a life interest for capital. Its new political system brought it into contradiction not only with humanity and culture, but also with its own spiritual basis. To uphold its dominance it suffered to decay what constituted its force and justification. This will avenge itself when in the contest of capitalisms for world power the highest perfection in technics is imperative, and its neglect cannot be made good by physical constraint. The great scientific and technical capacities of the German people, of its engineers, its scientists, its workers, who brought it to the front of industrial progress, were chained to the war chariot of big capitalism and, enhancing its fighting strength, were wasted and spoilt in this bondage.

National socialism, moreover, tried to impose its very theory upon science, in giving to nationalism the theoretical expression of the racial doctrine. Always German nationalism had taken the form of worship of the ancient Teutons whose virtues as a mirror for the effeminate Romans had been exalted by Tacitus. German authors had exposed the theory of the "Nordic" race, superior to other races and destined to dominate them, and nowadays represented by the Germans and some adjacent peoples. This theory was then blended with anti-semitism. The special capacities of the Jews for commerce and money dealing, for medicine and jurisprudence had, half a century ago already, aroused strong anti-semitic feelings among the petty bourgeoisie and in academic circles. Neither among the great bourgeoisie, that by its mastery of the industrial surplus value was any fear of Jewish finance, nor among the working class had they any importance. Anti-semitism was a sentiment of the lower middle class; but most adherents of national socialism came from these very circles. Jewish immigration from the East after the first world war, introducing its primitive trade methods of barter, and the appointing of Jews in political offices in the Weimar republic intensified the hatred and made anti-semitism the main creed of the most influential new leaders.

Thus racial theory became the central doctrine of national socialism. Real Germans were not all the German-speaking inhabitants of Germany, but only the "Aryans"—the same held good for surrounding peoples as the Scandinavians and the Dutch; the English were too much corrupted already by capitalism. The non-Aryan cohabitants, the Jews, had no rights; the allowance to settle they misused by assembling capital and by robbing and insolently suppressing the Aryans. So they were expropriated and the persecutions gradually increased to rough abuse and deliberate extermination.

National socialism by means of its political power forced this racial theory upon science. It appointed the spokesmen of the doctrine as university professors, and profusely procured funds for publishing books and periodicals for its vindication. That the amount of scientific truth in it is extremely meagre could be no hindrance. Capitalism in power always elevates to official science the doctrines that serve its purposes; they dominate the universities everywhere; but criticism and opposite opinions have the possibility to express themselves, albeit not from official chairs. Under national socialism, however, all critical discussion of the official doctrine was made impossible.

Still more grotesque was the extension of the racial theory to physics. In physics Einstein's theory of relativity was considered by almost the entirety of physicists as a most important progress of science, basis of numerous new developments. But Einstein was a Jew, and so anti-semitism took a stand against this theory. When national socialism came to power the Jewish professors, men of world fame often, were dismissed and expelled; the anti-Semitic opponents of relativity were hailed as the genial spokesmen of "German physics," the expression of sound and simple Aryan intelligence, against "Jewish physics," consisting in crooked theories contrived by Talmudian distortion of thought. It is easily seen that that "sound Aryan intelligence" is nothing but the simple-mindedness of petty burgher thought inaccessible to the deeper abstractions of modern science.

In the fight of German capitalism for world power anti-semitism was not needed, was rather a disadvantage. But it had no choice. Since the bourgeoisie had not dared to join the people's fight, 1848, to win domination, it had to surrender to the lead of other classes. First of the landed aristocracy with the Kaiser, who, by their stupid diplomacy, were responsible for the defeat in the first world war. Now of the petty burgher party and its leaders, who made this fad the basis of a policy that by evoking scorn and intense hatred all over the world, prepared for a new defeat.

From the beginning national socialism gave special attention to the farmers. The platform of any petty burgher party spoke of ridding the farmers from exploitation by mortgage and banking capital. Moreover, for the impending war it was imperative that Germany should feed itself and have sufficient raw materials. So an organization of agriculture, as essential part of the wholesale organization of production, was necessary. It was expressed in the nationalist socialist ideology of the farmer class, inseparably united with the soil, preservers of the racial strength of the forebears, the true "nobility of blood and soil." It had to be protected against the dissolving influences of capitalism and competition, and connected into the whole of planned production. Conforming to the reactionary forms of thought of the Nazi system was done by reviving mediaeval customs and forms of bondage abolished by the French revolution.

Thus mortgage was forbidden; the farmer was not allowed to invest foreign capital for ameliorations. If he wanted money for his farm he could go to the State offices, and thus his dependence on the State increased. In his farming he was subjected to a number of prescripts restricting his liberty. In the first place as to the products he had to cultivate; since agriculture had to feed the entire people, a difficult problem with the dense population, and still more so in war time, an exact fixation of needs and proceeds was necessary. The sale, too, was organized. The products had to be delivered to purchase offices, at prices fixed from above, or to agents visiting the farms. Theirs was the all-important task and duty: the feeding of the national community. This truth, however, they had to swallow in the form of complete subjection to Government measures sometimes even amounting to direct seizure of the crops. Thus the farmers, formerly free in, for better or worse, fighting their way through the vicissitudes of capitalism, were turned into serfs of the State. To meet the emergencies of big capitalism, mediaeval conditions, under flattering names, were restored for the farmers.

To the workers no less attention, though of a different kind, was given. For the great aim of conquering world power the internationally minded working class, fighting capitalism, splitting national unity, had first to be made powerless. So the first work of the revolution of 1933 was to destroy the social democratic and the communist parties, to imprison or banish their leaders, to suppress their papers, to burn their books and to transform the trade unions into national socialist organizations. Labor was organized not by the workers and for the workers, but by capital and for capital, through its new governing agents. The "labor-front," directed by State-appointed leaders, took the place of the unions where, formally at least, the workers themselves were master. Its task was not to fight the employers for improvement of working conditions, but the promotion of production. In the productive community, the factory, the employer was the leader and must be obeyed, unconditionally. The nationalist socialist leaders of the labor-front, often former officials of the unions, treated with the employer and brought forward complaints; but the latter decided.

It was not the intention of national socialism to make the workers helpless victims of employers' arbitrariness; the latter also had to obey the higher dictators. Moreover, for its great aim, the world fight, national socialism needs the goodwill, the devoted collaboration of all, as soldiers and as workers; so besides incessant propaganda, good treatment as far as possible, was serviceable. Where heavy exertions and extreme hardships were demanded from them the reward was praise of their performance of duty. Should they be cross and unwilling, hard constraint would make it clear that they were powerless. Free choice of their master has no sense any longer, since everywhere the real master is the same; the workers are transposed from one shop to another at the command from above. Under national socialism the workers were turned into bondsmen of State and capital.

How could it happen that a working class, appearing so powerful as the German one in the high tide of social democracy, almost ready to conquer the world, did fall into such utter impotence. Even to those who recognized the decline and inner degeneration of socialism, its easy surrender in 1933, without any fight, and the complete destruction of its imposing structure came as a surprise. In a certain way, however, national socialism may be said to be the regular descendant of social democracy. National socialism could rise to such power only on the shoulders of the previous workers' movement. By closer examination of the inner connection of things we can see that not only communism, by its example of State-dictatorship, but also social democracy had prepared the way for national socialism. The slogans, the aims, the methods contrived by social democracy, for the workers, were taken over and applied by national socialism, for capital.

First the idea of State socialism, consciously planned organization of the entire production by the centralized power of the State. Of course the democratic State was meant, organ of the working people. But intentions do not count against the power of reality. A body that is master of production is master of society, master of the producers, notwithstanding all paragraphs trying to make it a subordinate organ, and needs develops into a ruling class or group.

Secondly, in social democracy a leading bureaucracy already before the first world war was acquiring mastery over the workers, consciously aspiring at it and defending it as the normal social condition. Doubtless, those leaders just as well would have developed into agents of big capital; for ordinary times they would have served well, but for leaders in world war they were too soft. The "Leader-principle" was not invented by national socialism; it developed in social democracy hidden under democratic appearances. National socialism proclaimed it openly as the new basis of social relations and drew all its consequences.

Moreover, much of the program of social democracy was realized by national socialism; and that—an irony of history—especially such aims as had been criticized as most repulsive by the middle class of old. To bring order in the chaos of capitalist production by planned regulation always had been proclaimed an impossibility and denounced as an unbearable despotism. Now the State accomplished this organization to a great extent, thus making the task for a workers' revolution considerably easier. How often the intention of social democracy to replace the automatism of market and shop by a consciously organized distribution has been ridiculed and abhorred: everyone equally apportioned for normalized wants, fed and clothed by the State, all alike mere specimens. National socialism went far in the realization of this bogus. But what was meant in the socialist program as organized abundance is introduced here as organized want and hunger, as the utmost restriction of all life necessities in order that as much of productive force as possible remains for war materials. Thus the socialism the workers got was parody rather than realization; what in social democratic ideas bore the character of richness, progress and freedom, found its caricature in dearth, reaction and suppression.

The chief blame on socialism was the omnipotence of the State, compared with the personal freedom in capitalist society. This freedom, to be sure, often was no more than an ambiguous form, but it was something. National socialism took away even this semblance of liberty. A system of compulsion, harder than any slanderer ventured to impute to socialism, was imposed upon mankind by capitalism in its power and emergency. So it had to disappear; without liberty man cannot live. Liberty, truly, is only a collective name for different forms and degrees of bondage. Man by his bodily needs depends on nature; this is the basis of all dependencies. If life is not possible but by restraining of the free impulses they must be restrained. If productive labor can only be secured by submission under a commanding power, then command and submission are a necessity. Now, however, they are a necessity only for the succumbing capitalism. To uphold exploitation it imposes upon mankind a system of hard constraint, that for production itself, for the life of man, is not required. If a fascist system, instead of being shattered in world war were able to stabilize in lasting peace, a system of organized production providing as it pretended an abundance of all life necessities, even then it could not have lasted. Then by necessity it would perish through the inner contradiction of freeing mankind from the constraint of its needs and of yet trying to keep it in social slavery. Then the fight for freedom, as the only desire left, would be taken up with irresistible force.

The workers cannot foster the easy illusion that with a defeat in world war the role of national socialism is played out. The epoch of big capitalism is rife with its principles and instigations. The old world does not come back. Governments, even those styled democratic, will be compelled to interfere with production ever more. As long as capital has power and has fear, despotic methods of government will arise as formidable enemies of the working class. Not always in the open form of violent middle class or military dictatorships; they may also take the appearance of labor governments, proceeding from labor fights, perhaps even in the disguise or under the contradictory name of council governments. So a consideration, on broad lines, of their place and role in the development of society does not seem superfluous. A comparison with the rise of another new class, formerly the middle class, may offer an analogy, uncertain though, and surely to be used with caution, and with the reserve that now the pace of social evolution is much quicker, but has to go farther and deeper, than it was in former centuries.

The rise of the bourgeoisie took place in steps of gradually growing power. From the powerless burgesses of the early middle ages they lead to the merchants and guilds ruling their own towns, fighting the nobility and even vanquishing the knight armies in the open field; an essential element in the mediaeval world, yet only islands in an ocean of agrarian power. By means of the money over of the burghers the kings rise as masters above the other feudal powers, and institute centralized governments in their kingdoms. Their absolutism often is spoken of as a state of equilibrium, when the nobility was no longer, the bourgeoisie not yet strong enough for mastery; so a third power, protecting the privileges of the one and the trade of the other class, leaning upon them both, could rule both. Until, after new growth of trade and industry, the bourgeoisie is so much strengthened as to overthrow this rule and establish itself master of society.

The rise of the working class in the 19th century was the rise of a powerless, exploited, miserable mass into a class with acknowledged rights and with organizations to defend them. Their unions and their political parties may be compared somehow with the guilds and the town governments of the burgesses, an essential element in the all-powerful capitalist world. Whereas, however, the burghers could build up their money power separately, leaving the nobility with its landed property alone, the workers now, to build up their economic power, have to take the means of production from the capitalists, so that immediate fight cannot be avoided. Just as then in the further rise the old institutions, the independent town governments were destroyed and the burghers subjected by the biggest of the feudals, the princes, masters of the lesser aristocracy, so now the old organization of labor, unions and parties, are destroyed or subjected by big capitalism, thus clearing the way for more modern forms of fight. So there is a certain analogy between former absolutism and new dictatorship, a third power above the contending classes. Though we cannot yet speak of their equilibrium, we see that the new rulers appeal to labor as the basis of their system. It is conceivable that in a higher stage of the power of labor, camouflaged dictatorships may come up founded upon the support of labor, transient attempts to keep the workers in submission before their final victory.

Historical analogy may also be useful to show that development does not necessarily go along exactly the same lines everywhere. Later middle class mastery in Holland and England, by a fight against absolutistic attempts, developed out of the mediaeval urban privileges, without having lived under absolutism. In the same way now it might be that, whereas in some countries fascist dictatorships arise, in other countries the conditions are lacking. Then forms and conditions of the workers' fight will also be different. It is not well imaginable that in countries where personal liberty is firmly rooted in all classes, such as England and America, complete slavery could be established, though single measures of fascist character are possible. Capitalist domination there is founded on finer, more spiritual elements of power, more efficient than rough violence. Then the power of the workers for a long time will remain poor and unconscious; practical necessities will enforce partial steps in the direction of council organization, rather than a great revolutionary fight over fundamentals. The growth of clear consciousness of class and the organization of production are a far more extensive and laborious task, when the mind is filled with middle class ideas and when society is full of unorganized small trade.

In countries with strong fascist dictatorship, on the other hand, the heaviest part of the workers' task is the direct fight to overthrow it. There dictatorship has gone far already in clearing away small trade with its feelings of independence, as well as middle class ideas. The mind is bent already on organization of industry, the idea of community is present, though practice is a sham. The hard pressure forcing all into the same harness of servitude, regulating production. rationing consumption, uniforming life, evoke resentment and exasperation, only to be kept down by harder suppression. Because all physical power and an enormous spiritual power lie in the hands of the rulers, the fight demands from the workers the highest degree of devotion and courage, of clear insight and unity. The same holds good if capitalism should succeed in establishing one supreme dominating power over the entire earth.

The object of national socialist dictatorship, however, the conquest of world power, makes it probable that it will be destroyed in the war it unloosened. Then it will leave Europe ruined and devastated, chaotic and impoverished, the production apparatus adapted to war implements, entirely worn away, soil and man power exhausted, raw materials lacking, towns and factories in ruins, the economic resources of the continent squandered and annihilated. Then, unlike in the Germany of 1918, political power will not automatically fall into the hands of the working class; the victorious powers will not allow it; all their forces now will serve to keep it down. Whilst at the same time new rulers and leaders present themselves with promises and programs of a new and better order, and the allied armies are liberating the European continent for the exploitation by American capitalism. Then, in this economic, social and spiritual chaos it will fall to the workers to find ways for organizing themselves on class lines, ways for clearing up their ideas and purposes, ways for first attempts in reconstructing production. Wherever a nucleus of organization, of fight, of production is growing, wherever wide embracing connections are tied, wherever minds are struggling for clear ideas, there foundations are laid and a start is made for the future. With partial successes won in devoted fight, through strong unity and insight progressing by gradual steps, the workers must build their new society.

It is not possible as yet to foresee the coming forms of social strife and activity in the different countries. But we may say for certain that, once they understand it, the consciousness of their great task as a bright star will guide the workers through all the difficulties on their path. And that the certainty that by their work and fight they build up the power and unity of the working class, the brotherhood of mankind, will elate their hearts and brighten their minds. And that the fight will not end until working mankind has won complete freedom.

IV. The War

1. JAPANESE IMPERIALISM

The preceding chapters were composed in the first years of the war, 1941–1942, a summary of what past times of struggle provided in useful information for the working class, an instrument helpful in their further fight for freedom. Now, 1944, the war, begun as an attempt of German capital to wrench world power from the English bourgeoisie, has extended over the entire world. All the strains created by the growth of capitalism in different continents, all the antagonisms between new rising and old powerful bourgeoisies, all the conflicts and excitations in near and far away countries have coalesced and exploded in this truly world war. And every day shows how much deeper, more tremendous and more thorough than in any former war its effects will be, in America and Asia, as well as in Europe. Mankind in its entirety is involved, and the neutrals, too, experience its consequences. Every nation is implicated in the fate of every other nation, however remote. This war is one of the last convulsions in the irresistible process of unification of mankind; the class fight that will evolve from the war will make this unity into a self-directing community.

Besides Europe, its first scene, Eastern Asia has become a second, no less important, center of the war. In China war with Japan was already going on for some years when, by the outbreak of the war between America and Japan, it was included as a subordinate part in the world fight. This struggle in East Asia will have the same importance for the world's course as the fight in Europe. Hence its origins, as well as its tendencies, must be considered here somewhat more attentively.

The dense populations thronged together in the fertile plains of East and South Asia and the adjacent islands have long resisted the invasion of capitalism. With their number of nearly a thousand millions they constituted almost the half of mankind. Hence, as long as they remain in the condition of small agriculture and small handicraft, capitalism cannot be said to occupy the world, capitalism is not yet at the end of its task and its growth. The old powerful monarchies stiffened in their first contact with the rising capitalism of the 16th and 17th centuries, they kept off its intrusion and shut out its dissolving effects.

161

Whereas in India and the Indian islands commercial capital could gradually establish its sway, China and Japan could maintain themselves as strong military powers during some centuries. In the 19th century the military power of modern capitalism broke the resistance. The development of capitalism, first in Japan, now in China, was the origin, is the content and will be the outcome of the present world war.

In the 17th, 18th, and the first half of the 19th century Japan was a feudal-absolutist state separated from the outer world by strict prohibitional laws. It was governed by some hundred small princes [daimyos], each lord over his own realm, but all strictly subjected under the sway of the Shogun in the capital, formally the military chief for the nominal emperor, the Mikado in Kyoto, but practically the real ruler. The Shoguns, whose office was hereditary in the Tokugawa family, retained the daimyos in submission and kept internal peace during two and a half centuries. A strict feudal organization of four orders in society was maintained; but in the long run it could not prevent an inner development.

The basis of society was small farming, on lots mostly of only one or some few acres. Legally half the product had to be delivered to the prince, in kind (mostly rice), but often more was taken from the farmers. Above them stood the ruling and exploiting class of warriors, the samurai, forming the uppermost order ranged in a number of ranks, from the princes down to the common soldiers. They constituted the nobility, though their lowest most numerous ranks had only a small rice-income; they were a kind of knights, living around the castles of their lords. Since through the cessation of the internal wars of old their special office, fighting, was no longer needed, they had turned into a purely parasitic class, living in idleness or occupying themselves with literature and art–they were the producers of the famous Japanese art, afterwards so much admired in Europe. But they had the right to slay everyone of the lower orders they came across without being punished. Below the second order, the farmers, stood the lowest orders, the artisans and the merchants, who worked for the samurai, their patrons and customers; they earned money and gradually out of them arose a first species of bourgeoisie.

The basis of the system was heavy exploitation of the farmers; Japanese authors said the policy of the government consisted in leaving to the farmers so much that they neither could die nor live. They were kept in absolute ignorance, they were bound to the soil, which they could not sell, all ease of life was denied to them. They were slaves of the State; they were looked upon as machinery for production of the rice the ruling class needed. Sometimes the famished peasants rose in local revolt and obtained some redress, because the inept soldiers did not dare to oppose them. But hunger and misery remained the prevailing conditions.

Still, although the laws meant to establish a petrified immutability, conditions gradually changed. The extension of craft and commerce, the increase of the production of commodities, brought luxury into the towns. The ruling nobility, to satisfy their new needs, had to borrow money and became debtors of the merchant class, the highest daimyos, as well as the common soldiers. The latter, reduced to poverty, sometimes, notwithstanding the prohibition, escaped into other professions. In the 19th century their growing discontent crystallized into a systematic hostility to the system of government. Because they formed the most intellectual class and were influenced by some European ideas trickling through the narrow chink of Dutch commerce at Deshima, they were able to formulate their opposition in the nationalist program of "respect for the Emperor" as a symbol of national unity. So there were forces for change from feudal absolutism in the direction of capitalism; but they would have been too weak for a revolution, had not the big push from aggressive Western capitalism come to enforce admission.

In its first rise already, in the discovery of the entire earth in the 16th century, capitalism had knocked at the gates of Japan; it kindled wars between the feudal lords and princes; the spreading of Christendom over against Buddhism was an expression of the paralyzing disruption of the empire. A couple of consecutive strong Shoguns averted the danger by subjecting the rebellious lords to their centralized power; the foreigners were driven out, and with a booming blow—prohibition and extermination of Christendom—the gate was closed for two centuries and a half. Then modern capitalism in its world conquest again knocked at the gate, and with its guns forced it open. American and Russian men-of-war came in 1853, others followed, treaties for commerce were made with the Western powers. And now the old worm-eaten system of government broke down, the Shogunate disappeared, clans hostile to it got the upper hand, and through the "restoration" of 1868 established a strongly united state under the government of the Mikado.

This meant the introduction of capitalism. First the juridical basis for a middle-class society was laid: the four orders were abolished and all inhabitants became free citizens with equal rights. Freedom of trade, of living and travel, private property, also of the land, that could be bought and sold now, were established. Instead of the tiller of the soil paying half the product in kind, land taxes in money were laid upon the owner. The samurai lost their feudal privileges, and instead got an amount of money to buy a lot of land or to start a business; as artisans and employers they formed part of the rising bourgeoisie. The state officials, the army and naval officers, the intellectuals in the new society chiefly came from this samurai class. The upper ranks remained in power; part of the feudal princes now formed the Secret Council, which, behind the scenes directed government; their retainers, still linked together by the old clan ties, became cabinet ministers, generals, party chiefs and influential politicians.

So in Japan things were different from Europe. Capitalism did not come because a rising bourgeoisie vanquished the feudal class in a revolutionary struggle, but because a feudal class transformed itself into a bourgeoisie, certainly a performance worthy of respect. Thus it is easily understood that also under capitalism the feudal spirit, with its prejudices of ranks, its overbearing haughtiness, its servile respect to the emperor, persisted in the Japanese ruling class. The middle-class spirit of European capitalism was entirely lacking; Germany, that most resembles it, differs from Japan by the diversity there between the land owning nobility and the middle-class industrialists. Not till some dozens of years later a constitution was made, after the German model, with a parliament without power over the administration and the budget. Civil rights hardly existed, even on paper; government and officials had absolute power over the people. The peasants remained the deeply subjected, heavily exploited mass of starvelings; the substitution of capitalist for feudal pressure meant that they had to pay a lot of money in taxes or rent, that their land came into the hands of big landowners, that they could be evicted by withdrawal of the lease, that instead of the former known misery there came unforeseen ruin through unknown influences of market and prices. Peasant revolts were numerous after the first years of the Restoration.

Capitalism was introduced from above. Capable young men were sent to Europe to study science and technics. The government erected factories, in the first place armament works and shipyards; for military strength against the other powers was most urgent. Then railways and ships were built, coal mines constructed, afterwards the textile industry developed, chiefly silk and cotton, banks were founded. Private business was encouraged by subsidies, and state industries were turned over to private hands. In this way the government spent much money, got partly by taxes, partly by borrowing, or by the issue of paper money, which rocketted prices. This policy was continued later on; capital was fattened by government subsidies, especially navigation, with its ensuing artificial prosperity. The system often developed into sheer corruption; the new-made capitalist class, through the absence of inherited business maxims in its dealings, exhibited a brazen lack of ordinary honesty; plundering public funds for personal enrichment is considered a common affair. Even the highest officials and politicians take part in big enterprises and procure orders for them by means of political influence.

Large numbers of impoverished peasants flowed into the towns, to the factories, where a heavily exploited proletariat, almost without rights, accumulated in the slums, ravished through low wages (half a yen per day), long hours (14–16 hours), and child labor. State officials in the lower ranks, even intellectuals, engineers, marine officers are paid far lower wages than in Europe. The working classes in the country, as well as in the towns, lived in a state of hopeless misery, of squalor and despair, surpassing the worst conditions in Europe of olden times. In the textile industry there is a regular slave system; the farmers sell their daughters for a number of years to the factories, where they live intern under the most horrible unhygienic conditions; and after the contract expires they return in part only to their villages, bringing with them tuberculosis. Thus, Japanese production was cheap, and through the low prices of its trash could outbid Western products on the Asiatic market. On the basis of highly developed machine technics–complemented by extensive primitive home industry and the low standard of life of the workers–capitalist industry and commerce shot up powerfully; every ten years import and export were doubled. Though it did not equal America, England and Germany, it rose above most other countries. The number of industrial workers reached two millions in 1929; agriculture occupied less than half the population already. The workers lived in a state of partial slavery; only in machine industry and among the sailors was there a bit of organization. Strikes broke out, but were forcibly beaten down. Socialist and communist ideas, naturally finding their way under such conditions, were persecuted and exterminated ferociously. This fitted entirely in the system of police arbitrariness, of lack of personal rights, of brutal cruelty and lawless violence against their own, as well as against subjected alien people, which showed already the character of later fascism.

Imperialism, the big-capitalist politics of conquest, had no need to develop gradually here; from the first it belongs to the policy of introduction of capitalism from above. From the beginning militarism was the chief aim and ideal of the new system, first as a means of defense against the white powers, then as a means of conquest of markets and sources of raw materials. All the old fighting instincts, traditions of discipline and impulses of oppression of the former samurai class could exhibit themselves and revive in the military spirit of exalted nationalism. First by defeating in 1895 the mouldy Chinese power and conquering Korea and Formosa, it took its place among the big powers. Then its victory over the equally mouldy power of Russian Czarism in 1904, opened the way into the inner Asiatic realms. Now the Japanese rulers grew cockier and began to speak of Japan's world mission to lead East Asia and to free Asia entirely from the white domination.

This policy of conquest is often defended with the argument that the rapid increase of the population–a doubling in 35 years–that cannot find a sufficient living on the small lots of tillable soil in these mountainous islands, compels emigration or the increase of industrial labor for which markets and raw material must be available. Everywhere the rise of capitalism, with its abolition of old bonds and its increasing possibilities for living has brought about a rapid increase of population. Here, on the reverse, this consequence, considered as a natural phenomenon, is used as an argument for conquest and subjugation of other peoples. The real reason, however, of this policy of conquest, first of

Manchuria, then of the northern provinces of China, consists in Japan's lack of iron ore. All industrial and military power nowadays is based upon the disposal over iron and steel; hence Japan wants the rich mineral deposits of Jehol and Shansi. At the same time Japanese capital invaded China and set up factories, chiefly cotton mills, in Shanghai and other towns. And there a vision loomed of a future of greatness and power: to make of these 400 millions firstly customers of its industry, and then to exploit them as workers. So it was necessary to become the political master and leader of China. And most experts in Eastern affairs did not doubt that Japan, with its military power, its big industry, its proud self-reliance, would succeed in dominating the impotent and divided Chinese empire.

But here the Japanese rulers met with a heavy reverse. First with the unexpected tenacious resistance of the Chinese people, and then with a mightier opponent. Mastery over the markets and the future development of China is a life issue for American capitalism in its present state of development. Notwithstanding the most careful and extensive preparations Japan cannot match the colossal industrial resources of America, once they are transformed into military potency. So its ruling class will succumb. When the military power of Japan will be destroyed and its arrogant capitalist barons have been beaten down, then for the first time the Japanese people will be freed from the feudal forms of oppression.

For Japan this will be the dawn of a new era. Whether the victorious allies enforce a more modern form of government, or with the collapse of the suppressing power of a revolution of the peasants and the workers breaks out, in every case the barbarous backwardness in living standards and in ideas will have lost its basis. Of course, capitalism does not disappear then; that will take a good deal yet of internal and world fight. But the exploitation will assume more modern forms. Then the Japanese working class will be able, on the same footing as their American and European class-fellows, to take part in the general fight for freedom.

2. THE RISE OF CHINA

China belongs to those densely populated fertile plains watered by great rivers, where the necessity of a central regulation of the water for irrigation and for protection by dykes, in the earliest time already produced unification under a central government. It remained so for thousands of years. Under a strong and careful government the land rendered rich produce. But under a weak government, when the officials neglected their duties, when governors and princes made civil war, the dykes and canals fell into decay, the silted rivers overflowed the fields, famine and robbers ravished the people, and "the wrath of heaven" lay on the land. The population consisted chiefly of hard toiling peasants, carefully tilling their small lots. Through the primitive technics and the lack of cattle for ploughing, with the hardest labor during long days they could produce hardly more a than a bare existence. The slight surplus produce was taken from them by the ruling class of landowners, intellectuals and officials, the mandarins. Since usually more even was taken from them, they often stood on the brink of famine. The plains were open to the north, the Central-Asiatic steppes, from where warlike nomads came invading and conquering. When they conquered the land they became the new ruling class, formed a kind of aristocracy, but were soon assimilated by the higher Chinese civilization. So came the Mongols in the Middle Ages; so came in the 17th century the Manchus from the north-east, extended their empire in the 18th century far over Central Asia, but fell into decay in the 19th century.

In the numerous towns lived a large class of small artisans and dealers with a proletarian class of coolies below and the wealthy class of merchants above them. From the seaports, as well as on caravan routes to the West across deserts and mountains, the precious wares of Chinese origin: tea, silk and porcelain were exported, even into Europe. So there was a middle class comparable with the European as to free initiative in business. But in the Chinese peasants too lived the same spirit of independence and self-reliance, far stronger than in the Japanese, deeply curbed as they were under feudalism. If the oppression of the officials, tax farmers, landlords or usurers became too heavy, revolts broke out, increasing sometimes to revolutions, against which the possessing class sought protection from foreign military powers; in such a way the Manchus came into the country.

In the 19th century Western capitalism begins to attack and invade China. The strict prohibition of opium import led to a war with Britain, 1840, and to the opening of a number of ports for European commerce. This number increases in later wars and treaties; European merchants and missionaries invade the country, and by their use and abuse of their specially protected position incite the hatred of the population. Cheap European wares are imported and undermine home handicraft; heavy war contributions imposed upon China aggravate the tax burden. Thus revolutionary movements flare up, such as the Taiping insurrection (1853–1864), having its own emperor in Nanking, and the Boxer revolt, 1899; both were suppressed with the help of European military power, which showed itself as barbarian destroyers of old Chinese culture. When the war with Japan lays bare Chinese impotence, all the Western powers, including Japan, seize parts of it as "concessions," tearing it asunder in "spheres of influence." Foreign capital builds some few railways and installs factories in the great harbor towns; Chinese capital, too, begins to take part. And now the obsolete Manchu dynasty crumbles in 1911, and is replaced in name by a Chinese republic proclaimed in Nanking, in reality, however, by the rule of provincial governors and generals, the so-called "war lords," often upstart former bandit chiefs, who now with their gang of soldiers in continuous wars pillage the country.

For the rise of a Chinese capitalism the elements were present: a class of wealthy or even rich merchants in the cities, mostly agents of foreign capital, which could develop into a modern bourgeoisie; a numerous class of poor urban proletarians and artisans, with a low standard of life; and an enormous population as customers. Western commercial capital, however, was not a driving force towards a development to higher productivity; it exploited the primitive forms of home industry for commercial profit, and impoverished the artisans by its imports. Hence the dominating position of this Western capital, on the way to make China into a colony, had to be repelled through organization of the Chinese forces. This work of organization fell as their task to the young intellectuals who had studied in England, France, America or Japan, and had imbibed Western science and Western ideas. One of the first spokesmen was Sun Yat-Sen, formerly a conspirator persecuted by the Manchu government, a well-known figure in European socialist circles, then the first President in name of the Chinese republic. He designed a program of national unity, a mixture of middle-class democracy and government dictatorship, and after his death in 1925 he became a kind of saint of the new China. He founded the Kuomintang, the political organization and leading party of the rising Chinese bourgeoisie.

A strong impulse came from the Russian revolution. In 1920 students in Paris and workers (chiefly miners, railway men, typos and municipal workers) in Shanghai and Canton founded a Chinese Communist Party. Big strikes broke out against the mostly foreign employers, and by their exemplary solidarity the workers were able to get many of their demands conceded by the powerful capital; often, however, the fight led to bloody reprisals from the war lords. Now also the bourgeoisie took heart; in the next years the Kuomintang allied itself with the communist party and with Russia. Of course, the Chinese bourgeoisie did not profess any inclination to communist ideas; but it felt that such an alliance offered a lot of advantages. Merely by allowing them to shout for liberty and communism it gained the service of the most active groups of workers and enthusiastic young intellectuals for its purposes, and found skilled Russian organizers from Moscow as "advisers," to lead its fight and to instruct its cadres. Russia, moreover, gave it exactly the slogans it needed for its liberation from the grip of the all-powerful Western imperialism: the doctrine of world revolution against world capital, especially against its chief exponent, the English world power. Soon strictly enforced boycott and strike movements undermined European business and commerce; a sharp anti-foreigner excitation flooded the country; and from the interior, a terrified flock, came a stream of white missionaries, dealers and agents, fleeing to the seaports and the protection of the guns of the men-of-war. From Canton, 1926, an expedition went to the North, partly military conquest, partly intense nationalist propaganda campaign, "watering its horses in the Yang-tse River," chasing the war lords or compelling them to join, and uniting Central and Southern China into one state, with Nanking as its capital.

But now the long smouldering and ever again suppressed fight of the classes broke loose. The workers of the big towns, especially the industrial workers of Shanghai, the emporium of the East, took communism in its proletarian sense, as the workers' class fight. Their wages hardly sufficed to appease direct hunger, their working time was 14 to 16 hours daily; now they tried to raise their miserable conditions by striking, notwithstanding that Russian propaganda always had taught coalition with the bourgeoisie. The C.P. of China had been instructed from Moscow that the Chinese revolution was a middle-class revolution, that the bourgeoisie had to be the future ruling class, and that the workers simply had to assist her against feudalism and bring her into power. The C.P. had followed this lesson, and so had entirely neglected to organize and to arm the workers and the peasants against the bourgeoisie. It kept faith with the Kuomintang, even when this party ordered the generals to beat down the peasant revolts; so the communist militants were left at a loss, wavering between contradictory class sentiments and party commands. The mass actions that broke out in Canton and Shanghai were quenched in blood by the Kuomintang armies of Chiang Kai-shek, financed for that purpose by the Chinese and international bankers. A sharp persecution of communism set in, thousands of spokesmen and militants were slaughtered, the Russian "advisers" were sent home, the workers' organizations were exterminated, and the most reactionary parts of the bourgeoisie took the lead in government. These were chiefly the groups of rich merchants, whose interests as agents of foreign commercial and banking capital were bound to this capital and to the preservation of the old conditions.

Communism in the meantime had spread over the countryside. During all these years of anarchy the condition of the peasants had gone from bad to worse. By the landlords and tax collectors they were stripped to the bone; the war lords often demanded taxes for many years to come, and when they had been driven out by others who demanded the same taxes again, these were deposed safely in a foreign Shanghai banking house. Nobody took care of the canals and the dykes; through floods and the ensuing famine and pestilence uncounted millions perished. For some few pieces of bread the famished peasants sold their land to full-stocked hoarders and money lenders, and roamed as beggars or robbers through the land. Under such conditions communism, in its Russian bolshevist form of a workers and peasants republic, without capitalists, landlords and usurers, was hailed and made rapid progress in the most distressed provinces. At the same time it was extinguished in the towns, communism rose in the countryside as a mighty peasant revolt. Where it won power it began already to drive out the landlords and to divide up their land among the peasants and to establish Soviet rule. Part of the armies, consisting chiefly of workers and peasants, joined by their officers, mostly intellectuals sympathizing with the popular movement, revolted against the reactionary Kuomintang policy, and formed the nucleus of a Red Army.

The civil war thus ensuing was waged by the Kuomintang government as a campaign against the "communist bandits," who were branded with all kinds of atrocities—doubtless the rebellious peasants often were far from soft against their tormentors—and which had to be exterminated before unity of the nation was possible. From the side of the peasants it was a tenacious and heroic defense of their besieged chief territory in the south-eastern provinces Kiangsi and Hunan. Every year again from 1930 onward, the war of extermination is resumed with ever larger armies, and ever again it is frustrated by the superior skill, the indomitable courage and the self-sacrificing enthusiasm of the red troops that in careful and intrepid guerilla fighting had to win their very arms from the routed enemy regiments. Meanwhile, Japan makes use of this mutual destruction of Chinese military forces by occupying consecutively Manchuria and the Northern provinces.

What may be the reason that the Chinese bourgeoisie so ferociously made war upon the peasants and thereby squandered its military and financial resources? If we speak of the short existence of a Chinese bourgeoisie, we should bear in mind that this class differs considerably from the bourgeoisie of Europe, so that ideas instinctively associated with the latter class are not all applicable here. In Europe the rising bourgeoisie, a class of industrial and commercial employers and capitalists, in a social revolution, assisted by the peasants, had to break the political dominance of a landpossessing nobility. In China this antagonism is lacking; the bourgeoisie itself was the land-possessing class, and from herself came the ruling officials. On account of the lack of a rapidly rising industry the rich urban merchants and business men invested their money in land; and rent was as important a source of their income as profit; on the reverse landowners went into the town to set up a business. They combined the characters of two opposite European classes. Thus the peasants' fight found its most fitting expression in the communist slogan of fight against capitalism. In its character of landowners subjection and exploitation of the peasants was a life interest of the Chinese bourgeoisie; its deepest feelings were affected by the land expropriation of the red soviets. So the conservative elements of this class, who had first distrusted the Kuomintang as a disguised red organization, as soon as possible expelled the communists and made it an instrument of reactionary middle-class politics. They felt the lack of power on the part of the Chinese government to bring order into the chaos: so they sought support from the strongest anti-communist power, from Japan. Japan, aiming at dominance over the resources, the mineral riches and the labor power of China, came forward as the protector of the landowning interests against the rebellious masses. In every next treaty it imposed upon the Chinese government the duty to exterminate communism.

Against this conservative there was, however, an opposite trend, especially among the smaller bourgeoisie and the intellectuals. It anticipated and represented the future; it gave expression not to what the bourgeoisie had been till now, but to what it would be and should be. Its spokesmen realized that a wealthy class of peasants with purchasing power was the chief and necessary condition for a powerful development of capitalist industry in China. Their middle-class feeling understood instinctively that all these landowners and usurers represented a piece of feudalism, barring the way to the future development of China; and that a free landowning peasantry belongs to the middle-class world and would form its solid basis. Hence, next to and opposite to the conservative tendency there was a strong democratic stream of thought among the rising Chinese bourgeoisie. It was strongly nationalistic; the Japanese aggression, the seizure of precious provinces in the North, and the haughty brutalities of Japanese militarism filled it with indignation. It wished to end the civil war by concessions to the peasants in order to unite all force in a common resistance to Japanese imperialism.

Five years the extermination campaign lasted in Kiangsi, and, on a minor scale, in other provinces, without success. The communist armies were firmly rooted in the peasant population, among which they made extensive educational propaganda, and from which ever new forces came to join them. When at last their position against the besieging superior forces ably led by German military advisers, became untenable, they broke through the iron ring and invaded the South-western provinces. Then in 1934 the Red Army began its famous long march, over the highest, nearly unpassable, mountain passes, across the wildest and most dangerous rivers, through endless swampy steppes, through the extremes of heat and cold, always surrounded and attacked by better equipped superior White forces, until after heavy privations, heroic struggles and severe losses it arrived, a year later, in the North-western provinces, where in Shensi a new Soviet government was organized.

But now, in the meantime, tactics and aims had changed. Not against capitalism and landlords the communist fight was directed in the first place, but against Japan and Japanese imperialism. Before the start of their long march already the C.P. of China had proposed, publicly, to the Kuomintang to cease the civil war in order to fight in common the Japanese aggression, in which case it would stop the expropriations and respect the existing property rights, in exchange for social reform and democratic rights of the people. But this offer had not been regarded.

This change of tactics has been sharply criticized in other countries as an opportunistic renouncement of communist principles. Such criticism, however,

is based on the false supposition that the C.P. was a party of industrial workers exploited by big capitalism. The Chinese C.P., and still more the Red Army,
however, consists of rebellious peasants. Not the name stuck on a label outside,
but the class character determines the real content of thought and action. The
party leaders saw quite well that Japanese military power was the most dangerous threat to the Chinese peasants, and that a coalition of the Chinese bourgeoisie with Japan would make their liberation impossible. So it was imperative
to separate them and to direct all military and economic potencies of China
against Japan. To the red leaders the ideal of the future was a democratic middle-class China, with free peasants as owners, or at least well-to-do farmers of
the soil. Under communist ideas and slogans they were the heralds and champions of the capitalist development of China.

From these tendencies on both sides arose the new policy, in the dramatic
form of the capture, December, 1936, in Sianfu, of the gerneralissimo Chiang
Kai-shek by the government's own Manchurian troops, who wanted to fight the
Japanese rather than the Reds. The nationalist leader, in involuntary discours-
es with the communist leaders, could make certain that they were equally
nationalist and middle-class minded as himself, and were ready to put themselves under his command in a war with Japan. When, then, the civil war
ceased and the most reactionary leaders were turned out of the government,
Japan immediately drew the consequences and began war with a heavy attack
on Shanghai. China, with its undeveloped sleeping resources at first sight might
seem no match for the tremendous, carefully prepared war machinery of Japan.
But it had trained armies now, it was filled with a strong nationalist spirit, and
it got war materials from England and America. To be sure, its armies had to
give way, the government had to retreat to Chunking in the South-western
province of Szechuan, and Japanese troops occupied the Eastern towns. But
behind their back ever new armies of partisans stood up as guerilla and
exhausted their forces. Till, in 1941, after the war in Europe had gone on for
nearly two years, the long foreseen conflict between America and Japan broke
out in consequence of America's ultimatum that Japan should leave China.
Thus the Chinese war became part of the world war.

This world war means the rise of China as a new capitalist world power.
Not immediately as an independent power on an equal par with its allies,
Russia on the one, America on the other side, though it exceeds both in population. Its economical and political dependence on America, to which it is heavily in debt because of its war supplies, will mark the new future; American capital will then have the lead in building up its industry. Two great tasks are
standing in the forefront; the construction of railways and roads, combined
with the production of engines and motor cars, to modernize the primitive
expensive traffic; and introduction of mechanical power in agriculture to free
the human beast-of-burden and make its labor efficient. The accomplishment

of these tasks requires a big metal industry. China possesses all the resources necessary for capitalist development. It has coal, iron and other minerals, not enough to make it an industrial country for export as England or Germany, but enough for its own needs. It has a dense population with all the qualities necessary for capitalism: a strong individualism, painstaking diligence, capability, spirit of enterprise, and a low standard of needs. It has, moreover, a fertile soil, capable of producing an abundance of products, but requiring security by wide scientific care and regulation of the water, by constructing dykes and excavating and normalizing the rivers.

The ideals and aims for which the working masses of China are fighting, will of course not be realized. Landowners, exploitation and poverty will not disappear; what disappears are the old stagnant, primitive forms of misery, usury and oppression. The productivity of labor will be enhanced; the new forms of direct exploitation by industrial capital will replace the old ones. The problems facing Chinese capitalism will require central regulations by a powerful government. That means forms of dictatorship in the central government, perhaps complemented by democratic forms of autonomy in the small units of district and village. The introduction of mechanical force into agriculture requires the conjunction of the small lots into large production units; whether by gradual expropriation of the small peasants, or by the foundation of co-operatives or kolchozes after the Russian model, will depend on the relative power of the contending classes. This development will not go on without producing deep changes in the economic, and thereby in the social relations, the spiritual life and the old family structure. The dimensions, however, of things there, of the country, of the population, of its misery, of its traditions, of its old cultural life are so colossal, that an innovation of conditions, even if taken up with the utmost energy, will take many dozens of years.

The intensity of this development of economic conditions will stir the energies and stimulate the activity of the classes. Corresponding to capitalism the fight against capitalism will arise simultaneously. With the growth of industry the fight of the industrial workers will spring up. With the strong spirit of organization and great solidarity shown so often by the Chinese proletarians and artisans, even a rise more rapid than in Europe of a powerful working class movement may be expected. To be sure, the industrial workers will remain a minority compared with the mass of the agrarian population, equally subjected to capitalist exploitation, though in another way. The mechanisation of agriculture, however, will weave strong ties between them, manifesting itself in the community of interests and fights. So the character of the fight for freedom and mastery may take in many regards another aspect in China than in Western Europe and America.

3. THE COLONIES

When socialism grew up, half a century ago, the general expectation was that the liberation of the colonial peoples would take place together with the liberation of the workers. The colonies there and the workers here were exploited by the same capitalism; so they were allies in the fight against the common foe. It is true that their fight for freedom did not mean freedom for the entire people; it meant the rise of a new ruling class. But even then it was commonly accepted, with only occasional doubts, that the working class in Europe and the rising bourgeoisie in the colonies should be allies. For the communist party this was still more self-evident; it meant that the new ruling class of Russia looked upon the future ruling classes in the colonies as its natural friends, and tried to help them. Certainly the forces for colonial liberation were still weak. In India, with its 300 millions of people, industry and a class of employers gradually developed, giving the basis for an independence movement, that suffers, however, from the great diversity of races and religions. The 50 millions population of Java is well-nigh homogeneous, but entirely agrarian, and the opposition was till recently restricted to small groups of intellectuals.

These colonial peoples are no savages or barbarians, as the tribes of central Africa or the inhabitants of remote Indian islands. They live densely crowded in fertile areas with a highly developed agriculture. Often they have a thousand years old civilization; there is a separation between a ruling class of priests and nobility spending their portion of the total product in often refined artistic and spiritual culture, and the subjugated masses of heavily exploited peasants. Foreign warlike peoples invaded India and formed new upper social layers; incessant wars between larger and smaller princes checked the increase of the population. Agriculture was the chief occupation; because during many months agricultural labor had to rest, there was also an important cottage industry in the villages. This handicraft, artistic and highly developed, differing according to natural produce, raw materials and inherited endowments in different regions, produced a large amount of goods for export. Cotton goods, fine dyed cloths in many designs, silk wares, goldsmiths' and copper wares, beautifully decorated swords formed the contents of an extensive trade over Southern and Eastern Asia, and far to the West, even into Europe. Here the precious colored textile wares from the East, chiefly from Indian village industry, formed the main part of medieval traffic, produced the materials for the dress of princes, nobility and rich bourgeoisie, up to the 18th century, and brought a continuous flow of gold from Europe to India.

Against the invading European capitalism the Indian countries, mostly divided into small states, were soon powerless. The armed Western merchant vessels began to monopolize forcibly the entire trade of the Indian seas, with its enormous profits. Thereafter direct conquest and pillage brought the accumulated riches of Eastern treasuries into the hands of Western officials and adventurers, and contributed in England in the 18th century to form the capital needed in the industrial revolution. More important still was regular exploitation by enforced delivering of precious products—on the Molucca islands of spices, on Java of pepper, indigo, sugar—for which hardly anything was paid, a few coppers for what in Europe brought hundreds of florins. The population had to spend a great deal of its time and of its soil in these products for export, thus leaving not enough for their own food; famine and revolts were the result. Or heavy taxes were imposed upon the people of India, to procure high incomes for a parasitical class of English officials and nabobs. At the same time England employed its political power to forbid, in the interest of the Lancashire cotton industry, the export of Indian textile goods. Thus the flourishing Indian cottage industry was destroyed and the peasants were still more impoverished. The result was that in the 19th century, and even up to the present day, for the majority of the villagers life is a continuous state of hunger. Famines and pestilences, formerly unavoidable local occurrences, now take place in devastated larger regions and more often. But also in normal times in the villages and urban slums a state of misery reigns, worse than at any time in Europe.

The essence of colonial policy is exploitation of foreign countries while preserving their primitive forms of production or even lowering their productivity. Here capital is not a revolutionary agent developing production to higher forms; just the reverse. European capital is here a dissolving agent, destroying the old modes of work and life without replacing them by better technics. European capital, like a vampire, clasps the defenceless tropical peoples and sucks their life blood without caring whether the victims succumb.

Western science of course demonstrates that the domination of colonies by the Europeans is based on nature, hence is a necessity. The basis is formed by the difference of climate. In cool and moderate climes man can extort his living from nature by continuous exertion only; the temperature allows of assiduous hard working; and the inconstancy of the phenomena, the irregular change from storm and rain to sunshine stimulates the energy into restless activity. Labor and energy became the gospel of the white race; so it gained its superior knowledge and technics that made it master of the earth. In the hot tropical and sub-tropical countries, on the contrary, nature by itself or with slight labor bears abundant fruit; here the heat makes every continuous exertion a torment. Here the dictum could originate that to eat his bread in the sweat of his brow was the worst curse to man. The monotonous equality of the weather, only interrupted at the change of seasons, deadens the energy; the white people, too, when staying too long in the tropics, are subjected to these influences that render laziness the chief characteristic and Nirvana the highest ideal. These dicta of science doubtless are true, theoretically. But practically we see that the Indian and Javanese peasants till their soil and perform their handicraft with unflagging zeal and painstaking assiduity. Not, of course, in the nerve-racking tempo of modern factory work; economic necessity determines the character of their labor.

The Western bourgeoisie considers its rule over the colonies a natural and lasting state of things, idealizing it into a division of tasks profitable to both parties. The energetic intelligent race from the cool climes, it says, serves as the leaders of production, whereas the lazy, careless colored races execute under their command the unintelligent manual labor. Thus the tropical products, indispensable raw materials and important delicacies are inserted into the world's commerce. And European capital wins its well deserved profits because by its government it assures to the fatalistic aborigines life, security, peace and, by its medical service and hygienic measures, health, too. Suppose this idyll of a paternal government, honest illusion or deceptive talk of theorists and officials, to be as true as in reality it is impossible under capitalist rule, then still it would be faced by an insoluble dilemma: If by the cessation of wars, epidemics and infant mortality the population increases, there results a shortage of arable land notwithstanding all the irrigation and reclaiming that only postpones the conflict. Industrialization for export, properly speaking an unnatural way out for the most fertile lands, can give only temporary relief. Into such a final state every population that, ruled from above, is left to its own life instincts, must arrive. Every economic system develops its own system of population increase. If by an autocratic rule from above the feelings of responsibility are suppressed, then any active force of self-restraint and self-rule over the conditions of life is extinguished. The impending clash between increase of population and restriction of means of subsistence can find its solution only in a strong display of inner energy and will-power of a people, consequence of its self-reliance and freedom, or of an active fight for freedom.

In the later part of the 19th century and thereafter it is not the commercial capital in the first place that exploits the colonies. Capitalist enterprises come forth in ever greater numbers: partly agricultural and mining enterprises for cultivating rubber, coffee, tea, for winning oil, tin and other metals, partly industrial or mixed enterprises to work the tropical raw materials, such as textile or sugar factories. It is mostly European capital, drawing high profits from this exploitation. In India, where in such towns as Bombay lived a class of rich merchants, these also take part and constitute a first instance of a modern Indian bourgeoisie. This Indian industry consists well nigh exclusively of textile factories; and from all the textile goods consumed in India nearly 60 per cent is imported from England and Japan, 20 per cent comes from the cottage industry, and only 20 per cent is provided by Indian factories. Yet to exhibit and introduce aspects of modern work and life is sufficient inspiration to a nationalist movement, for throwing off the yoke of the Western rulers. Its spokesmen are the intellectuals, especially the younger generation, who are acquainted with Western science, and in opposition to it study and emphasize with strong conviction their own national culture. They feel deeply hurt by the racial haughtiness of the whites, who admit them in lower offices only; they come forward as the leaders of the oppressed masses, involving them into their fight for independence. Since the impudent riches of the rulers contrasts so sharply with the abject misery of the masses, this is not difficult. Though as yet the fight can only be peaceful propaganda, passive resistance, and non-co-operation, i.e., the refusal of collaboration with the English government, it alarms public opinion in England, inspiring so much apprehension in the rulers there that they resort to vague promises of self-government, and at the same time to sharp persecutions. The movement, of course, is too weak still to throw off the domination of Western capitalism. With the capitalist factories a class of industrial workers is coming into being with extremely low wages and an incredibly low standard of living. Strikes occurred against Indian, as well as against European employers. But compared with the immense population all this is an insignificant start, important only as indication of future development.

With the present world war colonial exploitation, as well as the problem of liberation, acquires a new aspect. Against the enormously increasing power of capitalism a fight for independence in its old meaning has no longer any chance. On the other hand, it is probable that from now on world capital under American hegemony will act as a revolutionary agent. By a more rational system of exploitation of these hundreds of millions of people capital will be able to increase its profits considerably; by following another way than the previous primitive impoverishing methods of plunder, by raising labor in the colonies to a higher level of productivity, by better technics, by improvement of traffic, by investing more capital, by social regulations and progress in education. All of this is not possible without according a large amount of independence or at least self-rule to the colonies.

Self-rule of the colonies, of India, and of the Malayan islands, has already been announced. It means that parliaments in Europe and viceroys sent from thither can no longer govern them despotically. It does not mean that politically the working masses will be their own masters, that as free producers they will dispose of their means of production. Self-rule relates to the upper classes of these colonies exclusively; not only will they be inserted into the lower ranks of administration, but they will occupy the leading places, assisted of course by white "advisers" and experts, to ensure that capital interests are served in the right way. Already from the upper classes of India a rather numerous group of intellectuals has proceeded, quite capable as ruling officials to modernize political and social life.

To characterize modern capitalist production as a system wherein the workers by their own free responsibility and will-power are driven to the utmost exertion, the expression was often used that a free worker is no coolie. The problem of Asia now is to make the coolie a free worker. In China the process is taking its course; there the workers of olden times possessed a strong individualism in tropical countries it will be much more difficult to transform the passive downtrodden masses, kept in deep ignorance and superstition by heavy oppression, into active well-instructed workers capable of handling the modern productive apparatus and forces. Thus capital is faced with many problems. Modernization of the government apparatus through self-rule is necessary, but more is needed: the possibility of social and spiritual organization and progress, based on political and social rights and liberties, on sound general instruction. Whether world capital will be able and willing to follow this course cannot be foreseen. If it does, then the working classes of these countries will be capable of independent fighting for their class interests and for freedom along with the Western workers.

To all the peoples and tribes living in primitive forms of production in Africa, in Asia, in Australia, it will, of course, mean all entire change of the world, when the working class will have annihilated capitalism. Instead of as hard exploiting masters and cruel tyrants, the white race will come to them as friends to help them and to teach them how to take part in the progressing development of humanity.

4. RUSSIA AND EUROPE

With this war Russia, the Federation of Socialist Soviet Republics, as it calls itself, has made its entry among the recognized capitalist powers. In the Western countries an entire change has taken place in valuation of and attitude towards Russia and bolshevism. Certainly, the first fear of a communist revolution and the accompanying calumnies had already died away gradually in the ruling classes. Yet they were not quite at ease about their workers, and since the talk of the C.P. on world revolution went on, reports of forged atrocities and real cruelties were a motive to exclude Russia from the community of civilized nations. Until they needed Russia as an ally against Germany; then sentiment made a turn, though at first only in the kind wish that both dictatorships might devour one another. Then there they met governing politicians, officials, generals and officers, factory directors, intellectuals, an entire well-dressed, civilized, well-to-do class ruling the masses, just as at home. So they were reassured. The church only kept aloof, because of the bolshevist anti-religious propaganda.

The similarity of political forms and methods of government in Russia and Germany strikes the eye at first sight. In both the same dictatorship of a small group of leaders, assisted by a powerful well-organized and disciplined party, the same omnipotence of the ruling bureaucracy, the same absence of personal rights and of free speech, the same levelling of spiritual life into one doctrine, upheld by terrorism, the same cruelty towards opposition or even criticism. The economic basis, however, is different. In Russia it is state capitalism, in Germany state-directed private capitalism. In Germany there is a numerous class of owners of the means of production, a bourgeoisie, which, because of the difficulty of the fight for world power, gave itself a tyrannical dictatorship; it is augmented by an increasing bureaucracy of officials. In Russia bureaucracy is master of the means of production. The conformity in the necessary forms of practical rule and administration, domination from above, gave them the same system of dictatorship.

There is similarity also in the character of their propaganda. Both make use of the ideology of community, because both represent organized against unorganized capitalism. As in Russia, the antithesis to old capitalism was expressed in the catchword of communism, so in Germany by socialism. These are the names under which, in extensive propaganda, the fight for their own power against the old capitalist powers is urged upon the masses as a fight against capitalism. Thus they present themselves as more than a mere nationalism, they proclaim new world principles, fit for all countries, to be realized by world-revolution and world war against the exponents of the old order, English and American capitalism. So they find adherents to their cause, followers of their party, within the country of their opponents, ready to undermine from within their power of resistance.

As similar hostile rivals they find a basis for their opposition in their origin and the consequent traditions. National socialism came to power as an agent of big capitalism, wiping out the old labor movement, in conscious sharp antagonism to the "Marxian" trends of social-democracy and communism. In their own country only it could proclaim itself a party of the workers and impose by terror-propaganda this trickery upon uncritical adherents. The Russian ideology proceeded directly from a revolution made by the workers under the communist banner, and appealed to Marxian doctrines that had been adapted to its cause; but in foreign countries only could it find belief that indeed it represented dictatorship of the workers. Here it could impose upon young people desirous to fight capitalism and exploitation, whereas national-socialism was considered everywhere as a genuine enemy of the workers, and found sympathy only among the upper and lower part of the bourgeoisie.

The foreign policy of the Russian revolution was a logical consequence of its basic ideas. Though a socialist community has no wishes but to live in peace besides other peoples, it is in danger of being attacked by capitalist states. Hence, it must prepare for war. Moreover, world revolution, annihilation of capitalism all over the world remains the supreme aim; only in this way, by liberating the workers elsewhere, the socialist state can secure its own freedom. So the socialist state arms and prepares for war, not only for defense, but also for attack. And with surprise naive idealists perceive that what seemed a haven of peace reveals itself a power for war. And they ask whether indeed compulsion by the sword can bring freedom to others.

The contradiction is easily explained. What is named state-socialism discloses itself as state-capitalism, the rule of a new exploiting class, bureaucracy, master of the production apparatus, as in other countries the bourgeoisie. It, too, lives on surplus value. The larger its realm, its power, the larger its share, its wealth. Thus, for this bureaucracy war assumes the same significance as for the bourgeoisie. It takes part in the world contest of powers, on the same footing as other States, but with the pretension to be the world-champion of the working class. And though in view of the allied governments it cannot make too much show of it, and temporarily even silences the Comintern, yet it knows that in all foreign countries communist parties are working on its behalf. Thus the role of Russia in and after the war begins to depict itself. Behind the old now deceitful aims of extending the realm of communism stands the reality of extending the own international power. If the German bourgeoisie tries to steer its course in the track of England and America, the working class, prevented during long years from finding its own new way, may produce communist parties as agents of Russian hegemony over the Mid-European regions.

This policy and position among the other capitalist powers has its basis in an inner change of policy in Russia itself. State capitalism has consolidated its power in and through the war, the completion of the preceding development. Since the revolution there was a continual struggle between the socially important groups. First, State bureaucracy, with the Communist Party as its organ, being master of the industrial production, in a hard fight subdued the peasants in its campaign of founding the kolchoses. Besides them, however, stood the army officers and the numerous technical experts and officials in the factories, commonly called the engineers. They had an important function as technical leaders of the production, they had their own union, and were mostly non-party men. The well-known trials of engineers on forged charges of sabotage were an episode in the silent struggle; they were condemned not because they had committed the imputed crimes, but for intimidation and to forestall any attempt at independent political action. In the same way in the trial of General Tukhachevsky and other officers all elements from whom independent action was feared, were shot and replaced by others. Thus the political bureaucracy remained master, but it had to regard the other groups.

The war made a unification of all these forces necessary, and at the same time possible, on the basis of a strong nationalism aspiring to expansion. In the preceding years some so-called reforms had been proclaimed, though by the absence of free speech and free press they had no meaning for the working masses; they now could afford an opportunity for non-party men to take part in the governing apparatus. Party rule and Comintern was pushed into the background. Now under a firmly consolidated ruling class the masses, as in every capitalist state, could be led to the front in well-disciplined gigantic armies.

At the same time the war has brought about an increase of the spiritual influence of bolshevism in Western Europe. Not among the bourgeoisie; now that organized big capitalism is becoming master of the world it has not the least inclination to make way for state capitalism. Not very much among the workers; in the beginning the recognition perforce of the communist parties by the governments may increase its credit among workers dominated by nationalism; but its support of government policy, however masked by a seeming of wild opposition talk, will soon discredit it among the fighting masses of the working class. Among the Western intellectuals, however, Russian bolshevism attracts ever more attention.

Under the rule of big capitalism it is the class of intellectuals that has the technical lead of production, and the spiritual lead of society in its hands. Now it begins to ask—in so far as it is not entirely occupied by its narrow personal job—why shareholders and stock jobbers should have the upper command over production. It feels itself called upon to lead social production as an organized process, to throw off the dominance of a parasitical bourgeoisie and to rule society. It is divided, however, in a series of higher and lower ranks, arranged after usefulness or what else; they form a ladder on which, in mutual rivalry, one may ascend by ambition, capacities, favor or cunning. The lower and badly paid ranks among them may join the fight of the working class against capital. Its higher and leading elements, of course, are hostile to any idea of mastery by the workers over the process of production. Their prominent thinkers and learned scholars, often refined or ingenious spirits, strongly feel their superiority threatened by the phantom of a general "levelling." The intellectual class feels quite well that its ideal of social order cannot exist without a strong power apparatus, to keep down private capital, but chiefly to keep down the working masses. What they want is a moderate dictatorship, strong enough to resist attempts to revolution, civilized enough to dominate the masses spiritually and to assure a rational liberty of speech and opinion to the civilized; anyhow, without the rough violence that made national socialism the object of hatred all over Europe. A free road to the talented, and society led by the intellectual elite, such is the social ideal rising in this class.

This they see realized to a fair extent, though mixed up with barbarous remnants, in the Russian system. And the Russians have exerted themselves to promote such ideas. Soon after the revolution already scientific congresses were organized where the assembled scholars from all countries were regally entertained—though there was dearth in the land—and got the most favorable impression of the young enthusiasm and the fresh energy bestowed by the new-shaped society upon science and technics. Of the Solovki camps, where the deported peasants and workers are ill-treated till they perish, of course, nothing was shown to them, nor did they know of the deadly hard labor of millions of victims in the icy wilds of Siberia; probably not even the ordinary "black workers" in the factories did they meet with. Such inspiring experiences could not but strongly impress the younger Western intellectuals; what trickled through about atrocities was easily effaced by the splendor of increasing production figures in the world-wide propaganda of the C.P. And now the military successes of the Russian armies enhance the image of Russia as a vigorous civilized modern State.

So we may surmise something about the future of Russia and Bolshevism in Europe. In its antagonism to the Western powers of private capitalism, England and America, its ideology may serve as a valuable weapon to undermine the solid power of their bourgeoisie, by rousing, in case of need, working class opposition against her. As a recognized respectable party the C.P. will try to win posts of influence in politics, either in competition or in collaboration with social democracy; by a seeming show of sparkling opposition talk it seeks to gather the workers in its fold, to deter them from taking their own road to freedom. As it does already now, it will try, by a quasi-scientific propaganda among intellectuals, to win them over to some bolshevist kind of dictatorial government, and adorn it, may be, with the mark world-revolution.

More direct and important will be the Russian influence upon Central Europe. In the wake of the annihilation of military power comes economic slavery. To impose as much as possible of the burdens on the defeated foe, through the necessity of restoration and compensation of the immeasurable wanton destruction and pillages by the German armies, not only all property, so far as it is left, will be seized, but also all the peoples in so far as they are left, will be harnessed under the yoke of hard labor. The victors probably will not, as after the first world war, leave to the German bourgeoisie the possession of the production apparatus and the rule of the country.

Before, then, an effective fight for their cause will be possible to the Central European workers, a deep change in their thinking and willing must take place. They are faced not only by the formidable physical power of victorious world capitalism, but they will also encounter extreme difficulty in resisting the spiritual forces of Bolshevism on the one side, nationalism on the other side, to find the way clear to their class task. In this fight they must involve the Russian workers. Russian State capitalism, as well, has been exhausted and ravaged by the war; to restore itself it will have to lay a harder pressure upon the workers. So the Russian workers will be compelled to take up the fight for freedom, for liberation out of slavery, as a new great task, the same as the workers all over the world.

5. IN THE ABYSS

The second world war has thrown society into an abyss deeper than any former catastrophe. In the first world war the contending capitalisms stood against one another as Powers of old form, waging war in old forms, only on a larger scale and with improved technics. Now the war has reversed the inner structures of the States, and new political structures have arisen; now the war is a "total war," into which all forces of society are linked up as its subordinate means.

In and through this war society is thrown back to a lower level of civilization. That is not so much because of the immense sacrifices of life and blood. During the entire period of civilization—i.e., the period of written history and of the division of society into exploiting and exploited classes, between the primitive tribal life and the future world unity of mankind—war was the form of the struggle for existence. So it is quite natural that the last world fights, before the final consolidation drawing along all people, should embrace greater names and be more bloody than any former war.

What makes this retrogressive is first the regress from military and juridical norms that in the 19th century gave a certain appearance of humanity to warfare. The enemies were nominally considered as equal humans and soldiers, political rights of vanquished or occupied countries were recognized, national sentiments respected; civilians usually stood outside the fighting. In international treaties on "the laws of war" these principles were endorsed, and however often violated, they stood out as international law, that could be appealed to against the arbitrariness of a victor. Total war tramples on all these scraps of paper. Not only are all supplies seized and all industry is put into the service of the conqueror, not only are prisoners of war set to work for the enemy, but on an ever larger scale all people from occupied regions are forcibly, in a real slave hunting, dragged off to work in the German war industry. So, by producing arms for the foe, they are constrained to aid him against their own nation; at the same time relieving the enemy's workers for service at the front. Now that war is a matter of industrial production, slave labor becomes one of the foundations of warfare.

It is natural that in the occupied countries—half of Europe—resistance sprang up, and it is natural that it was suppressed severely, even when it consisted only in tentative first traces. It is not natural, however, that in the repression such a height of cruelty was reached, as first applied in the rough mishandling and extermination of the Jewish citizens and then extended to all national opposition. The German soldier, himself an unwilling slave of the dictatorial apparatus, develops into a master and instrument of oppression. As a filthy contamination the habits of violence and outrage spread over the continent, wakening an immense hatred against the German occupants.

In former wars occupation of a foreign country was considered a temporary situation, and international law expressed it in this way, that the occupant was not allowed to change anything in the fundamental law of the country, and only took the administration in its hands insofar as war conditions necessitated it. Now, however, Germany interfered everywhere in the existing institutions, trying to impose the national-socialist principles, pretending it was the beginning of a new era for the entire Europe in which all the other countries as allies, i.e., vassals, had to follow Germany. Underlings it found in the small number of foreign adherents to its creed, and the larger number who saw their chance now; they were made rulers over their compatriots and exhibited the same spirit of wanton violence. The same spiritual tyranny as in Germany itself is imposed; and especially in the Western countries, with their large civil liberties, this arouses an increasing embitterment, that found expression in underground literature. Neither the silly fiction of the unity of the Teutonic race nor the argument of the united continent of Europe made any impression.

The fall into barbarity is due, firstly, to the destructive power of modern war machinery. More than in any previous time all industrial and productive power of society, all ingenuity and devotion of men is put into the service of the war. Germany, as the aggressive party, set the example; it perfected the air weapon into bombers that destroyed, with factories of war supplies, the surrounding city quarters. It did not foresee at the time that the steel production of America many times surpassed that of Germany, so that the system of destruction, once that America would have transformed its industrial into military power, would fall back with multiple vehemence upon Germany itself. In the first world war much lamenting was heard about Ypres being destroyed and some French cathedrals damaged; now, first in England and France, and then on a larger scale in Germany, towns and factory quarters, grand monuments of architecture, remnants of irretrievable mediaeval beauty, went to rack and ruin. Week after week the wireless boasted of how many thousands of tons of explosives were thrown upon German towns. As an instrument of terror to bring the German population upon its knees, or to rouse the desire for peace into resistance to the leaders, these bombardments were a failure. On the contrary, through the exasperation over the wanton destruction and killings a disheartened population was bound the firmer to its rulers. They rather gave the impression as if the Allied rulers, sure about their industrial and military superiority, wished to prevent a revolution of the German people against the national-socialist rulers which would have led to milder peace conditions, preferring to beat down German attempts at world power once and for all by a downright military victory.

Besides the material, the spiritual devastation perpetrated among mankind represents no smaller fall into barbarity. The levelling of all spiritual life, of speech and writing to one prescribed creed, and the forcible suppression of any different opinion has grown in and through the war into a complete organization of falsehood and cruelty.

Censoring of the press had already proved necessary in former wars to prevent sensational news harmful to the warfare of the country. In later times, when the entire bourgeoisie felt keenly nationalist and closely bound to the government, the papers felt it their duty to collaborate with the military authorities in upholding morale by optimistic statements, in criticizing and abusing the enemy, and in influencing the neutral press. But censorship became more needed than before to suppress resistance on the part of the workers, now that the war brought a heavier pressure of long hours and of shortness of provisions. When propaganda is needed, artificially to rouse in the people enthusiasm for war, counter propaganda revealing the capitalist background of the war cannot be tolerated. So we see in the first world war the press turned into an organ of the army staff, with the special task to uphold the submissiveness of the masses, as well as the fighting spirit.

In the present war this may still represent the state of things on the Allied side; but on the other side it is far surpassed by the adaptation to war conditions of the already existing department of propaganda, with its staff of artists, authors and intellectuals. Now its system of directing opinion, raised to the utmost perfection and extended over Europe, reveals its full efficiency. By stating its own case as the case of highest right, truth and morals, by relating every action of the foe as an act of weakness, or of baseness, or of embarrassment, an atmosphere of faith and victory is created. It proved itself capable of transfiguring the most obvious defeat into a brilliant success, and to represent the beginning of collapse as the dawning of final victory, and thus to inspire stubborn fighting and to postpone the final collapse. Not that people accept it all as truth; they are suspicious of anything they hear; but they see the resolution in the leaders and feel powerless through lack of organization.

Thus the German masses are the victims of a system growing more violent and more mendacious as ruin approaches. So the destruction of the power of German capitalism will be accompanied by the aimless destruction and new slavery of the German people, not by its rise to a new fight for a new world of real freedom.

As a destructive catastrophe, the reign of national-socialism passed over Germany and the surrounding countries. A torrent of organized cruelty and organized falsehood has flooded Europe. As a poisonous taint they have infected mind, will and character of the peoples. They are the mark of new dictatorial capitalism, and their effect will long be felt. They are not a chance degeneration; they are due to special causes characteristic of the present times. Whoever recognises as their deepest cause the will of big capital to keep and to extend its domination over mankind, knows that they will not disappear with the end of the war. Nationalism excited to red heat everywhere, imputing all this to the bad racial character of the foe, thereby rousing stronger national hatred, will always be a fertile soil for new violence, material and spiritual.

The fall into barbarity is not a biological atavism to which mankind might be subjected at any time. The mechanism of how it came to work lies open to the view. The reign of falsehood does not mean that what is said and written is all lies. By emphasising part of the truth and omitting other parts the total can turn into untruth. Often it is combined with the conviction of its truth on the part of the speaker. Doubtless, it holds for everybody that what he says is never the objective, material, all-sided truth, but always subjective truth, a colored personal, one-sided image of reality. Where all these subjective, personal, hence incomplete, partial truths compete, control and criticise one another, and where most people thereby are compelled to self-criticism, there arises out of them a more general aspect which we accept as the nearest approach to objective truth. If, however, this control is taken away and criticism is made impossible, whilst only one special opinion is put forward, the possibility of objective truth entirely vanishes. The reign of falsehood finds its essential basic in the suppression of free speech.

Cruelty in action often is accompanied by ardent devotion to new principles, that is, irritated by its failure to make progress rapidly enough. In normal society there is no other way than patient propaganda and the thorough self-education in working out arguments. If, however, dictatorship gives to the few power over the many, then, excited by the fear of losing this power, it tries to obtain its aims through increasing violence. The reign of cruelty finds its essential basis in the dictatorial power of a minority. If we wish that in the coming times, in the fight of classes and peoples, the downfall into barbarity be prevented, these are the things we must oppose with all energy; dictatorial power of a small group or party, and suppression or limitation of free speech.

The storm now sweeping over the earth has raised new problems and new solutions. Besides the spiritual devastation it brought spiritual renovation, new ideas in economic and social organization, most conspicuous among them ideas on new forms of suppression, dominance and exploitation. These lessons will not be lost to world capital; its fight will be more tenacious, its rule stronger by using these new methods. On the other side in the workers a stronger consciousness will dawn of how completely their liberation is bound up with the opposite factors. Now they feel in the body how much the reign of organized falsehood hampers them in gaining the simplest inkling of the knowledge they need, how much the reign of organized terror makes their organization impossible. Stronger than ever before the will and the strength will arise in them to keep open the gates to knowledge by fighting for freedom of speech against any attempt to restrict it; to keep open the gate to class organization by refusing and repelling any attempt at forcible suppression, in whatever guise of proletarian interest it may present itself.

In this second world war the workers' movement has fallen much deeper than in the first. In the first world war its weakness, so sharply in contrast with former pride and boasting, manifested itself in that it was dragged along, that deliberately, by its own will, it followed the bourgeoisie and turned into underlings of nationalism. This character persisted in the next quarter of a century, with its idle talk and party intrigue, though gallant fighting in strikes occurred. In the present war the working class had no will of its own any more to decide on what to do; it was already incorporated into the entirety of the nation. As they are shuffled to and fro over factories and shops, uniformed and drilled, commanded to the fronts, mixed up with the other classes, all essence of the former working class has disappeared. The workers have lost their class; they do not exist as a class any more; class-consciousness has been washed away in the wholesale submission of all classes under the ideology of big capital. Their special class-vocabulary: socialism, community has been adopted by capital for its dissimilar concepts.

This holds good especially for Central Europe, where in former times the workers' movement looked more powerful than anywhere else. In the Western countries there remains a sufficient amount of class feeling soon to find them back on the road to fight in the transformation of war industry to peace industry. Encumbered, however, with the heavy load of old forms and traditions, leading to battle in the old forms, it will have some difficulty to find its way to the new forms of fight. Still, the practical needs of the struggle for existence and working conditions will, more or less gradually, compel it to put up and clarify the new aims of conquering the mastery over production. Where, however, dictatorship has reigned and has been destroyed by foreign military power, there under new conditions of oppression and exploitation, a new working class must first take its rise. There a new generation will grow up, for whom the old names and catchwords have no meaning any longer. Certainly, it will be difficult under foreign domination to keep the class feeling free and pure from nationalism. But with the collapse of so many old conditions and traditions, the mind will be more open to direct influence of the new realities. Every doctrine, every device and catchword will be taken, not at its face value, but at its real content.

More powerful than before, capitalism will tower after the war. But stronger also the fight of the working masses, sooner or later, will arise over against it. It is inevitable that in this fight the workers will aim at mastery over the shops, mastery over production, dominance over society, over labor, over their own life. The idea of self-rule through workers' councils will take hold of their minds, the practice of self-rule and workers' councils will determine their actions. So from the abyss of weakness they will rise to a new unfolding of power. Thus a new world will be built up. A new era is coming after the war, not of tranquility and peace, but of constructive class fight.

V. The Peace

1. TOWARDS NEW WAR

Hardly had Berlin fallen, hardly had the German power been annihilated, when in the American press well nigh unanimously a new war cry arose, proclaiming Russia the new enemy. With all the armies still in the field, a panic of new war spread over the exhausted tormented world. The new weapon, the atomic bomb, that had turned into dust two big industrial towns and killed at one stroke a hundred thousand people, struck terror into the hearts of civilised mankind and made the Americans realize their own insecurity. "There is no secret, and there is no defense," was the verdict of the atomic physicists who had constructed the bomb; in a couple of years every government can have them made, and they can be carried across the oceans or easily smuggled into America. An intensive campaign in the "Security Council of the United Nations" for eliminating the threat was started. America proposed to establish an international, supernational board or authority, sole master of dangerous material all over the world, qualified to inspect manufacture in every country. The Russian Government refused to admit such a committee with such powers into its territory and demanded that first America should destroy all its atomic bombs and give up its supremacy.

Why could not the Russian Government agree to an international control? Russian scientists, speaking for their rulers, said that Russia, the only country free from capitalism, must keep strictly to its sovereignty, cannot take part in a capitalist world unity, cannot suffer its socialism to be corrupted by capitalist-minded inspecting authorities. One would say that to open up their happier and progressive way of life to the view of the rest of the world should only propagate their economic system. So the Russian rulers' true reason for shunning a close contact of their subjects with the peoples of freer private capitalism must be that there is, besides war secrets, too much to conceal. During and after the war so many more details have come to light about conditions in Russia: the general low standard of living of the masses, the wide divergence between low wages of the workers and high salaries of the political and technical leaders, the concentration camps, where ten or more millions of people are starved and worked to death under the most horrible working conditions. The existence of this immense army of slave-laborers testifies that besides the much praised highly technical sector of Russian economy there is a large sector consisting of unskilled forced labor of the lowest level of productivity. It means a state of economic backwardness, not suspected before beneath the glorifying figures of five-year plans and stackhanovism, an inner weakness beneath the apparent progress. Whereas organization and skilful planning, according to either admiring or hostile socialist opinion in the Western world should imply a higher form of production system, the effect seems to be frustrated to a high degree by the secret police, essential instrument of dictatorship, that ever endangers the security and state of life of any member of the technical and bureaucratic officialdom.

Russia and America are not only rivals in that they both are in need of the oil abundance in the Near East. Moreover, Russia has to fear the power of America. The yearly production of steel in 1945 for America was 80 millions of tons, for Russia (after the fourth five-year plan) 24 millions; for coal these figures are 575 and 250 millions of tons. This shows the relative industrial strength, that cannot be compensated by Russia having 170 millions against America 130 millions of people. And now America transformed its industrial power into military and political power. This political power finds its ideological expression in the call for world-unity. "One world or none" was the panic cry of the atomic scientists when aghast they saw the consequences of their work; if this terrible new power is not fettered through international unity, it will destroy mankind itself. But it stands to reason that in any world organization of "united nations" the most powerful will dominate the others. The Russian rulers fully realize that to consent to the establishment of a superpower with large competencies means subjection under the most powerful of the associates, under American capitalism. They refuse.

So both prepare for war. Is it inevitable? All we can see and consider is what deep-seated forces lie at the root of this threat. It is to America in the first place that we have to turn. Here private capitalism is in full development, here socialism is insignificant, practically absent in politics, here planned economy and State direction of production was only a short-lived war necessity, soon replaced by free enterprise. All the conditions and phenomena of former free capitalism in Europe, especially in England and Germany, repeat themselves here, now on a far bigger scale. In 1923 already American production exceeded that of total Europe; at the beginning of the war, notwithstanding nine millions of unemployed, it produced more than in any former year. Then during the war the production increased enormously, as well on account of the greater number of workers as of a rapid rise in technical productivity; so that, despite the tremendous production of war materials, it was not necessary to impose strict limitations on the people's consumption, as was the case in European countries. War is always a golden time for capitalist profit, because the State, as buyer, pays willingly the highest prices. In America it was a gold rush as never before; war profits were not in terms of millions, but of billions of dollars. And the end of the war that devastated the production apparatus of Europe, sees America with a production apparatus more than fifty per cent larger than at its beginning, with an industrial production twice as large as that of the rest of the capitalist world. For this increased capacity of output a market must be found. This is the problem facing American capitalism.

An inner market might easily be found by giving a larger share to the working class, thus increasing their buying capacity. But this course, a cutting of profits, capitalism cannot take. It is convinced that the workers, if they can provide a fourth-hand car and a refrigerator, are well off and have nothing to desire. The essence of capital is to make profit.

So foreign markets have to be found. First there is devastated Europe. Its production apparatus has to be restored by American exports made possible through big loans. Part of it is already American property, and for what nominally remains European property heavy interest will have to be paid to American finance. European economy stands under direct control of American supervision agents who will see to it that the loans are spent in such a way that Europe cannot develop into a serious competitor. In Europe American capital finds a working class with much lower standard of life than that of the American workers, hence promising bigger profits than at home. But this is only possible if first of all its labor power is restored by sending as relief gifts of food, clothes, fuel, to the hungry impoverished peoples. It is investment at long, promising profits only in the long run. Moreover, it is here confronted with Russia trying to extend its exploitation system over Central and Western Europe.

Then there is China, the most promising market for American products. But here American capitalism has done its very best to spoil its own chances. In the civil war it supported the capitalist government against the red peasant armies, with the sole result that the American officers and agents turned away with disgust from the incapable rapacious Kuomintang rulers; that the peasant armies could neither be defeated nor win entire power, so that the permanent civil war brought chaos and prevented recovery. The natural sympathy of American capitalist rulers towards exploiting classes in other parts of the world, and its equally class-born hostility against popular movements, makes them blind to the fact that only out of the latter the basis for strong economic development may arise. Thus an entire reversal of policy would be necessary. The fact that the communist armies are backed by Russia intensifies American antagonism towards the Chinese people's masses, thus preventing China from becoming a market for American export.

Then there is Russia, the U.S.S.R., in extension and population a continent in itself, after the U.S.A., the second realm of the world in industrial development under one State government, with immense sources of the most valuable raw materials, the second gold producer of the world, abounding in fertile land, with a rapidly increasing population estimated within twenty years to reach up to 250 millions. It is closed to foreign commerce; an iron wall isolates it from any foreign influence. American capitalism, so much in need of markets for its outpouring mass of products can it suffer such a wall to exist without trying to break it open? It waged a war for "liberty"; liberty means free commerce and intercourse all over the world. It is not to be expected from the mightiest capitalist class that it should tolerate exclusion from a third part of the industrially developed world.

Moreover, American capitalists are confident that against the impact of even peaceful commerce Russian economy will not be able to hold out, but will gradually give way to private ownership. So, apparently, think the Russian rulers; they refuse to expose their skilfully constructed higher organization of planned economy to the corrupting influences of private capitalism.

Thus the conditions for a deep-seated conflict are given. By its very nature American private capitalism is, fundamentally, the aggressor; Russian state-capitalism has to defend its position. Of course, defense often has to consist in attacking; in any war preparation each party imputes aggression to the other. So Russia tries to establish a protecting fringe beyond its borders and tries to extend its domination over Europe. Moreover, in all capitalist countries it has an organization of devoted adherents and agents, allured by the revolutionary traditions of 1917, convinced that organized state-directed economy means socialism, firm in the expectation of an approaching economic crisis that will upset the system of private capitalism.

Among expert economists, too, there is a widespread opinion that world industry, that is, especially American industry, is to face a heavy crisis. Its productive capacity, its output of products is so large that there is no market for it. So, after the first peace boom supplying the deficiencies of the war years, there will come a heavy slump, with large unemployment and all its consequences. Strictly speaking, it is a continuation of the 1930–33 slump, after which no real recovery until 1940 took place. Then the war provided an enormous market for a rapidly expanding production, a market never choked because all products were rapidly destroyed. Now that the war is over the capitalist class again faces the pitiful situation that the world cannot absorb its products. Is it to be wondered at that once more its thoughts turn to those golden years of high profits when death and destruction of uncounted human lives brought in such a rich harvest? And that even great parts of the workers, narrow capitalist-minded as they are, think of that time only as years of high wages and exciting adventure?

War as a market can be partly substituted by war preparation as a market. Armaments already occupy a notable part of the productive force of Society. For the budget year 1946–47 America's military budget amounted to 12 billions of dollars. Compared with an estimated total yearly national product of 180 billions it may not look impressive; but compared with an American peacetime export of seven billions it gains in importance. The bulk of production is always destined for home consumption of food, clothes, tools, machinery, etc.; the fringe of export and extension is the active force that stimulates the entirety of production, increasing the need for productive apparatus and labor hands, who, in their turn, need commodities; under capitalism each extra demand from outside tends to raise, directly and still more indirectly at a much enhanced rate, the extent of production. The continued demand for war materials to be destroyed and to be replaced continually because in a few years they are superseded by new inventions, may act as a force postponing the impending industrial crisis.

It is highly questionable, however, whether such a rate of war preparedness can last indefinitely. Though theoretically it seems possible that two lots of slave-drivers, practising different methods, but not so very different in deepest character, when viewing the risks, may prefer to come to terms with one another, it does as yet not look probable. The American capitalist class, knowing that at the other side of the iron curtain war preparations go on in the same feverish tempo, trusting that at the moment America is the strongest in war technics, driven by the desire to have the entire world open to international trade, believing in America's mission to make the world into one unity, might in view of the allurements of war well be expected to overcome its fear of seeing its big cities turned into dust by atom bombs. And then hell again breaks loose over mankind.

Is war inevitable? Is not war an anachronism? Why should man, able to discover atomic processes, not be able to establish world, peace? Those who pose this question do not know what capitalism means. Can there be world peace when in Russia millions of slaves are worked to death in concentration camps, and the entire population lacks freedom? Can there be world peace when in America the kings of capital keep the entire society in subjection and exploitation without being faced by any trace of a fight for social freedom? Where capitalist greed and capitalist exploitation dominate world peace must remain a pious wish.

When we say that, hence, war is inseparable from capitalism, that war can only disappear with capitalism itself, this does not mean that war against war is of no use and that we have to wait till capitalism has been destroyed. It means that the fight against war is inseparable from fight against capitalism. War against war can be effective only as part of the workers' class war against capitalism.

If the question is raised whether it is possible to forestall a threatening war, it is pre-supposed that there is a conflict between government, invested with power and authority on war and peace, and the masses of the population, especially the working class. Their voting power is without effect since it works only on election day; parliaments and Congresses are part of the ruling Power. So the question comes down to this: Have the workers, and in a wider sense the people's masses, at the moment of danger the possibility, by other than parliamentary means, to enforce their peace-will upon the war-preparing rulers? They have. If such a will actually lives within them, if they are prepared to stand with resolute conviction for their aim. Their form of fight then consists in direct mass-actions.

A government, a ruling class cannot go into war with the people unwilling and resisting. Therefore a moral and intellectual preparation is no less necessary than a technical and organizational preparation. Systematic war propaganda in the press, in broadcasting, in movies, must waken a bellicose spirit and suppress the instinctive but unorganized spirit of resistance. Hence it is certain that a decided conscious refusal on the part of the people's masses, demonstrated in outspoken widely heard protest, can have a determining influence upon the governmental policy. Such a protest may appear first in mass meetings voting sharp resolutions. More efficient will be the protest if the masses go into the streets demonstrating; against their ten and hundred thousands all riot acts and court injunctions are meaningless. And when these are not sufficient, or are suppressed by military violence, the workers and employees in traffic and industry can strike. Such a strike is not for wages, but to save society from utter destruction.

Government and the ruling class will try to break the resistance with all means of moral and physical suppression. So it will be a hard fight, demanding sacrifices, steadfastness and endurance. The psychological basis for such fight is not at once present in full vigour; it needs time to develop, and does so only under heavy spiritual strain. Since the middle classes always tend to vacillate between opposite moods, capitalist greed expressing itself in nationalist aggressiveness, and fear for destruction, from them stubborn resistance cannot be expected. The fight, therefore, takes the character of a class fight, with mass strikes as its most powerful weapon.

In the 19th century the idea of a universal strike at the outbreak of war, as well as that of a general refusal to take up arms, was propagated, especially by the anarchists; it was meant as a direct impediment to mobilization and warfare. But the power of the working class was far too small at the time. In the first decade of the 20th century, when an imperialist war became ever more threatening, the question of how to prevent it became urgent among European socialists. In the German socialist party there were discussions about mass strikes, and the idea gained ground whether mass actions could be used against war. But the party—and union—leaders opposed all such actions because they feared that in that case Government would suppress and annihilate their laboriously built-up organizations. They wished to restrict the workers' movement to parliamentary and trade union action. In 1912, when again war loomed near, an international peace congress was held at Basle. Under solemn bib-bam of the bells the delegates entered the cathedral, to listen to fine speeches from the most prominent leaders on the international unity and brotherhood of the workers. Part of the delegates wished to discuss ways and means how to oppose war; they intended to propose resolutions calling up the workers of all countries for discussion and mass action. But the presidium said no; no discussion was allowed. Whereas now the splendid demonstration of unity and peace-will, it said, would impress and warn the war-mongers, the discussions exposing our dissensions about the ways of action would encourage the militarists. Of course, it was just the reverse. The capitalist rulers were not deceived by this show; they at once sensed the inner weakness and fear; now they knew they could go on and that the socialist parties would not seriously oppose the war. So the disaster took its inevitable course. When in 1914, during the last days of July, working masses demonstrated in the streets of Berlin they felt uneasy, because the socialist party failed to give energetical directions; their calls were drowned in the louder national anthems of the bourgeois youth. The war started unhampered, with the working class organizations tied firmly to its chariot.

Basle had been a symbol, a test, a crossroad. The decision taken there determined all further events, the four years of murder over Europe, the catastrophe of all moral and spiritual progress, and then beyond, Hitlerism and the second world war. Could it have been otherwise? The Basle result was not chance, but a consequence of the actual inner state of the workers' movement: the supremacy of leaders, the docility of the masses. Social developments depend on the deeper general power relations of the classes. But just as in geography small structure details of watersheds determine whether the water flows to one or to another ocean, so small hardly noticed differences in relative strength at definite moments may have decisive effects on the course of events. If the opposition in the socialist parties had been stronger, more self-confident; if at the time in the workers the spirit of independent action had been stronger; if, hence, the Basle congress had been compelled to discussion and thus had brought more clearness, when the war, surely, would not have been prevented. But from the onset it would have been crossed by class fights, by internal strife within each country breaking up national unity, exalting the workers' spirits. Then the history of the later years, the state of socialism, the relations of the classes, the conditions of society would have been different.

Now again society at large, and the working class especially, stands before the same question: can the war be prevented? Of course, there are differences;

then the bourgeoisie was mostly unaware of the danger, whereas now it is itself full of apprehension; then the working class was well organized in a socialist party proclaiming itself hostile to imperialist policy, and the deadly foe of all capitalism, whereas present day America shows nothing of the sort. It is not certain whether this is only weakness. The Russian workers are entirely powerless; they lack the liberties which the American workers enjoy and may use in their fight: freedom of speech, of press, of discussion, of organization, of action. So, in any case, it is up to the American working class to decide whether as obedient instruments they will help to make their capitalist masters all-powerful masters of the world, or whether, by making war against war, they will enter for the first time into the war against capitalism, for their own freedom.

2. TOWARDS NEW SLAVERY

The second world war has devastated Europe. In Germany nearly all towns have been turned into ruins and rubbish by American bombers, where 60 million people, starving and naked, have to live as savages in their holes. In France, Italy, Holland, Poland, England, large parts have been devastated in the same way. More vital still than this visible lack of housing is the destruction of the production apparatus. Under the industrial system of capitalism the production apparatus, the factories, machines, traffic are the backbone, the basis of life. Under primitive, pre-capitalist conditions of simple agriculture the soil secures life. Under capitalism-in-ruins agriculture, retrograde as it is, cannot provide sufficient food for the industrial millions, and ruined industry cannot provide tools and fertilizers to restore agriculture. So Europe, after the war, as first and main task, faces the problem of recovery.

Recovery, reconstruction, was the watchword proclaimed and heard everywhere. It meant more than simply reconstruction of the production apparatus, the construction of new machines, ships, trucks and factories. It meant reconstruction of the production system, of the system of social relations between capital and labor, the reconstruction of capitalism. Whereas during the war ideas arose and were heard of a new world to come after the war, a better world of harmony, social justice and progress, even of socialism, now it was made clear that, practically, capitalism and exploitation were to remain the basis of society. How could it be otherwise? Since during the war the workers acted only as obedient servants, soldiers to vanquish their masters' enemies, with never a thought of acting for their own freedom, there can be no question to-day of any change in the basic principle of society, capitalist exploitation.

This does not mean restoration of old capitalism. It has gone forever. Conditions have changed. Capitalism is in distress. We are poor. Where productive force has been destroyed so thoroughly, it stands to reason that there must be scarceness of all life necessities. But there is more to it. Poverty is not equally distributed. As President Truman lately stated, wages had risen less and profits had risen more than the prices. The poor are poorer now; the rich are richer than before. This is no chance result of temporary conditions. To grasp its meaning we have to consider the deeper economic basis of the new social conditions. Formerly, in ordinary times, the gradual renovation of the productive apparatus at the rate in which it was used up or became antiquated, took a certain regular percentage of the entire labor of society. Now the mass destruction demands a mass renovation in a short time. This means that a larger part of the total labor has to be spent on the production of means of production, and a smaller part is left for consumption goods. Under capitalism the means of production are the property of the capitalist class; they are renovated out of the surplus-value. Hence more surplus-value is needed. This means that a larger share of the produce has to fall to the capitalist class, a smaller share to the working class. As capitalist opinion in the middle class literature expresses it: For recovery of prosperity the first condition is production of capital, accumulation of profits; high wages are an impediment to rapid recovery.

Thus the main problem of capitalist policy since the war is how to increase the surplus-value by depressing the standard of life of the workers. Automatically this happens already by the steady rise of prices, a consequence of the continuous issue of paper money under scarcity of goods. So the workers have to fight ever again for increase of the nominal wages, have ever again to strike, without attaining more than that the wages slowly, at a distance, follow the increasing cost of living. Still there may be a willingness among individual employers—in view of the shortness of labor power—to pay more than the contracted scale of wages; so the State intervenes in the interest of the entire capitalist class. First by means of the institute of mediators. These state-appointed mediators, formerly designated to arbitrate in case of wage disputes, now have the function of imposing standard wages, maximum wages not to be surpassed by any employer. It now happens that in a strike the employer is willing to pay more wages, but the State forbids it. Or the government proclaims a general wage-pegging which, in view of the rising prices, means a continuous lowering of life standard. Thus the strike against individual employers or employers' unions becomes meaningless; each strike is directed and must be directed consciously against State power.

Trade unions, too, now acquire a new function. They are directly interposed as officially recognized institutions that negotiate and make treaties, in the name of the workers, with the governmental and capitalist bodies. Government gives legal sanction to the decisions of the union; this means that the workers are bound morally and legally to the contracts made by the union leaders considered as their representatives. Formerly it was the workers themselves who in their assemblies had to decide on the new working conditions;

they could, by their vote, accept and reject them. Now this semblance of independence, of at least formal free decision in bargaining, is taken from them. What the union leaders in conference with government and capitalists arrange and agree upon, is considered law for the workers; they are not asked, and should they refuse, all the moral and organizational power of the union is used to force them into obedience. It is clear that unions as formally self-ruling organizations of the workers with chosen leaders are far more apt to impose the new bad working conditions than would be any power institute of the State. Thus the trade unions are made part of the power apparatus dominating the working class. The union is the salesman of the labor power of the workers, and in bargaining in conference with the State officials sells it to the employers.

This does not mean, of course, that now the unions and their leaders in every case consent to the capitalist demands. Thereby their authority would soon break down, as is actually the case to a certain degree now. Their attitude, moreover, often depends on political considerations, whether they stand entirely at the side of the Government, as in England, or are hostile against the Government, as in France. The trade union leaders in France, belonging to the C.P., hence agents of the Russian rulers, have not the least interest now to sustain the French capitalist class and its government, as they did some years ago when they took part in government themselves and stood hostile against the workers' strikes. Thus the fight of the workers against impoverishment is used by the political parties as a subordinate means in the struggle between the Western system of private capitalism and the Russian system of state capitalism.

The problem facing European capitalism, however, has a still wider scope. It is not only a matter of wages; it is the question whether, after this breakdown of the economic system, the working masses are willing to rebuild it. Capitalism knows that "labor only can save us." Hard work and low wages are the conditions for recovery. Will the workers, who remember the hard life under capitalist exploitation before the war, consent to a still harder life in order to restore that state of things? They may, if they can be convinced that it is for a better world that they now exert themselves, for a world of freedom for their class, for socialism. Socialism is the magic word able to transform sullen rebels into ready co-operators.

In broad layers of the middle class the conviction awoke that socialism, in one way or another, was needed for recovery; in most countries socialist ministers took office, socialist and communist parties dominated the parliaments. In England the slogan read: "Labor only can save us"; a large combined middle class and workers' vote gave an overwhelming majority to the Labor Party that in former governments had shown its capitalist reliability. Where a downright capitalist government would have been unable to suppress forcibly the resistance of the workers and to enforce the new hard living conditions upon them, a Labor Government was the only escape.

England, indeed, was in a critical condition. The second world war had exhausted its capital of foreign investments, the interest of which formerly directed a stream of unpaid consumption goods into the country. Uncle Shylock had given his generous aid only after his hard-pressed Ally had delivered most of its assets—notwithstanding the fact that the war essentially had served to destroy America's most dangerous rival to world domination, a Germany disposing of the resources of the entire European continent. England had to give up a large part of its colonies, it could hardly bear the expenses of playing the part of a Big Power any longer. Also we see the English bourgeoisie lose its old self-reliant feeling of confidence; its foreign policy, e.g., in the Near East, shows signs of diffidence. The privileged position formerly occupied by the British working class, having its share in England's exploitation of the world, had gone. Now the Labor Party faced the task of clearing the bankrupt estate.

Socialism, however, was not to be simply make-believe. A good dose of Socialism was really needed to restore capitalism. Some of the basic industries of capitalist production, as coal mining and railway traffic, as a consequence of private ownership encumbered with an entirely antiquated lack of organization, constituted a ridiculous muddle of inefficiency. To a well-developed capitalist production good organization of such basic branches as coal, steel, traffic, is just as necessary as that of post and telegraph; so nationalization is a capitalist necessity, to which the name socialization is given. Though there is nothing revolutionary in it, former governments were too full of respect for private enterprise to satisfy those general needs; a "socialist" Labor Government was needed to establish capitalist efficiency. When now the miners complain that they find no difference in treatment between the former mine owners and the new Coal Board they have to consider that the reform was not made for them, but for capitalism. It was not an attack on capitalist property; the coal mine shares—of doubtful quality—were replaced by Government Bonds; this manipulation has in no way lessened the exploitation of the workers.

The State has to assume functions in the production apparatus that formerly were the domain of private enterprise. This does not yet mean state-capitalism, as in Russia, but only state-directed capitalism, somewhat as it was in Nazi-Germany. And there are more points of resemblance. Capital is scarce in post-war Europe, as it was in Germany after the first war. The strictest economy is necessary. No more than under German fascism can it now be left to the free will of the capitalist class to spill the available national capital by importing luxuries or materials for the production of luxuries. To rebuild the production apparatus of the country Government has to take in hand the control and command of all imports an exports, of all transport of values across the frontiers. International trade then cannot be left to private merchants; the governments negotiate trade pacts, often strictly bilateral, on quantities comprising the bulk of food supplies and the industrial produce of the entire country. What Nazi-Germany introduced as the new totalitarian system of trade is now imitated by all the European States, an emergency measure here, just as it was there. But the character of the emergency is different; there it was to spare forces for a new assault toward world conquest, to prepare for world war; here it is to stave off starvation and revolution, a result of world war. Every government has to import foodstuffs from abroad—grain production in Europe by deterioration of the soil and lack of hands having diminished to only half or two-thirds of its pre-war amount—lest the hungry population should revolt and bring the C.P. into power. But they must be paid by the export of industrial products withheld from their own people; or by loans from America, tying Western Europe with the bonds of debt slavery to the master of the world's gold.

So the State has a far greater power now than before. It is the consequence of war destruction. This does not mean, however, that it is a temporary abnormal state of things. Nobody believes that hereafter old private capitalism can return. The increasing size of enterprises, the interconnection of world economy, the concentration of capital demand planning and organization; though now and then it needs catastrophes to enforce these tendencies. These post-war conditions form a transition, an introduction to a new world, the world of planned capitalism. The State rises as a mighty power above society. It dominates and regulates economic life, it directs planned production, it distributes food and other life necessities according to its judgment of primary needs, it distributes the surplus-value produced by the workers among the owners of capital; it directs more or less even the spiritual food, having distributive power over the paper needed for the printing of books. In its organization the political parties are its bickering office-of-publicity holders, and the trade unions are part of its bureaucracy. And, most important, the totalitarian State incorporates the working masses into its social organization as the obedient producers of value and surplus-value. This is performed by calling planned capitalism by the name of socialism.

This is not simply usurpation of a name. A simple word, a deceitful name, has no such power. The name is the expression of a reality. Socialism was the watchword of the suffering and fighting workers in the past century, the message of their liberation, the magic word occupying their hearts and heads. They did not see that it meant only an imperfect liberation, the rule of their leaders as new masters, disposing over production apparatus and product. Socialism was the program of the leaders and politicians they sent into the parliaments there to fight capitalism and exploitation. The goal of socialism, after the conquest of State power, was the organization of production, planned economy, transferring the productive apparatus into the hands of the community, represented by the State. Now that in the 20th century capitalism in emergency needs planned economy, direction and organization of production through State power, the old slogan of the workers just fits in with the new needs of capitalism. What had been the expression of their modest hopes for liberation becomes the instrument of their ready submission under stronger slavery. All the traditions of former aspirations, sacrifices, and heroic struggles, binding socialist workers to their creed and their party and condensed in the name socialism, now act as fetters laming resistance against the growing power of the new capitalism. Instead of clearly seeing the situation and resisting, blindfolded by the dear traditional slogans, they go into the new slavery.

This socialism is for Europe; it is not for America, nor for Russia. It is born in Europe; it has to save capitalist Europe. Why did Europe succumb into such utter powerlessness? It has outside Russia, 400 million people, more than the U.S.A. and the U.S.S.R. together, it is rich in raw materials for industry, rich in fertile land; it had a highly developed industry and a well-instructed population disposing of an abundance of capital. Why, then, such a lack of capitalist power? Because Europe is divided up in a dozen nationalities, speaking several dozens of languages, and so is driven by fierce centuries-old antagonisms and national hatreds. At the rise of capitalism these nations were the right size for economic units; now that capitalist efficiency needs larger units, of continent size, Europe is at a disadvantage against the new powers America and Russia. Its inner inextinguishable enmities and wars called in those mightier rivals who trampled it down, physically and economically. What at the end of the Middle Ages happened to the Italian towns, which had been the birthplaces of burgher power and early capitalism, but which, torn by their mutual feuds and hatreds, could not establish a larger national unity, and so were, as battlefield, trampled by the French and the Spanish armies and subjected to mightier foreign powers—now happened to Europe on a larger scale. European capitalism is now the victim of that nationalism that once was its force. When after the first world war President Wilson, as the arbiter of Europe, proclaimed the principle of national self-determination this was the very means to keep Europe powerless, divided up into a host of independent, mutually fighting parts. It is quite natural that now socialist politicians propagate the idea of one consolidated socialist Europe; but they are too late; Europe is being partitioned already into an Eastern and a Western block. The idea itself of trying to make socialist Europe a third world power bridling the aggression of the others, belongs to the realm of middle class ideology that sees only contending nations, of continent size now; this ideology means the salvation of European capitalism.

Looking from a general point of view we may say that the development of the productive forces of society renders inevitable their social organization into one well-planned entirety. It may take place in two different ways. One is the way of capital, making State power the directing power of the production, making managers appointed from above the commanders of labor. It leads to totalitarianism in different degrees, the State extending its regulative power over ever more realms of human and social life. It leads to dictatorship, more or less camouflaged by parliamentary or sham democratic forms. Such dictatorship does not necessarily assume the brutal forms we have seen in Germany and Russia, with an all-powerful secret police keeping all classes in its cruel grip. For the working class the difference between Western democratic and Eastern dictatorial forms of Government is not essential, economically; in both it is subjected to exploitation by a ruling class of officials that commands production and distributes the produce. And to stand over against the State as the all-powerful master of the production apparatus, means loss of a good deal of that limited amount of free action by which it could formerly resist the demands of capital.

The other way is the way of the working class, seizing social power and mastery over the production apparatus.

3. TOWARDS NEW FREEDOM

The second world war has inaugurated a new epoch. More than the first world war it has changed the structure of the capitalist world. Thereby it has brought a fundamental change in the conditions of the workers' fight for freedom. These new conditions the working class has to know, to understand, and to face. It has, first, to give up illusions. Illusions about its future under capitalism, and illusions about an easy way of winning freedom in a better world of socialism.

In the past century, the first epoch of the workers' movement, the idea of socialism captured the mind. The workers built up their organizations, political parties, as well as trade unions, and attacked and fought capitalism. It was a fight by means of leaders; parliamentarians as spokesmen did the real fighting, and it was assumed that afterwards politicians and officials should do the real work of expropriating the capitalists and building up the new socialist world. Where reformism pervaded the socialist parties it was believed that by a series of reforms they would gradually mitigate and finally transform capitalism into a real commonwealth. Then at the end of the first world war hopes ran high about a near world revolution led by the communist party. By proclaiming strict obedience of the workers towards the leaders under the name of discipline, this party believed it could beat down capitalism and establish state socialism. Both parties denounced capitalism, both promised a better world without exploitation, under their rulership. So millions of workers followed them, believing they would defeat capitalism and liberate the proletariat from slavery.

Now these illusions have broken down. First about capitalism. Not a mitigated, but an aggravated capitalism faces us. It is the working class that has to bear the burden of capitalist recovery. So they must fight. Ever again strikes flare up. Though successful in appearance, they do not succeed in staving off want and misery. Against the formidable power of capitalism they are too weak to bring relief.

Not illusions about party communism–such could hardly have existed; because the C.P. never concealed its intention to establish a despotic rule over a subordinate working class. This goal stands squarely opposite to the workers' goal of being free masters of society themselves.

There were, too, illusions about socialism and unions. Now the workers discover that the organizations they considered as part of themselves stand as a power against them. Now they see that their leaders, political and union leaders, take side with capital. Their strikes are wild-cat strikes. In England Labor holds the State office for capitalism-in-need, and the trade unions are inserted as part of the apparatus of the State. As in the Grimethorpe strike a miner said to a reporter: "As usual, we are united and every one is against us."

This, indeed, is the mark of the new time. All the old powers stand against the workers, driving, sometimes cajoling, mostly denouncing and abusing them: capitalists, politicians, leaders, officials, the State. They have only themselves. But in their fight they are firmly united. More firmly, more unbreakably than in former contests, their mutual solidarity forging them into one solid body. Therein lies an indication of the future. To be sure, such small strikes cannot be more than a protest, a warning, to reveal the mood of the workers. Solid unity in such small units can be no more than a promise. To exert pressure upon the government they must be mass strikes.

In France and Italy, where the government tried to maintain wage-pegging without being able to prevent a rise of prices, mass strikes flared up, now indeed consciously directed against the government; combined with stronger forms of fight, with shop occupation, seizure by the workers of the offices. It was not, however, a pure class action of the workers but at the same time a political manuever in party strife. The strikes were directed by the central committee of the trade unions (C.G.T.), dominated by the Communist Party, and had to serve as an action of Russian politics against the Western governments. Thus from the onset there was an intrinsic weakness in them. The fight against private capitalism took the form of submission to state capitalism; hence it was opposed by those who abhorred state capitalist exploitation as a worse condition. So the workers could not arrive at real class unity; their action could not display as real massal class action; their great aim of freedom was obscured through servitude to capitalist party slogans.

The fierce antagonism sprung up at the end of the war between Russia and the Western powers has changed the attitude of the classes towards Russian communism. Whereas the Western intellectuals take side with their capitalist masters against dictatorship, large parts of the workers once more see Russia as their partner. So the difficulty for the working class to-day is that it is involved in the struggle of two world powers, both ruling and exploiting them, both referring to the exploitation on the other side in order to make them obedient adherents. In the Western world the Communist Party, agent of Russian state capitalism, presents itself as the ally and leader of the workers against home capitalism. By patient, petty work in the organizations it shoved itself into the leading administrative places, showing how a well-organized minority is able to dominate a majority; unlike the socialist leaders bound to their own capitalism it does not hesitate to put up the most radical demands for the workers, thus to win their favor. In countries where American capitalism retains in power the most reactionary groups, the C.P. takes the lead of popular movements, as the future master, to make them allies of Russia should they win dominance. If in America itself the working masses should come to mass actions against new war, the C.P. will immediately join and try to make the action a source of spiritual confusion. On the reverse, American capitalism will not be slow to present itself as the liberator of the enslaved Russian masses, hereby to claim the adherence of the America workers.

This is not a chance situation of today. Always capitalist policy consists in dividing the working class by making it adhere to two opposite capitalist parties. They feel by instinct that in this way the working class is made powerless. So the more they are alike, two lots of profit-seeking exploiters and office-seeking politicians, the stronger they emphasize their often traditional artificial differences into sounding slogans simulating fundamental principles. So it was in home politics in every country, so it is now in international politics, against the working class of the world. Should capitalism succeed in establishing "one world" it certainly would discover the necessity to split into two contending halves, in order to prevent unity of the workers.

Here the working class needs wisdom. Not solely knowledge of society and its intricacies, but that intuitive wisdom that is growing out of their plain condition of life, that independence of mind that is based upon the pure principle of class struggle for freedom. Where both capitalist powers try to win the working masses by their noisy propaganda and thus to divide them, these have to realize that theirs is the third way, the fight for their own mastery over society.

This fight arises as an extension of their present small attempts of resistance. Up till now they struck separately; when one factory or industry went on strike the others looked on, apparently uninterested; so they could only worry the rulers who at most appeased them with small concessions. Once they perceive that the first condition to enforce their demands is mass unity of action they will begin to raise their class power against State-power. Up till now they let themselves be directed by capitalist interests. Once they understand that the other condition, not less primary, is to keep the direction in their own hands by means of their delegates, their strike committees, their workers' councils, and do not allow any leaders to lead them, they will have entered the road to freedom.

What we now witness is the beginning of breakdown of capitalism as an economic system. Not yet visible over the entire world, but over Europe, where it took its origin. In England, in Europe, capitalism arose; and like an oil-spot it extended ever wider over the world. Now in this centre we see it decay, hardening into despotic forms to stave off ruin, showing the now flourishing new sites, America, Australia, their future.

The beginning of breakdown: what was supposed to be a matter of the future, the limitedness of the earth as an impediment to further expansion of capitalism now manifests itself already. The slow increase of world trade since the first world war indicates the slackening tempo, and the deep crisis of 1930 has not been vanquished by a new prosperity. The slackening at the time did not enter into the consciousness of man; it could only be made out afterwards in statistical figures. Today the breakdown is conscious experience; the broad masses of the people feel it and know it, and in panic try to find a way out.

The breakdown of an economic system: not yet of a social system. The old dependencies of the classes, the relations of a master and a servant class, the basic fact of exploitation as yet are in full vigour. Desperate efforts are made to consolidate them. By transforming the chance economy into planned economy, by increasing State-despotism, by intensifying the exploitation.

The beginning of breakdown of an old system: not yet the beginning rise of a new system. The working class is far back, compared to the master class, in recognizing the changed conditions. Whereas the capitalists are active in transforming old institutions and adapt them to new functions, the workers stubbornly adhere to traditional feelings and actions, and try to fight capital by putting their trust in agents of capitalism, in unions and parties. Surely the wild strikes are first indications of new forms of fight. But only when the entire working class is permeated by the new insight into the significance of self-action and self-rule, the way to freedom opens out.

The breakdown of capitalism is at the same time the breakdown of the old socialism. Because socialism now turns out to be a harsher form of capitalism. Socialism, as inherited from the 19th century, was the creed of a social mission for the leaders and politicians: to transform capitalism into a system of State-directed economy without exploitation, producing abundance for all. It was the creed of class struggle for the workers, the belief that by transferring government into the hands of these socialists they would assure their freedom. Why did it not happen? Because the casting of a secret vote was too insignificant an effort to count as a real class-fight. Because the socialist politicians stood single-handed within the entire capitalist fabric of society, against the immense power of the capitalist class being master of the production apparatus, with the workers' masses only looking on, expecting them, little squad, to upset the world. What could they do otherwise than run the affair in the usual way, and by reforming the worst abuses save their conscience? Now it is seen that socialism in the sense of State-directed planned economy means state-capitalism, and that socialism in the sense of workers' emancipation is only possible as a new orientation. The new orientation of socialism is self-direction of production, self-direction of the class-struggle, by means of workers' councils.

What is called the failure of the working class, alarming many socialists, the contradiction between the economic breakdown of capitalism and the inability of the workers to seize power and establish the new order, is no real contradiction. Economic changes only gradually produce changes in the mind. The workers educated in the belief in socialism stand bewildered now that they see that the very opposite, heavier slavery, is the outcome. To grasp that socialism and communism now both mean doctrines of enslavement is a hard job. New orientation needs time; maybe only a new generation will comprehend its full scope.

At the end of the first world war world revolution seemed near; the working class arose full of hope and expectation that now its old dreams would come true. But they were dreams of imperfect freedom, they could not be realized. Now at the end of the second world war only slavery and destruction seem near; hope is far distant; but, a task, the greater aim of real freedom looms. More powerful than before, capitalism rises as master of the world. More powerful than before the working class has to rise in its fight for mastery over the world. More powerful forms of suppression capitalism has found. More powerful forms of fight the working class has to find and use. So this crisis of capitalism at the same time will be the start of a new workers' movement.

A century ago, when the workers were a small class of downtrodden helpless individuals, the call was heard: proletarians of all countries unite! You have nothing to lose but your chains; you have a world to win. Since then they have become the largest class; and they have united; but only imperfectly. Only in groups, smaller or larger, not yet as one class-unity. Only superficially, in outer forms, not yet in deep essence. And still they have nothing to lose but their chains; what else they have they cannot lose by fighting, only by timidly submitting. And the world to be won begins to be perceived dimly. At that time no clear goal, for which to unite, could be depicted; so their organizations in the end became tools of capitalism. Now the goal becomes distinct; opposite to the stronger domination by state-directed planned economy of the new capitalism stands what Marx called the association of free and equal producers. So the call for unity must be supplemented by indication of the goal: take the factories and machines; assert your mastery over the productive apparatus; organize production by means of workers' councils.

Further Reading
(Compiled by Robert F. Barsky)

Ackerman, Frank. ed. *The Changing Nature of Work*. Washington, DC: Island Press, 1998.

Ahrens, Werner. "Works Councils in the Industrial Provinces: Eight Case Studies of Relations Between Management and Production in the Factory." [Betriebsraete in der industriellen Provinz. Acht Fallstudien ueber bertriebliche Herrschafts und Produktionsverhaeltnisse.] *Sociologia Ruralis* 22.2 (1982), 197–198.

Albeda, Wil. "Between Harmony and Conflict: Industrial Democracy in the Netherlands." *Annals of the American Academy of Political Social Science* 431 (1977) : 74–82.

— "Changing Industrial Relations in the Netherlands." *Industrial Relations* 16.2 (1977) : 133-144.

Albrecht, Sandra L. "Forms of Industrial and Economic Democracy: A Comparison of Prevailing Approaches." *Mid-American Review of Sociology* 8.2 (1983) : 43–66.

Altmann, Norbert, Peter Binkelmann, and Klaus Dull. "New Forms of Employment: Managerial Polices and Employee Interests. [Neue Arbeitsformen, betriebliche Leistungspolitik und Interessen der Beschaftigten.] *Soziale Welt* 33.3-4 (1982), 440–465.

Altmann, Norbert, and Klaus Dull. "Rationalization and Participation: Implementation of New Technologies and Problems of the Work Councils in the FRG." *Economic and Industrial Democracy* 11.1 (1990): 111–127.

Antipev, Anatoliy Grigorevich. "Work Group Council in the System of Collective Administration." [STK v sisteme upravleniya kollektivom.] *Sotsiologicheskie Issledovaniya* 16.5 (1989): 70–73.

Anweiler, Oskar. *The Soviets: The Russian Workers, Peasants, and Soldiers Councils, 1905-1921. [Die Ratebewegung in Russland, 1905-1921.]* Trans. Ruth Hein. New York: Pantheon Books, 1975.

Ascher, Abraham. "'Radical' Imperialists Within German Social Democracy, 1912-1918." *Political Science Quarterly* 76(4) (1961): 555–575.

Bayat, Assef. *Workers and Revolution in Iran: a Third World Experience of Workersí Control*. London: Zed, 1987.

Balfour, Campbell, ed. *Participation in Industry*. London: Croom Helm, 1973.

Bellace, Janice R. "The European Works Council Directive: Transnational Information and Consultation in the European Union." *Comparative Labor Law Journal* 18 (1997), 325–361.

Bellamy, Richard and Darrow Schecter. *Gramsci and the Italian State.* New York: St. Martinís Press, 1993.

Bernstein, Paul, and Bonnie Burrow. *Training Workers for Democratic Management: Findings on the European Experience.* Society for the Study of Social Problems (SSSP), 1979.

Bertram, Hans. "Transformation Process: Commission for the Study of Social and Political Changes in the New Federal Republic of Germany (KSPW). [Transfromationsprozesse: Die Kommission fur die Erforschung des sozialen und politischen Wandels in den neuen Bundeslandern (KSPW).]" *Diskurs* 7.1 (1997) : 59–63.

Boekelman, Marinus Antonius M. The Development of the Social and Political Thought of Anton Pannekoek, 1873-1960: From Social Democracy to Council Communism. Thesis, University of Toronto, 1980.

Boggs, Carl. "Marxism, Prefigurative Communism, and the Problems of Workersí Control." *Radical America* 11-12.6-1 (1977–1978), 98–122.

Bologna, Sergio. "Class Composition and the Theory of the Party at the Origin of the Workers- Councils Movement." Trans. Bruno Ramirez. *Telos* 13 (1972): 4–27.

Bolweg, J. F. "Reflections on the C.O.P. Experiments in Participation. [Reflecties rond de C.O.P. experimenten medezeggenschap.]" *Mens en Onderneming* 31.1 (1977), 45–66

Boreham, Paul, and Richard Hall. "Trade Union Strategy in Contemporary Capitalism: The Microeconomic and Macroeconomic Implications of Political Unionism." *Economic and Industrial Democracy* 15.3 (1994), 313–353.

Bradley, Keith and Alan Gelb. *Cooperation at Work: The Mondragon Experience.* Heinemann Eductional Books, 1983.

Bricianer, Serge. *Pannekoek and the Workers' Councils. [Pannekoek et les conseils ouvriers.]* Trans. Malachy Carroll. Saint Louis: Telos Press, 1978.

Brinton, Maurice. *The Bolsheviks and Workers' Control, 1917 to 1921, The State and Counter-Revolution.* Solidarity, 1970.

Broekmeyer, M. J., ed. *Yugoslav Workersí Self-Management. Proceedings of a symposium held in Amsterdam, 7–9 January, 1970.* Dordrecht, Reidel, 1970.

Bronfenbrenner, Kate, ed. *Organizing to win: new research on union strategies.* Ithaca: ILR Press, 1998.

Burns, Tony. "Joseph Dietzgen and the History of Marxism." *Science & Society* 2002 66(2): 202–227.

Carby-Hall, J. R. *Worker Participation in Europe.* Croom Helm; Roman and Littlefield, 1977.

Clegg, Ian. *Workersí Self-Management in Algeria.* New York: Monthly Review Press, 1971.

Coates, Ken, ed., et al. *The New Worker Co-operatives*, Spokesman Books, 1976.

Coates, Ken, and Tony Topham, eds. *Workers' Control: A Book of Readings and Witnesses for Workers' Control.* MacGibbon & Kee, 1968; Panther, 1970.

Comisso, Ellen Turkish. *Workersí Control Under Plan and Market: Implications of Yugoslav Self-management.* New Haven, CT: Yale UP, 1979.

Congdon, Tim. "The Economics of Industrial Democracy." *New Society* 34.682 (1975), 255–257.

Daniels, Robert Vincent, ed. Introduction. *Documentary History of Communism and the World: From Revolution to Collapse.* Trans. Robert V. Daniels. Hanover: University Press of New England Press, 1994.

Danik, Claude. "Trade union politics." *Canadian Labor and Employment Law Journal* 5 (1996), 117–121.

Dankabaar, Ben. "New Production Concepts, Management Strategies and the Quality of Work." *Work, Employment and Society* 2.1 (1988):25–50.

de Zwaan, Frans H. "A Works Council. [Een Ondernemingsraad.]" *Mens en Onderneming* 28.3 (1974), 145–162.

— "How Well does the OR Work? [Hoe Goed Doet de OR Het?]" *Mens en Onderneming* 28.4 (1974), 216–231.

Dolgoff, Sam, ed. *The Anarchist Collectives: Workers' Self-Management in the Spanish Revolution* (1936–1939). Free Life Editions, 1974.

Einemann, Edgar. *Research by the Concerned for a Human Future of Work.* International Sociological Association (ISA), 1986.

Falkner, Gerda. "European Works Councils and the Maastricht Social Agreement: Towards a New Policy Style?" *Journal of European Public Policy* 3.2 (1996), 192–208.

Fincham, Robin, and Grace Zulu. "Works Councils in Zambia: The Implementation of Industrial Participatory Democracy." *Labor and Society* 5.2 (1980) : 171–190.

First Dilic, Ruza. "On E. Sicardís Reflections. [O Razmisljanjima E. Sicarda.]" *Sociologija sela* 12.1 (1974) : 92–94.

Fisera, Vladimir, ed. *Worker's Councils in Czechoslovakia, 1968-9: Documents and Essays.* London: Allison and Busby, 1978.

Frege, Carola M. "Workers' Commitment to New Labor Institutions: Comparing Union Members in East and West Germany." *European Journal of Industrial Relations* 4.1 (1988): 81–101.

Furstenberg, Friedrich. "The Regulation of Working Time in the Federal Republic of Germany." *Labor and Society* 10.2 (1985), 133–150.

— "West German Experience with Industrial Democracy." *Annals of the American Academy of Political and Social Science* 431 (1977) : 44–53.

Gerber, John Paul , *Anton Pannekoek and the Socialism of Workers' Self-Emancipation, 1873-1960.* Dordrecht; Boston; Amsterdam: Kluwer Academic; International Institute of Social History, 1989.

Gerber, John. "From Left Radicalism to Council Communism: Anton Pannekoek and the German Revolutionary Marxism." *Journal of Contemporary History.* 23(2) (1988): 169–189.

Gevers, P. "From the Company Council...to the Workers' Council? A Dilemma That the Belgian Workers Movement Must Solve." [Du conseil díentreprise...au conseil des travailleurs? Un dilemme pose au mouvement ouvrier.] *Recherches Sociologiques* 8.2 (1977), 189–210.

Gluckstein, Donny. *The western Soviets: workers' councils versus parliament, 1915–1920.* London: Bookmarks, 1985.

Gramsci, Antonio. *Antonio Gramsci: pre-prison writings.* Richard Bellamy, ed. Trans. Virginia Cox. Cambridge: Cambridge University Press, 1994.

Greenberg, Edwards S. "The Consequences of Worker Participation: A Clarification of the Theoretical Literature." *Social Science Quarterly* 56.2 (1975), 191-209.

Guérin, Daniel. *Anarchism.* Introduction by Noam Chomsky. Monthly Review Press, 1970.

Hansen, Erik. Marxists and Society: The Emergence of Marxian Social Theory in the Netherlands, 1894-1914. Journal of European Studies 64(4), 1976: 262–285.

Hassencamp, Alfred, and Hans Jurgen Bieneck. íTechnical and Organizational Changes and Design of Working Conditions in the Federal Republic of Germany." *Labor and Society* 8.1 (1983) : 39–56.

Herrigel, Gary. "Works Councils: Consultation, Representation and Cooperation in Industrial Relations." *American Journal of Sociology* 102.4 (1997), 1205–1208.

Hethy, Lajos. "Plant Level Participation in Hungary." *Osterreichische Zeitschrift fur Soziologie* 13.1 (1988): 38–49.

Hinton James. *The First Shop Stewardsí Movement.* London: G. Allen & Unwin, 1973.

Horkheimer, Max. "The Authoritarian State." *Telos* 15 (1973): 3–20.

Hovels, Ben W. M., and Peter Nas. "Works Councils in the Netherlands: Some Findings from an Empirical Survey." *Netherlands Journal of Sociology* [*Sociologia Neerlandica*] 13.2 (1977) : 107–124.

"Industrial Democracy in Europe: Differences and Similarities across Countries and Hierarchies." *Organization Studies* 2.2 (1981), 113–129.

Jacoby, Sanford M. "Current Prospects for Employee Representation in the U.S.: Old Wine in New Bottles?" *Journal of Labor Research* 16.3 (1995), 387–397.

Kalecki, Michal. *Socijalizm, fuinkcjonowanie I wieloletnie planowanie.* [*Socialism–functioning and long-run planning.*] Jerzy Osiatynski,ed. Trans. Bohdan Jung. Oxford: Oxford University Press, 1992.

Kaufman, Bruce E and Morris M. Kleiner, ed. *Employee Tepresentation: Slternatives and Future Directions.* Madison, WI: Industrial Relations Research Association, 1993.

Keman, Hans. *The Development of Industrial Democracy in the Netherlands since the Second World War: From Corporatism to Co-Counseling?* International Sociological Association (ISA), 1986.

Klandermans, B., and N. Terra. "A Works Council Consults Its Supporters: The Mobilization of Union Members. [Een centrale ondernemingsraad raadpleegt zijn achterban: de mobilisatie van vakbondsleden voor een advies.]" *Mens en Onderneming* 34.5 (1980), 392–412.

Kleiner, Morris M., and Young-Myon Lee. "Works Councils and Unionization: Lessons from South Korea." *Industrial Relations* 36.1 (1997): 1–16.

Kochan, Thomas A., and Harry C. Katz. "Collective Bargaining, Work Organization, and Worker Particpation: the return to plant level bargaining." *Labor Law Journal* 34 (1983), 524–530.

Kolaja, Jiri. "A Yugoslav Workersí Council." *Human Organization* 20.1 (1961): 27–31.

— "New Data on Worker Self-Administration." *American Journal of Economics and Sociology* 39.4 (1980), 415–417.

Kolaja, Jiri Thomas. *Workersí councils: the Yugoslav experience.* New York: Praeger, 1965.

— *Workers' Councils: The Yugoslav Experience.* London: Tavistock Publications, 1965.

Koopman Iwema, Agnes M. "Power, Motivation and Codetermination." *Netherlands Journal of Sociology [Sociologia Neerlandica]* 19.2 (1983), 199–204.

— "Workers' Council Laws in Germany and the Netherlands. [De Ondernemingsraad in Duitsland en Nederland: Wetgeving en Praktijk]." *M and O* 36.4 (1982), 327–347.

Kreissig, Volkmar. *Employee Participation and New Forms of Management in East Germany and Russia.* International Sociological Association (ISA), 1998.

— *German Unification and New-Old Issues of Industrial Relations.* International Sociological Association (ISA), 1994.

Lammers, Cornelis. "Problems and Achievements of Self Management in Yugoslavia. [Problemen en Prestaties van het Joegoslavisch Zelfbestuur.]" *Mens en Maatschappij* 48 (1973), 139–151.

— Pauline L. Meurs, and Ton A. Mijs. "Direct and Indirect Participation in Dutch Firms and Hospitals." *Organization Studies* 8.1 (1987): 25–38.

— and Ada van der Hoogte. *The Role of Dutch Employersí Associations with Respect to Legislation on Industrial Democracy.* International Sociological Association (ISA), 1986.

Lammers, D. J., J. H. T. H. Andriessen, A. A. Mijs, and P. L. Meurs. "Do Worker Councils Have a Chance in Dutch Hospitals? [Maakt de ondernemingsraad in het Nederlandse ziekenhuis een kans?]" *Mens en Onderneming* 34.2 (1980) : 88–104.

Lauc, Ante. "Influence of the Working Class and Some Means of Increasing Working Class Influence. [Utjecaj Radnicke Klase I Neki Putovi Povecanja Utjecaja Radnicke Klase.]" *Sociologija* 14.4 (1972), 625–641.

Lecher, Wolfgang, and Stefan Rub. "The Constitution of European Works Councils: From Information Forum to Social Actor?" *European Journal of Industrial Relations* 5.1 (1999): 7–25.

Lecher, Wolfgang, and Ulrike Sieling Wendeling. "New Developments in the Discussion of Co-Determination in Europe." *Labor and Society* 4.1 (1979) : 80–98.

Looise, Jan Cornelis. "Employee Representation at the Crossroads: Trade Unions and Works Councils in Changing Industrial Relations. [Werknemersvertegenwoordiging op de tweesprong: Vakbeweging en vertegenwoordigend overleg in veranderende arbeidsverhoudingen.]" *Dissertation Abstracts International* 50.4 (1989), 624-C.

Looise, Jan C., Jan De Leede, and Ulke Veersma. *The Effects of Changes in Organization and Work on Works Councils.* International Sociological Association (ISA), 1998.

Majchzakowa, Irena. "The Workersí Councils in Poland." *Archives Internationales de Sociologie de la Cooperation et du Developpement* 2 (1957): 146–155.

Mangold, Werner. *Aspects of Social and Political Consciousness of German Industrial Workers.* International Sociological Association (ISA), 1978.

Mapadimeng, Simon M. "Workplace Representaion through the Workplace Forums in Contemporary South Africa: Opportunities and Constraints." *Society in Transition* 29.3-4 (1998): 93–103.

Markey, Ray, and Jacques Monat, eds. *Innovation and Employee Participation Through Works Councils: International Case Studies.* Brookfield: Ashgate Publishing Company, 1997.

Marsden, David *Ward. "West European Developments in Industrial Democracy."* Free Inquiry in Creative Sociology 8.1 (1980) : 1–5.

Matuszak, Grzegorz. "Workers' Opinions about the Reward and Punishment of Workers in an Industrial Enterprise. [Opinie zalogi o wyroznianiu I karaniu pracwnikow w przedsiebiorstwie przemyslowym.]" *Przeglad Socjologiczny* 33 (1981), 321–330.

McGlynn, Clare. "European Works Councils: towards industrial democracy?" *The Industrial Law Journal* 24 (1995) : 78–84.

Melman, Seymour. *After Capitalism: From Managerialism to Workplace Democracy.* NY: Knopf, 2001.

Miller, Douglas. "The Industrial Representation of Labor Unions in the Federal Republic of Germany. [Die betreibliche Prasenz von Gewerkschaften in der Bunderepublik Deutschland.]" *Soziale Welt* 30.3 (1979), 328–353.

Mohamed Halfini S., and Sandbrook, Richard. eds. *Empowering people: Building community, civil associations and legaliity in Africa.* Toronto: Centre for Urban and Community Studies, University of Toronto. c1993. Proceedings of an International Conference of Civil Association held in Arusha, Tanzania, August 1991.

Monat, Jacques. "Participation and Political Structure." *Labor and Society* 8.4 (1983) : 371–378.

Mourianx, Rene. "Strategies and Events: The Form of the CGT from 1936 to 1968. [Strategies et événements: la forme de la CGT de 1936 a 1968.] *French Politics and Society* 14.4 (1996): 15–22.

Mulder, Mark. "The Seizable Power. [De Grijpbare Macht.]" *Acta Politica* 8.2 (1973), 133–152.

Noble, David. *America by Design: Science, Technology, and the Rise of Corporate Capitalism.* NY: Knopf, 1977.

— *Forces of Production: A Social History of Industrial Automation.* NY: Knopf, 1983.

Obradovic, Josip. "Distribution of Participation in the Process and the Making of Decisions on Themes Linked With the Economic Functioning of Enterprises. [Distribucija Participacije u Procesu Donosenja Odluka na Temama Vezanim uz Ekonomsko Poslovanje Poduzeca.]" *Revija za Sociologiju* 2.1 (1972): 15–48.

Obradovic, Josip. "Participation-Research Results and Theory. [Participacija–Rezultati Istrazivanja I Teoretski Model.]" *Revija za Sociologiju* 4.1 (1974): 29–54.

Obradovic, Josip. "Workers' Participation: Who Participates?" *Industrial Relations* 14.1 (1975): 32–44.

Pollert, Anna. *Labor Movements in Transformation in Post-Command Economies: The Case of Central Eastern Europe.* International Sociological Association (ISA), 1998.

Pontusson, Jonas. "Works Councils: Consultation, Representation and Cooperation in Industrial Relations." *Contemporary Sociology* 26.3 (1997), 338–339.

Popovic, Mihailo V. "Can the Working Class Control the Total Process of Social Reproduction? [Moze li radnicka klasa da ovlada celokupnom drustvenom reprodukcijom?]" *Sociologija* 28.1-2 Jan–June (1986): 1–10.

Preusche, Evelyn. *Workis Councils in East Germany between Cooperation and Conflict.* International Sociological Association (ISA), 1994.

Rahnema, Saeed. "Works Councils in Iran: The Illusion of Worker Control." *Economic and Industrial Democracy* 13.1 (1992) : 69–94.

Rasnic, Carol D. "Germanyís statutory works councils and employee codetermination: a model for the United States?" *Loyola of Los Angeles International and Comparative Law Journal* 14 (1992), 275–300.

Rudolf, Stanislaw. "Intergrating Activities of the European Community Regarding Worker Participation Issues (European Company Councils). [Dzialania integracyjne wspolnoty europejskiej w zakresie partycypacji pracowniczej (Europejskie Zakladowe).] *Przeglad Socjologiczny* 43 (1994), 185–199.

Samuels, Warren J. "Reflections on the Intellectual Context and Significance of Thorstein Veblen." *Journal of Economic Issues* 29.3 (1995), 915–922.

Sandbrook, Richard, and Mohamed Halfani, eds. *Empowering people: building community, civil associations and legality in Africa: proceedings of an International Conference of Civil Associations held in Arusha, Tanzania, August 1991.* Toronto: Centre for Urban and Community Studies, University of Toronto, 1993.

Scheinecker, Martina. "Between Personnel and Management. Work Organization and Flow of Information amoung Members of Works Councils. [Zwischen Belegschaft und Unternehmensleitung. Arbeitsorganisation und Infromationsfluss im Betriebsratskollegium.]" *Osterreichische Zeitschrift fur Soziologie* 13.1 (1988) : 98–99.

Schnabel, Claus, and Joachim Wagner. "Industrial Relations and Trade Union Effects on Innovation in Germany." *Labor* 8.3 (1994), 489–503.

Schulten, Thorsten. "The European Works Councils: Prospects for a New System of European Industrial Relations." *European Journal of Industrial Relations* 2.3 (1996), 303–324.

Schurer, H. Anton Pannekoek and the Origins of Leninism. *Slavonic and East European Review* 41(97) (1963): 327–344.

Shaw, Jo. "Works councils in German enterprises and Article 119 E.C.." European Law Review 22 (1997), 256–262.

Shipway, Mark. *Anti-Parliamentary Communism: The Movement for Workers' Councils in Britain, 1917–45.* Basingstoke: Macmillan, 1988.

Sirianni, Carmen. *Workers Control and Socialist Democracy: the Soviet Experience.* London: NLB, 1982.

Smart, D. A. *Pannekoek and Gorter's Marxism.* London: Pluto Press, 1978

Stanzani, Claudio. "European Work Councils: The Critical Aspects of Participation. [I comitati aziendali europei: aspetti critici di partecipazione.]" *Sociologia del Lavoro* 68 (1998), 219–228.

Stern, Robert N., and Nada Zupan. *Before the Flood: Legal Structure and the Practice of Self-Management in a Yugoslavian Workers' Council, 1973–1989.* American Sociological Association (ASA), 1991.

Streech, Wolfgang. "Industrial Citizenship under Regime Competition: The Case of the European Works Councils." *Journal of European Public Policy* 4.4 (1997), 643–664.

— "Neither European Nor Works Councils: A Reply to Paul Knutsen." *Economic and Industrial Democracy* 18.2 (1997), 325–337.

Sturmthal, Adolf Fox. *Workers Councils: A study of Workplace Organization on Both Sides of the Iron Curtain.* Cambridge: Harvard U P, 1964.

Tallard, Michele. *Bargaining over New Technology and New Forms of Democracy in the Firm.* International Sociological Association (ISA), 1990.

Tanasijevic, Vera, and Zivojin Kojic. "Quantity of Information Available to Workers on the Rights of Workersí Conferences. [Obavestenost radnika rudnika, topionice I rafinacije bakra Bor o pravima zbora.]" *Socioloski Pregled* 10.1-3 (1976): 35–45.

Teulings, A. W. M. "A Political Bargaining Theory of Co-Determination An Empirical Test for the Dutch System of Organizational Democracy." *Organization Studies* 8.1 (1987): 1–24.

— "Representation of Workers Interest and Consultation in the Dutch Works Council." *Socilogia Neerlandica* 5.2 (1970) : 80–102

— "Representing Employee Interests: Works Councils and the Rank and File: Representation Strategies and Avoidance Rituals." *Economic and Industrial Democracy* 9.2 (1988), 179–195.

— H. J. L. Voets. "The Function of the Works Council. [Het Functioneren van de Ondernemingsraad.]" Mens en Onderneming 25.2 (1971), 108–119.

Thimm, Alfred L. *The False Promise of Codetermination: The Changing Nature of European Workers' Participation.* Toronto: Lexington Books, 1980.

Toth, Andras. "The Invention of Works Councils in Hungary." *European Journal of Industrial Relations* 3.2 (1997), 161–181.

Turner, Lowell. "Works Councils: Consultation, Representation , and Cooperation in Industrial Relations." *Industrial and Labor Relations Review* 50.4 (1997), 707–708.

Vanek, Jan. *The Economics of Workersí Management: A Yugoslav case study.* London: Allen and Unwin, 1972.

Van der Bruggen, A. L. A., and J. F. den Hertog. "Workersí Participation at the Departmental Level. [Werkoverleg op afdelingsniveau]." *Mens en Onderneming* 30.6 (1976), 334–353.

van Holle, Roland. "Twenty-Five Years of Works Council in Belgium. [Vijfentwintig jaar Ondernemingsraden in Belgie.]" *Mens en Onderneming* 28.4 (1974), 232–247.

Van Hoorn, Th. P., and H. C. Dekker. "Social Reporting at a Crossroad? [Sociale verslaggeving op een tweesprong?]" *Mens en Onderneming* 31.3 (1977), 127–199.

Vinogradov, V. *Workersí Control Over Production: Past and Present.* Moscow: Novosti Press Agency Pub. House, 1973.

Visser, Jelle. "Works Councils and Unions in the Netherlands: Rivals or Allies?" *Netherlands Journal of Social Sciences* 29.1 (1993): 64–92.

Weston, Syd, and Miguel Martinez Lucio. "Trade Unions, Management and European Works Councils: Opening Pandoraís Box?" *International Journal of Human Resource Management* 8.6 (1997), 764–779.

Wheeler, Sally. "Works Councils: Toward Stakeholding?" *Journal of Law and Society* 24.1 (1997): 44–64.

Windmuller, John P. "Industrial Democracy and Industrial Relations." *Annals of the American Academy of Political and Social Science* 431 (1977) : 22–31.

— "Perspectives in Dutch Labor Relations." Mens en Onderneming 24.2 (1970), 136–141.

Wirth, David A. "Trade Union Rights in the Workersí State: Poland and the ILO." *Denver Journal of International Law and Policy* 13 (1984/1985), 269–282.

AK Press
674-A 23rd Street
Oakland, CA 94612-1163
USA
(510) 208-1700
www.akpress.org
akpress@akpress.org

AK Press
PO Box 12766
Edinburgh, EH8 9YE
Scotland
(0131) 555-5165
www.akuk.com
ak@akedin.demon.uk

The addresses above would be delighted to provide you with the latest complete AK catalog, featuring several thousand books, pamphlets, zines, audio products, video products, and stylish apparel published & distributed by AK Press. Alternatively, check out our websites for the complete catalog, latest news and updates, events, and secure ordering.

Printed in the USA
CPSIA information can be obtained
at www.ICGtesting.com
JSHW012049140824
68134JS00035B/3341

9 781902 593562